no cloak
no dagger

GRACE STODDARD

No Cloak No Dagger

Published by Wheatmark®
610 East Delano Street, Suite 104
Tucson, Arizona 85705 U.S.A.
www.wheatmark.com

International Standard Book Number: 978-1-60494-144-9
Library of Congress Control Number: 2008935796

There are no secrets that time does not reveal. Jean Racine
Brittanicus 1669

notes from the author

ALTHOUGH THE AUTHOR IS not Keith Armstrong, his story will be told in the first person in order to more effectively portray his thoughts, emotions, and memories. No Cloak No Dagger is being written for all those who have gone before, and will come after who dedicate their lives to the love of country and who are for the most part unrewarded and unknown, and in memory of Armstrong's two sons who died under tragic circumstances.

acknowledgement

THERE MUST BE A special place for a husband who exhibits patience, support and unequivocal understanding while his wife spends many months consumed with the life of another man. I must thank my daughter who is always available to explain a new technique on the computer, and at Wheatmark, the unseen, but supportive Grael Norton and Susan Wenger.

introduction

INTELLIGENCE HISTORY ... THE factual history of spying ... is very hard to write. Documents lie: entire files are left behind in an archive with the intent of misleading later generations of researchers. Those bound by the Official Secrets Act must remain silent. Unlike James Bond, who knows everything and conquers all with magical devices and disdain for both his enemies and his superiors in Whitehall, undercover work is not glamorous; it is dangerous, and unrewarding. This book is being written to dispel some myths and relate a story: the story of a man who was involved from his teen years during WWII until forced retirement years later. The story is true, but some names and places have been changed.

chapter 1

LONDON WILL ALWAYS BE London: grey, drizzling, gloomy with a slim possibility that some sun will shine for a while, but there were obvious changes, too. Badly scarred by the Blitz, there were burned out buildings, collapsed flats, and hardly a street without a gaping hole where a bomb had hit. Batteries of anti-aircraft machines were in Hyde Park, camouflaged huts and trucks in Grosvenor Square, and barrage balloons were tugging at the end of steel cables. Big Ben still stood looming over it all.

Streets were crowded with soldiers in uniform, business men in bowler hats, bobbies, and girls going to and from work. Food rationing was tight and clothing coupons were scarce. The big red buses still rolled and the taxis still hooted. London was battered, but not beaten.

I left SOE headquarters in Dorset Square that day in good spirits. One of my friends had persuaded me to go with him to the Belgian Embassy where, he said, two very attractive girls were more than ready to go out with two young British Officers wearing the uniform of the Royal Army Service Corps. The uniforms were camouflage for our real identities: soldiers chosen to be trained as saboteurs to be dropped into Nazi- occupied Europe.

I was aware that a blind date had its hazards, but I was willing to risk it. Tall, blond, blue eyed and one hundred and seventy pounds of mostly muscle, I had been recruited by Special Operations Executive. My friend and I were just a couple of teenagers hoping to meet some girls. This was not to be my lucky day. Inside the embassy my friend's girl was waiting for him, but my date had found better things to do. Those two went off and left me to deal with my disappointment.

As I was leaving I noticed a girl at the switchboard. She was lovely, with auburn hair, deep blue eyes, and regular features.

Clearly she did not like my staring at her and said sharply, "Qu'est qu' il y a Monsieur?" (What do you wish?)

I started to explain my reason for being there and suddenly asked if she would have a drink with me when her work permitted.

Without hesitation she declined saying that she did not accept such invitations from strangers. The switchboard buzzed and I left, but not before asking the military guard for her name. It was de Roche, Arlette de Roche. Yes, she was Belgian and had fled from the Nazis with her family.

The next day I called the embassy and took a deep breath when she answered. I identified myself as the British Officer who had spoken to her yesterday and would she care to hunt for some lunch with me? (In those days unless you ate at a military mess or canteen you did have to hunt.) She answered that she did not know. If I came around would she think about it until then, I persisted? A long silence: "Peut-être," she said. (Perhaps)

She did go out with me that day and we did find some lunch. Later we sat in the churchyard of Saint Paul's Church in Knightsbridge. We talked about ourselves. I told her how I had enlisted at seventeen, knowing I would be conscripted soon. I told her about my family in Cornwall. I said nothing about SOE.

She told me about being born in Katanga where her father had mining interests. She had grown up there, learning to ride and shoot, outdoors most of the time, an upbringing that accounted in part for her extraordinary physical assurance and confidence. In the mid thirties her family returned to Belgium where she went to a convent school until the Nazis came.

Her family did not bother to hide their hatred of the invaders and when her older sister was arrested, and never heard from again, the family made plans to escape. In a daring escapade they attempted to cross the water at night in a row boat. Fortunately they were picked up by a Grimsby Trawler and taken to safety in England.

Now she lived with her family in an apartment in Belgrave Square. No, she was not content to sit at a switchboard and was about to join FANY(First Aid Nursing Yeomanry). No, she did not have a boyfriend.

The minutes sped by and she had to return to work. I walked

her back to the embassy and by the time we reached the front doors I was in love. Arlette seemed such a superior person that I could not imagine her ever being interested in me, but as I was leaving, she smiled and agreed to see me again.

We were together every moment we could find. I made no secret of the fact that for me, other people ceased to exist. Late one afternoon, standing by the flowers in Green Park, Arlette told me that she loved me, too.

I was sent for more training to Wanborough manor and by a remarkable coincidence Arlette was there, too. Recruiters from SOE had approached her, and like mine, her uniform was a cover. She was really FANY(S) for Special. I should not have been surprised that SOE would find her. She was young, strong, intelligent, and intensely patriotic. Above all, she was Belgian: a perfect candidate for French or Belgian section. She was recruited and she would serve even though she knew much better than I what the dangers were.

The training at Wanborough Manor was intense. For instance we were sent into pitch dark cellars of the ancient building to find and defuse explosive devises. We had to learn many different forms of deception: how to learn to walk, dress, and eat the way people did in other countries, or for instance how a Polish farmer might sound while trying to speak French or Flemish. We were taught psychology. We were taught how to tell by the tone of voice if someone was betraying you or how to look for a flicker of an eye under the same circumstances.

From the beginning, Arlette impressed our instructors as she was an expert with fire arms, could shinny up a tree as fast as a squirrel, and put down an adversary as quickly as any man. Her skills in the classroom were outstanding. Everyone admired her and we wondered how anyone so feminine could be so tough.

Our feelings were beginning to be apparent and I knew I had better tell our commanding officer how we felt about each other. We were not supposed to have romantic relationships. He looked at me thoroughly and I was sure this would be reported to London. We were waiting for the order to transfer one of us, but it never came. I don't think this was due to any tender heartedness at Whitehall, but probably it was thought best to keep it in the family where we could be watched under the all seeing eye of SOE.

There were few places at Wanborough where we could be alone. Sometimes we sat and talked in an empty staff car and sometimes in the chapel.

One warm, summer day we took the train to Cambridge. We rented a punt and drifted along the Cam. We had brought our lunch and a portable gramaphone. Arlette had an amazing collection of records and was especially fond of Glenn Miller. I had grown up surrounded by music and it was important to us both.

I remember the day well: the angry swan that hissed at us, the way Arlette laughed uninhibitedly and teased me about the English being so undemonstrative, too restrained. Together we sang "Deep Purple" not knowing then how prophetic the words were.

That day the war seemed far away. We talked of marriage, the pros and cons. We could not predict the end of the war and decided not to wait. We thought our superiors would not approve and certainly not Arlette's parents. Why would they want this extraordinary daughter of theirs to marry a boy she met by chance? An Englishman? An Anglican? And this is exactly how they did react, but when Arlette made up her mind she had a will of iron. In the end they consented.

When I told my commanding officer in London what we planned he tried to dissuade me. "You are much too young for marriage," growled Colin Gubbins. I maintained that if I was old enough to fight for the King then I was old enough to marry. Scowls, but no prohibition.

We were married in Saint Paul's Church with her parents and my best man as the only attendees. The priest hurried through the service and kept pushing his glasses back up from the end of his nose. My new in-laws stood tall and quiet beside each other.

We were all laughing as we came out of church. Arlette and I had been given a weekend pass. "Compassionate leave," my CO said. "Only a short weekend, I regret. Call it passionate leave."

We hailed a passing taxi and the five of us managed to squeeze into the back. We told the driver we had just been married and wanted to go to the Ritz Hotel to celebrate. He took us there, all smiles, and when we arrived I offered him a pound note. He waved my hand away and said, " 'Appy years ahead, Sir and Lady. Lor luv you, Sir.

This one is on the 'ouse." As he drove off I could see him wiping his eyes with a red handkerchief.

Somehow we would survive the war and our love would last for long years ahead.

chapter 2

ENGLAND BETWEEN TWO WARS was a peaceful, happy place in which to grow up. Manners and customs had not changed since the Victorian era and children knew what was expected of them and there was comfort in following the rules.

I was born in the spring of 1924, the middle of five children: two brothers and two sisters. Our family home was a big, rambling farmhouse that stood near many ancient manor houses in Cornwall. We children played hide and seek among the many ruins, stalked one another in the rolling countryside, rode behind the hunt, and traversed the neighborhood in pony and trap. We were Cornish gentry with the considerable status that comes with heritage and ancestry in the complicated British class system. I spent much of my time with our old vicar of whom I was very fond. He was gentle and warmhearted and I spent more time in church than any other member of the family and thought that someday I might become an Anglican parson. That influence has never left me and my strong faith became a large part of my survival tools later on.

My Victorian father, Robert Keith Armstrong, was a senior member of a banking chain: a hard-working, strong-minded man who I both admired and feared and whose approval I always sought. As a man of high principles he was a stern taskmaster. Whatever the cause there always seemed to be a gulf between my father and me.

He could trace his ancestry to a foot soldier from Guernsey who came across the Channel with the Conquerer, as did many of William of Normandy's men. Over one hundred years later a descendant was living in Somerset holding various manors of the abbey of Glastonbury. After him came a Knight who fought with King Edward the First against Robert the Bruce at the Battle of Falkirk in 1209. Another was a captain in the Royalist Army and had to flee to France until the monarchy was restored in 1660.

Many forebears were humble farmers in Cornwall or Somerset, but there were enough heroes on the family tree to make a deep impression on a growing boy and cause him to wonder if he could ever measure up to ancestral figures like Sir Richard Grenville or Sir Francis Drake.

My father was endowed with a quick mind and prodigious energy. He worked ceaselessly in his garden. I can recall all of us setting out cabbage plants by torchlight and we were expected to be just as hard working and uncomplaining as he. There was little praise for work well done; it was just expected. Although there was a gardener and a farm hand, other chores included sawing logs, gathering firewood for our many fireplaces, cleaning out stables, feeding and tending the farm animals. (I milked the goats.) Although my father was careful with pocket money, he did buy me a pony, but I had to forego a saddle until I could learn to ride bareback. When the beautiful saddle was finally given to me I had a hard time adjusting to it.

My mother, the former Elizabeth St. Aubyn, was of Irish, Cornish, and German background. She was warm, charming, temperamental, and very gifted musically. I can remember as a young boy the thrill of watching rehearsals of the local operatic group and being so proud of my mother's abilities. The theater has had an appeal for me ever since. My mother was extremely psychic with an uncanny ability to perceive events taking place elsewhere, or to catch glimpses of the future: what her Celtic ancestors would have called 'second sight.'

My paternal grandfather and I were very close. I was always happy when I was able to visit my grandparents in Somerset. I spent so many long summers there that at one point they were concerned that I was picking up the local accent. There was a sleepy little railway station at Ilminster and I savored the feeling of warmth and acceptance that awaited me there. I also visited an aunt and uncle in Crewkerne where they had a farm supply store. At the station in Crewkerne I would be met by a horse drawn cab with a door at the back, glass windows, and a quilted satin ceiling. Behind my uncle's house was a garden with a fig tree that grew up against the wall. We would sit there for hours in the calm of the English countryside. On Sunday, on the other side of the wall, the bells of the ancient church would be rung. In wonder, I would watch the bell ringers in their Sunday best, jackets off, sleeves rolled up, hats still on, pull on the heavy ropes which carried them up to the belfry ceiling and down again. I was sure someday one, or all would disappear and be snatched into Heaven.

In the early days, because of the lack of praise from my father in any area, I lacked confidence and did poorly at the local grammar school. I had the word "impossible" written across one of my reports and dreaded the reaction at home fearing it would only confirm his opinion of me. Soon after, my grandfather came to my rescue and offered to send me to a good public (private) school in Yorkshire: Ambleton. It was a boarding school of excellent reputation, not quite in the class of Eton or Harrow, but solid enough concerning tradition and standards. The main object of all such schools was to accept young barbarians and teach them gentlemanly behavior so they could eventually become leaders. If this could not be accomplished through teaching, then beating was considered an appropriate alternative. It has been said that there was a streak of sadism in British public schools in those days, and largely, I think the charge is true. Caning was a standard form of punishment. It required young boys to receive strokes with a four foot bamboo cane, sometimes on bare skin. It certainly was a procedure likely to awaken any latent cruelty in the flogger, and it probably had sexual overtones as well.

Many years later, we joked that attending a good English public school prepared one for anything the Germans or Communists could dish out.

I missed those happy days in Somerset when I suddenly found myself as a ten year old "new boy" at Ambleton. My early years there were plagued by illnesses: the worst was appendicitis followed by peritonitis. The convalescence made it difficult for me to participate in sports, and thus deprived me of that all important road to popularity and acceptance in school life. As a student I was average, but showed great aptitude in languages and mathematics.

The Headmaster, The Reverend Canon Paul Andrew Scott, was cold and forbidding. At least he seemed so to me. He had his favorites, usually those who shined in the classroom or on the rugby field and his list of "special boys" did not include me.

The senior boy, in my time, was a fierce individual who obviously enjoyed his privilege. He was annoyed by the fact that during my convalescence I was ineligible for punishment. When I improved and the ban was lifted he decided to make up for lost time. For some minor infraction I was summoned to the senior dormitory, told to drop my pajama bottoms, bend over and hold the lowest rung of the bed. Then the senior boy gave me eight blows as close together as he could. Blood ran down my legs and the pain was terrible. The senior boy held out his hand to shake as if to say, "No hard feelings." This was the traditional finale to beatings, but to me it was the final insult. A wave of rage came over me and I smashed him hard in the face.

I stood there shaking and then went back to my own dormitory where the other boys gathered around after seeing my bloody pajamas. They wanted to see the damage, crying out, "Good heavens," and "What a beast." "You had better see matron, Armstrong." Instead of showing my wounds I went into the bathroom and soaked my bottom in alternately hot and cold water. I went to bed and slept on my face all night.

The next morning there was a definite buzz going around at breakfast. Soon after I was summoned to the Headmaster's study. He gave me four light strokes after scolding me for striking the senior boy. "Bad form, Armstrong." With a flash of defiance I said I would do it again if given cause. Canon Scott looked at me in amazement and dismissed me. After that he seemed to treat me with a little less scorn and sarcasm. The senior boy was made to apologize also, but his eyes flashed resentment. I suppose he has long since forgotten me. I have not forgotten him.

Of course there were happy memories, too: singing in our productions of Gilbert and Sullivan, and fishing in the small river that flowed past the school. Our English Literature teacher was a fierce Scotsman and he taught me to box and I learned how important it was to defend myself.

I didn't appear to be a rule breaker, but the inner imp in me took great delight in attempting to 'bypass' some of the regulations and not get caught. We were not permitted to leave the school without permission which was seldom granted. There was a drainpipe that was perfect for shimmying down. Once I went to visit a girl who lived in town and did a little harmless flirting. On other occasions I joined an old poacher who offered to take me on rabbit hunting forays by moonlight. We managed to catch one or two of the scampering little ones with wire snares. When I climbed back to the dormitory it was often within ear shot of some unsuspecting faculty. This ability to move swiftly and quietly served me well later.

As we moved toward the end of term in the early years of the war, many of the senior boys were joining the service. Although I was a bit younger and had not finished school I was encouraged to follow their lead. I know the Headmaster was glad to be rid of me. Later when he was consulted about my ability as an officer I am sure he was the main reason for my being denied.

First I tried the Royal Navy thinking my chances were better at becoming an officer, but I was turned down. Then I decided to join the Royal Army Service Corps and try again. The RASC was not the most glamorous branch of the Army, but I thought my chances of a commission were better there. Again: turned down. My self confidence was at an all time low. I had been to a good school, spoke with an unmistakable public school accent, and had spent three years in Officers Training Corps and thought myself more eligible than many others who were being accepted.

On the day I joined the service I prayed that I would be shown the way and accept whatever God had planned for me.

chapter 3

ONE MORNING I HAD just parked the lorry when I heard a tap on the window. Startled, I looked around to see a Captain standing there. I didn't know him, but he seemed to know all about me.

"Someone who has been to a good school and had three years of Officer Training Corps should be doing more than repairing equipment," he said. "There is more important and exciting work to be done and I'll tell you about it if you're interested."

I was eager to hear what the Captain had to say. I had considered my work in the RASC important to the war effort if certainly not glamorous, but from childhood I had been impressed by the exploits of ancestors and here was a chance to impress my father and join those illustrious ranks. How could I know that it would be decades before my family would know anything of what I had done in the war and even after?

The Captain said that he belonged to an organization called SOE(Special Operations Executive). It had been formed under the Ministry of Economic Warfare, but had special functions of its own. If I would be willing to undergo a series of interviews and tests I might become a member of SOE. My duties would be explained later. I was not to discuss our conversation with any living soul: not to any of the men in camp; not to my family; not to friends. Talking about any of this would have dire consequences. I assured him I would not breathe a word to anyone. What choice would I have made had I known that this secrecy and subterfuge would haunt me for the rest of my life? More to the point; did I have a choice? I had no idea why I had been selected. I was not told that losses among agents inserted into Europe were so high that SOE was being forced to recruit green soldiers like me.

Soon I was summoned to Lansdowne House in Berkeley Square

for interviews. I was asked all sorts of questions about myself, my family, my interests in sports, languages, all about my school, my emotional makeup, special aptitudes, etc. Shortly I was told that I was no longer a lorry driver, but for one day a civilian working for the Ministry of Economic Warfare. Then I immediately became a Subaltern(Lieutenant) in SOE.

During the testing period I had a very surprising invitation for lunch at the Savoy Hotel with a Lieutenant Colonel Claude Dansey. I did not know at the time that he was second in command in the branch of the Secret Service known as MI6 (Military Intelligence). In time he became an influential friend and mentor who played an important part in my life. That day he was just a stranger, who for some unknown reason had invited me to lunch.

Claude Dansey was tall, lean, with a clipped mustache, and stern eyes that looked through steel rimmed glasses. He had a staccato way of speaking and often ended a statement by barking a question: "D'you see? D'you understand?" He was accompanied by another officer who said very little, but seemed to be making mental notes all during lunch. My attention was easily diverted to the food as it was rare in those days to have anything matching the fare at the Savoy. I know that I ate heartily and consumed everything set before me even though I was nervous about the meeting.

Dansey said, "I know that you have been approached by SOE. If you are accepted by SOE I have a very special and secret assignment for you, d'you see?"

Connected to MI6 was a section called 'Z' one function of which was to keep a constant watch on all activities of SOE. If I joined SOE Colonel Dansey wanted me to be a part of the Z surveillance team. I would make reports to him on everything I experienced and observed. I did make these reports to him until the spring of 1944. I am unaware of any significance to my reports. Again, I was to tell no one. If I did talk ... "you won't live very long, d'you understand? You'll go out feet first, d'you see?"

I did see and I sure did understand! I was being asked to spy on an organization to which I did not yet belong for another organization about which I knew very little. How could they trust a teenage boy to do this kind of work? They most likely thought that I would never be suspected and was so full of my new importance that I would follow directions to a *T*.

Special Operations Executive had been created in the summer of 1940. The original purpose was economic sabotage of the German war effort. It called for the rapid training of agents for infiltration into countries controlled by the Nazis. Some of the agents were recruited from the flood of refugees who came pouring into Britain after the fall of France. It was inevitable that some of these foreigners would be Nazi agents seeking to infiltrate our Intelligence branches and some native born Britons became traitors, too. As a naive teenager I knew nothing about this.

SOE had sections devoted to almost all the occupied countries and I was assigned to F Section. F stood for French, and was an assignment that pleased me because of my love for, and familiarity with, the language and my success with it in school. N Section was for Holland (Netherlands), B for Belgium and so on. It was later that I learned of the Nazi infiltration into N Section. It became a major scandal that was hushed up and never revealed to this day. The fact that I know the details of its existence is one of the major causes of my ongoing problems.

For the next six weeks I underwent special training with constant emphasis on secrecy. Again I was ordered not to communicate with my family. In due time they would receive letters from me really written by others. Phony addresses and even censor marks were used. This presented no problem for SOE because they had recruited the best forgers that British jails had to offer.

Each trainee was given a code name because real names were never used and we were forbidden to ask any questions about background, etc. My code name became Vapor because of a comment made early in training. One of my officers said, "Armstrong's like a puff of smoke. You know he is around, but he always seems to disappear quickly."

The training was intense. Ways had been devised to test courage and control under stress. We might be sent into the London Underground and made to walk the tracks until a train appeared and then dodge into a recess in the wall or flatten along the rails hoping that a projection would not catch our clothing and drag us to certain death.

We were taught to pick locks, cross rooftops in the dark, break into houses, follow other trainees without being detected, and evade pursuers. We studied silhouettes of enemy and friendly aircraft. Our memories and powers of concentration were always being honed. We played one parlor game as a tool for memory improvement. Objects were placed on a table and we had a brief time to study them. Then the table was covered and we had to make a list of all that we could remember from the table.

Trainees were required to assume new identities and memorize every detail of our imaginary background. Sometimes we were quizzed in the middle of the night and wakened from a deep sleep with a bright light in our eyes: What's your name, where are you from, what's your mother's name, what kind of dog do you have at home, who was your Latin teacher?" The questions were supposed to be answered quickly and perfectly.

One day I was sent to Northumberland House in London and asked to sign the Official Secrets Act. There are many pages to this document, but signers only see the first page where the signature goes. Signing was not a choice. It is an obligatory step for working for the government in any capacity regardless where one is on the scale of importance. I was not concerned with the content of the OSA because I knew that I was, always would, and always have been loyal to the Crown.

Soon after Arlette and I were married we were separated. She continued her training in Britain and I was sent to a secret training camp in Canada. It was a grim place on the shores of Lake Ontario and the most secret of SOE installations. It was simply known as Camp X.

We were flown there in an aircraft with Air Training Auxiliary women pilots. I am not sure if it was said with relief, disbelief, or smugness when my seat mate told me he had been released from a British prison. Did he wonder if I too had been chosen from the pool of prisoners? I said nothing and no more information was forthcoming from him.

Situated to the north of Lake Ontario and bordered on other sides by miles of uninhabited wilderness, Camp X looked barren and forbidding. Approaches from all sides were guarded by British commandos skilled in all quick and lethal means of deterrent.

Our instructors were 'other ranks' (non-com)who told us sternly,"Your officer status does not impress us. You are here to be transformed into top notch killing machines."

We were sent into the wilds alone and without any provisions to survive and return to camp with some pre-determined object. We swam, in full uniform, from one point to another in freezing waters. The object was to survive the attacks of swimmers sent to harass us. I used my water-soaked boots and recently strengthened arms and legs to fight off the attackers.

Training involved learning how to derail or blow up trains; how to dodge bullets and move so quickly that one could disarm the enemy before he could pull the trigger. Speed was constantly stressed and, luckily, I was more agile than most. No mercy was shown and I saw two men killed while I was at Camp X: one drowned in the icy waters of Lake Ontario and the other was shot because live ammunition was used in some training exercises.

The hardest training to endure were the mock interrogation sessions. These were thought to be good preparation for the possibility that we might be captured. The sessions were long and brutal and the pressure never let up. Those who cracked or failed tests disappeared. Some may have been eliminated from the program; others may have been sent to an establishment in Crieff in Scotland. There they would have been held until the end of the war because they knew too much of SOE and its training methods. They knew the location of Camp X and its activities and that had to be kept quiet.

Although I was very fit, strong, and agile, the expectations were extremely high. As the days went by I was not sure if I would pass. Still I was not weeded out. Many, many times since I have wondered when and why it was decided that I was one of those selected to be among the agents chosen to be dispensable. Was it when I was questioned and tested at Lansdowne House? Was it when I was first chosen to be a recruit in SOE? Was it at Wanborough Manor? Or still later at Camp X? Was it when all the training had ended or even later than that? I will never know. Somewhere along the line my fate had been determined.

Miraculously, most of us survived Camp X and the day came for our return home. I descended from the plane aware that I was a totally different man physically. I was not really aware of the emotional changes that had been programmed onto me: a rejection of all normal and conventional values. Ethics? A form of weakness. Compassion? It just gets in the way. Dirty tricks, lies, deceptions? Of course. Murder? If necessary. Loyalty? There is only one loyalty: to the Crown.

I was given a few days' leave: time to spend with Arlette and a quick visit to my parents. When they heard that I had been given a clerk's job the disappointment on my father's face was very obvious. Not only did I keep my true assignment from them, but also that I was married.

My training in Canada had taught me to endure pain, live off the land, move silently and travel with a full pack over open land without being detected. Now I would learn the more deadly aspects of espionage.

Near Christmas I was sent to another SOE facility at Beaulieu, the estate of Lord Montagu at the edge of the New Forest. This was an expanse of land with forests, old growth trees, a lake, and protected by royal command for at least ten centuries. The forest had been vast until many trees were felled to build ships for Sir Frances Drake and others. Several out-buildings had been transformed into bleak dormitories and I was surprised when told that I had been assigned to N Section, not F as I had been before.

Like my mother, I am sensitive to psychic phenomena. Usually I keep such manifestations to myself because people are suspicious of such claims. You are thought to be imagining things or just plain odd, but these things do occur to some people. Near our headquarters was a ruined abbey and one night as I was passing I distinctly heard the sound of chanting. For a moment I thought it might be some form of choir practice in one of the nearby churches, but it had such an out of time quality that I knew it was not. Then as I stood there I perceived … not saw … a dim procession of cowled monks passing. The whole experience lasted only a few seconds, but it was not my imagination. I kept this to myself, but later heard of others experiencing this ghostly chanting and procession. You may or may not believe in the supernatural, but I know what I saw and heard.

The training at Beaulieu lasted several weeks and was as intense as at Camp X, but in other ways it was very different.

One night, after dinner, my instructor drew me aside and said, "You have learned to be a killer, Vapor, but have you ever killed a man?"

Before I could answer he said, "We have arranged to remedy that."

A prisoner from Dartmoor, a convicted murderer serving a life sentence, had been brought to camp. Armed with two knives he would be released in an hour or two near the woods and told that another armed man would be waiting for him. If he could kill this person he was assured his freedom. (I knew that to be a lie.) My assignment was simple: kill or be killed. Jut one more test. If I passed there would be praise from my instructors. If not ...

I was taken to the spot where I was to wait: an open glade not far from a pond. Although the criminal would know where I was, I didn't have his location.

My first reaction was fright. The second was surprise that the powers that be in SOE would have spent so much time, effort, and money on my training only to have me killed by a convict. This strange assignment went beyond all that I had ever believed, and yet seemed consistent with what had been pounded into me for the past several months.

When I moved into the dark forest my heart was pounding furiously and I had to take deep breaths to calm myself. We had been taught how to use knives quickly and deliberately: no wild slashing, no frantic stabbing. Just one clean thrust. I could use both hands equally well. I had prepared my knives by winding the handles with cord that had been soaked in water until they were rough and had a sure grip. I told myself over and over that if I did kill the convict it would be self preservation and not murder.

I moved silently through the cold, damp woods to a point where a path entered the clearing and stood with my back against a tree. As I listened for any noise I realized that the tree gave my back protection, but inhibited my vision. I crawled into a notch about ten feet from the ground. In Canada we had been taught to crouch in this position for hours and those hours passed in agonizing slowness. I thought of Arlette and wondered what she would be told if I died here.

As dawn broke I still heard nothing and saw nothing. I had thoughts of stalking him, but decided against it. My muscles ached from loss of circulation. I wondered how long I should wait and what would happen if I had no encounter at all. Would I be accused of cowardice?

As he was upwind of me, I smelled the man before I saw him. At last I made him out. He was tall and slight and had blond hair. He looked left and right and then came across the clearing and as he passed beneath me I leaped for him. It was an awkward angle and my feet hit his shoulders. He went down and I heard him gasp. I went down too, but was up quicker and was able to parry his first thrust. As I sprang away from him I saw a blinding light as his elbow caught me in the eye.

A knife fight that must end in killing is an ugly thing, but this one did not last very long. Neither of us said a word. We circled each other, knives held low, but as he lunged I caught his wrist and pulled him forward so that I could kick him and throw him over my head to the ground. Before he could recover I was on him: my left knee in the small of his back and my left forearm under his chin. I had driven the knife in my right hand into the ground and grabbed his hair to pull his head back as I swiftly drew the other knife from right to left across his throat. There was a gurgle and rush of blood as the life went out of him. I dropped the dead weight, and shaking, stood up and saw the blood all over my arms and clothes. I looked down and saw his knives wrapped in cord just like mine. I moved away and was violently ill.

Soon I was aware of three men coming into the woods. One was the Colonel of Dutch Section in charge of our training at Beaulieu. One was the 'other rank' who had given me this mission and the third I didn't recognize. The Colonel came to me and said, "Well done!" as if I had just made a good bat in cricket. The other two came forward with a long pole and a length of rope. They tied the body to the pole at both ends and hoisting the pole on their shoulders, walked off as if they had just bagged a deer.

Like a nanny addressing a fretful child, "Come along now and let's get you cleaned up and have a look," said the Colonel.

I followed along silently: relieved, thankful, and aware of the approbation of the others.

A carefully folded tarp had been placed next to one of the outbuildings waiting for whomever it would envelope. I was taken inside and my bleeding wrist was tended to. My bloody clothes were taken away and I took a hot shower, a luxury not allowed in camp. I went to bed and fell into a deep sleep where I should have dreamed of hooded monks, and bloody knives, but I slept soundly and wakened to resume the training as if nothing had happened.

I don't know how many, if any, other SOE trainees ever had the same experience. For their sakes I hope none. The episode was never mentioned again even though I am sure it went on my record and into my confidential file.

chapter 4

FOR A SOLDIER THERE can be no planning. You are just a cog in a giant machine. You go where you are told, do what you are told, and have very little time to think. I could remember killing the convict, but there was little time to think about it: it was a test and I had passed.

After the course at Beaulieu, all training was being conducted on a crash basis. I was given a brief leave and then sent to parachute school at Ringway near Manchester. First we jumped from a tower and then from low flying airplanes, usually at night and often in the rain. I found the tower drops the most nerve racking; the ground seemed to come up at you with a rush and it was difficult to control the chute when falling such a short distance. Sometimes we were dropped, with full pack, into an ice cold lake, then unhooked our harness and swam ashore.

We were taught how to roll from a plane as it was moving on the ground. We were expected to be able to exit this way because the stubby Lysander would only touch down briefly without stopping, let us exit, and keep going for a quick takeoff. We wore helmets and special suits with padding and neck protection. I was deployed this way only once.

With that training behind me I was returned to SOE Headquarters in Dorset Square to wait for my assignment. I had already been assigned to N Section in stead of F. No explanation was offered and I wondered if it was to separate Arlette and me. By now I had learned not to question anything.

One day a Lieutenant Colonel came to see me. After watching me for a few minutes he said, "Well, my boy, this is a very special day for you. One you will never forget. You are going to see the PM."

I stared at him in disbelief. Why on earth would Winston

Churchill want to see an obscure teenage Subaltern in SOE? I had no time to think about it. We were driven off in a staff car along Whitehall toward Downing Street. It was a cool morning with traces of the early rain still on the streets. We arrived at No.10 and a bobby watched as our driver opened the door for us. I stepped out and followed the Lt.Colonel as we were both saluted by the armed sentry at the door. When the door was opened we moved onto a hallway and I found it difficult to believe that all this was happening. I knew my face was flushed and suddenly my collar was much too small.

We were kept waiting only a few minutes when a door opened and a rather small man came forward wearing a dark pinstriped suit and a polka dot bow tie. He was not more than five and a half feet tall and I was amazed at the size of this man who I thought of as the giant who practically held the fate of Britain in his hands. He was pudgy, with a pink complexion, and had sharp eyes under wispy brows. He held some papers in one hand and had a cigar clamped between his teeth. He nodded to the Colonel and took me into a room and closed the door. We were alone.

In a rasping voice that seemed half growl, the prime minister said that he was glad to meet one of his best agents; "really one of the very best." He had a different way of speaking. "Really" sounded like "weally", but I was too nervous and curious to be concerned with speech. As I had been rather average throughout training, how could I be considered one of he best? This praise being heaped on me seemed too exaggerated.

Churchill went on to say that he had a mission for me: a mission of the utmost importance and the utmost secrecy. Again those often heard words: "no one was to know, I could not discuss it with anyone." I would be dropped into Holland taking with me a memorized coded message for the Dutch resistance. "You will be dropped into Gelderland, the south of Holland," he said almost fiercely. "You may be required to bring information back. If you fail, you may never be heard from again. If you succeed," his face broke into a smile, "all of us will be in your debt."

A wave of uncertainty and self doubt swept over me. "But, Sir, I don't speak Dutch."

"Well, my boy, you have two weeks to learn."

Of course, I did not learn much. I was told that the sortie would be carried out at the full moon later that month. Then I was given the message that had to be memorized. It was not very long and I repeated it to him. Part of it concerned the flooding of the lowlands to immobilize the Panzers when the invasion day arrived; the other part concerned figures that I didn't comprehend.

I left No. 10 feeling ten feet tall. I told no one about my meeting, even Arlette. Less than two weeks remained before the full moon and there was much to be done including learning a few phrases of Dutch. Enormous pains were made to establish a plausible fictitious identity. It was decided that I would be a Polish laborer. My identity cards had to be perfect. My clothing had to be of continental origin and even the dust in my cuffs had to be from Polish soil. Eye glasses had to be in keeping with the style of the area and so did the fillings in my teeth. I had only one filling which was removed and replaced in the Polish style of dentistry: one of the first areas that the Gestapo checked in their hunt for spies and saboteurs. The dentist also removed a perfectly good molar to replace it with a false tooth. This was to be filled with a lethal amount of cyanide. This tooth was called an American style screw tooth. It could be chewed on quite safely, but if ground together laterally the tooth would break open and the cyanide would be released. Thus if an agent was captured and tortured beyond endurance his captors would be frustrated by his quick suicide. Agents had been carrying cyanide for years, but sometimes were captured and searched before getting to the capsule in time. This tooth was considered a more efficient tool and I was warned not to become too weak from torture before I could activate the poison.

Some unfortunates, selected to give disinformation to the enemy if captured, tried this tooth only to find out that it was empty. I was one of those with an empty tooth, but didn't know it until a long time later. I did know that I had a very sore jaw that seemed to heal much too slowly and I did not chew very well. If Arlette noticed she said nothing. Perhaps she was familiar with the procedure.

It was an intense life that we lived in wartime London. The air raids continued and at night we heard sirens and could see the searchlights sweeping through the sky over the blacked out city. Arlette and I had a small flat. We knew that the future was unpredictable and it gave our time together a very special meaning. We rarely went to theater or the cinema, but stayed home and spent many hours listening to, and singing along with music on the little wind-up gramophone: Bittersweet, Indian Love Call, and For You Alone ... Caruso's first song sung in English. Decades have passed and I can still remember her: tall, slim, well tanned, dark hair cut short in regulation length and bright blue eyes.

We could not talk to each other about our work, so we talked of the future. Arlette wanted very badly to return to the Congo where her family still owned land. She knew that her father would help me find work. She assured me that I would love it there and she extolled its virtues and the unspoiled quality of it all. The memories of Africa had never left her and she cared little for what was left behind in Belgium. She considered the Congo her real home.

The more I learned about her family's escape, the more my admiration for them grew. They had returned from the Congo only a short time before the Germans overran Belgium and their hostility for the invaders must have been too obvious to be ignored. Arlette's older sister was picked up for questioning and never heard of again. The rest of the family decided to escape before it was too late.

Their plan was to get across the English Channel in a sixteen foot boat, hoping to evade Nazi patrols and be picked up by a British vessel as they neared the coast of England. When she told me about it I was astounded. "Surely that was suicide!"

"Yes," she said, "but it was suicide to stay."

The group had provisions and warm clothing, but were soon soaked with icy spray. They all tried to encourage each other by talking about the freedom they would soon find once on shore. Then miraculously, a British patrol boat (a Grimsby Trawler) appeared out of the mist, spotted them, and picked them up. Eventually, after thorough investigations, the family were allowed to settle in London in an enclave of other Belgian refugees in Belgrave Square.

Arlette had an icy hatred of the Nazis: she called them 'sales Boches' (dirty Huns). I remember her standing in our little kitchen cooking breakfast and telling me quietly that if giving her own life would hasten the end of the war by one hour she would gladly do it.

The days were swiftly coming to an end for our time together and a plane was waiting on a secret airfield in Sussex to carry me away during the full moon.

chapter 5

THE SECRET AIRFIELD IN Bedfordshire was heavily guarded. I was taken there just a few days before the full moon. In England clear weather is not anything on which one can depend, and we could only hope for breaks in the clouds to insure visibility for the signal lights at the drop area. What remains in my memory is the little parachute hut in the far corner of the field. It was only about ten by twelve feet with a shelf running around three sides that was stacked with a dozen or so parachutes. A Royal Air force Sergeant was in charge of fitting them and always said,"God bless Sir, and good luck."

The night came when the weather gods gave us a green light and I stood near the Halifax, parachute in place, my adrenaline pumping, and my jaw throbbing from the "new" tooth. The interview with Churchill left me with the impression that my mission could make a considerable contribution to the war effort ... and might be my only chance to do so!

Another Sergeant stood beside me and said that he would tap me on the shoulder when it was time to jump. "Then move very quickly," he said and I nodded silently.

After midnight we took off for the relatively short flight to Holland. We flew low to avoid enemy radar and I could see the calm waters of the English Channel below. Ahead we could see searchlights from the Coast of Belgium crisscrossing the dark sky. Two of them made a 'v' sign and I took this as a good omen ... Churchill's famous symbol. The pilot seemed to weave back and forth in the searchlights until he found a gap. He advanced his throttle and flew through the gap until a circle of lights appeared. I felt the two taps, stood in the hatchway for a moment and out I went. I counted to three and my chute opened with the familiar shock. There was little time to control my drop as it was important for the pilot to fly as low as was safely

possible to avoid enemy sightings and so that the winds at higher
elevations would not alter my course. I saw the flares below and when
I had almost landed they were extinguished. A moment later I landed
with a jolt and felt strong hands taking my chute and my flight suit
which were buried and covered with leaves. I was already in my Polish
clothing. We were in a forested area which was very unusual for
Holland. Someone whispered a code and I answered appropriately.
Then something was said in Dutch which I didn't understand and I
was hustled into a car with three others. The engine must have been
very fine-tuned because it hardly made a noise as we continued down
dark roads with our lights out. As we went I was praying (and I am
sure so were the others) that no German patrols would find us. We
spoke very little; only one man spoke any English.

Little did I know then, because of the many agents that had
fallen into the waiting arms of the Nazis, that my safe arrival was
not what was anticipated in England. No one was sure on which
side the betrayers were. It was expected that I would be captured,
tortured and give the information (false I found out). The powers
that be were sure I would break. Bad luck for them; good fortune for
me. After the war there were inquiries after inquiries and many of us
thought we knew who the traitor or traitors were, but the betrayals
were hushed up and to this day the information is kept in deep file.
The public must not know that all was not perfect in the Intelligence
community!

I was taken to a safe house near Arnhem where I was told that the
man to whom I was to deliver my messages would appear. He was a
member of the Orde Dienst, the command structure of the Dutch
Resistance. In the meantime I was shown my hiding place under the
floorboards. There was one board that was on a well concealed pivot
and this was used to allow me to crawl in. Many Dutch houses have
a space between the ground floor and the ground and this was to be
my home for the time being. It was dark, cold, and frequented by
rats and I was thankful for my heavy overcoat. The decor left a little
to be desired: wall hangings were cobwebs and the 'carpet' brown
and smelly. I could hear noises upstairs: language that I had only a
glimmer of understanding, doors opening and closing and the usual
sounds of human activity as the occupants went through their day.

The owners apologized for the lack of blankets because every so often the Germans came on 'wool patrols' taking blankets for themselves. I was to use this hole during the daylight hours and could come up at night. I was passed food ... mostly bread and thin soup. When I did come up I had to be ready to dart down quickly in case of patrols coming in the small hours, but it was always a relief to have a change of scene and a little exercise.

The members of the group who were sheltering me reminded me of East Anglia farmers: square built, taciturn, tough, and solid. The German grip on Holland was very tight and the Dutch were determined not to give in to their occupiers. They fought back silently. Many were caught and executed and some were taken to concentration camps. The rest fought on doggedly waiting for the liberation that they were sure would come.

The leader of the group finally contacted me. I remember seeing a pair of lips through the boards and hearing the code that had been given to me. In silence he received the information I had for him. He told me it would be difficult, no impossible, for me to return to England. Nazi patrol boats had closed the ports, and it was too risky for a Lysander to taxi in. He told me that German Intelligence seemed to know of SOE plans in advance. Drops of ammunition constantly fell into Nazi hands and too many agents were picked up and, at gun point, made to transmit radio messages back to England. Even when the messages contained pre-arranged warning signals they were ignored, or perhaps suppressed by someone in SOE.

I was dismayed and disheartened. In England I had been assured that once I had made contact I could be withdrawn quickly. Since I was now relegated to a longer stay in Holland I asked Orde Dienst if I could work with them. I told them of my training in sabotage and demolition and they could always use more men. I waited several days before being notified that I could help. Twice German patrols entered the house and once had a dog with them. I lay motionless while the dog sniffed around the floor, but the owners had spread something along the boards to inhibit the dog's sense of smell. The Luftwaffe police did not find me this time.

Eventually I participated in two operations. One was blowing up a troop train; the other was the destruction of a power station.

Both were very dangerous, but carefully planned and I was relieved to escape boredom and inaction.

The train would consist of a locomotive, three coaches, and two large wagons with slatted sides for carrying animals or freight. Due to Teutonic efficiency we knew the train would pass at a specific spot at a specific time. The tracks were patrolled by guards, but others in the Resistance would eliminate them. Our job was to plant three explosive charges on the tracks where they would be detonated simultaneously: two heavy ones at either end of the train and one in the middle.

We had blackened our faces with soot from the fireplace, wore dark clothing, tight leather gloves, and rubber soled shoes. When the time was right we moved into a waiting car that took us on a circuitous route to a point about one hundred yards from the ambush site. The plastic charges were heavy: perhaps forty or fifty pounds each. We carried them through thick underbrush on a moonless night, but it is amazing how one's eyes can adjust quickly to the dark.

We worked in a triangle: three men to a group responsible to one another. The man at the top of the triangle was the lookout able to signal by flashlight in case of danger or a change in plans. The man on the right was responsible for placing the explosives in position. The one on the left carried the heavy spool of wire and was responsible for the actual detonation at exactly the right moment. We reached the tracks and planted the explosives. We backed off quickly unwinding the wire until we were about eighty yards away. We waited.

I was only doing what I had been trained to do, but I remember the excitement as I heard the distant sound of the train. As predicted it was right on time and we could see the train as it passed over the first charge. When it was in the right place over all charges I pressed the detonator plunger. Suddenly there was a huge sheet of fire. As we raced for our car we could see wheels, timbers and bodies flying through the air. The scene was utter chaos and no one could have survived. We made it back to the safe house where I tried to wash my face although it was hard to remove soot with cold water and poor soap. I was given a bowl of delicious hot soup and we all shared the exhilaration of a successful mission. A somber note reached us the next day: two cars had held Jews headed for the camps. Perhaps their deaths were a merciful alternative to what they were to experience. It troubled me a great deal after the war, even though by then I knew only too well what awaited them in one of those camps.

We had to accept that reprisals would be swift and merciless. After a raid such as ours the Gestapo might chose a street in some nearby town, hammer on the door of the first house, drag out the eldest son, take another victim from the next house and so on until they had enough. The captives were marched to the center of town and executed and often the inhabitants were forced to watch. The irony was that this demonstration did not stop the sabotage: it simply increased the zeal of the resistance movement. The Dutch were never cowed and they remembered. In many places in Europe one can see the names of street signs combined with the names of those who were victims of Nazi reprisals.

The attack on the power station was a more complex operation requiring more men. The others, all Dutch, reminded me of the other Dutchmen who gave the British such a hard time in the last century during The Boer War. Night after night, hiding in the cellar of another house, we listened carefully to the plans for the raid. Dutch cellars can get wet and damp, but this one was large and dry as it was the crypt of an old manor house whose owners were willing to risk their freedom to let us use it. We sat on the tombs of long dead ancestors lined against the wall where we worked out every detail: who would kill the sentries, who would cut the wires, who would place the explosives, how we would escape. The plan was rehearsed many times

Due to my training I was allowed to share command with a tall man named Piet who was born in the Dutch Indies where he had been a planter. Piet stood six feet four, yet his size did not prevent him from moving silently and swiftly. He was twenty-eight and at the time I thought that quite old.

Churchill had declared that we were to harass, destroy, and "set Europe ablaze." This mission was designed to do precisely that. Our target was between Rosendaal and Velp. Closely guarded and surrounded by minefields, it was a primary source of electricity for the German military machine. Two roads, wide enough for a heavy vehicle led east and west through heavy undergrowth to the power station.

There were two rings of security; the outer one was guarded by the Volkstrum (home guard). It was about five hundred and fifty yards from the power station. Usually the Volkstrum were men too old or unfit for active duty, but we heard that these had been hand picked. Six of them patrolled the outer ring working from sentry boxes. The inner ring had five sentries, usually working closer together. There were two towers, but the searchlights on them had been turned off so attention would not be drawn to the installation. There was a sentry in each tower. On the west was a small stream with a wooden bridge. The whole compound was surrounded by a wire fence and heavy locked gates. Our men who had been surveilling the station told us that an officer inspected every six hours during the day and every four hours at night. We learned that the sentries sometimes disobeyed orders and lit cigarettes. We knew that the glow of a cigarette can determine the position of the smoker from forty yards away because, if you watched carefully, you could tell which way the smoker was facing. The sentry boxes were elevated as an advantage for the Germans. That night it worked to our advantage.

Two sentries at each end of the road were armed with sub machine guns and would have to be dealt with first and simultaneously. It was agreed that Piet and I would deal with the sentry on the west. If all went according to timing all thirteen sentries would be dead within five minutes. Then we could carry out the rest of the plan.

It was going to be a brutal operation. During those days I accepted death as a close companion to life. I accepted my own death not just as a possibility, but as a probability. Everything was expendable: equipment, property, homes, and lives. The eliminating of an enemy sentry was not considered taking a life, but as a necessary step towards victory and eventually peace.

Our arms varied. I carried a German sub machine gun known as a Schmeisser MP-2811, and a PO-8 Lugar, a gun known for its accuracy even at considerable distances. Some of us had hand grenades, but the essential weapon was a commando knife with a double sided six inch blade. It was razor sharp and grooved lengthwise for easy withdrawal. Our transportation had German markings and the driver was dressed as a German soldier with all the necessary credentials. Although there were always patrols, we were not challenged.

We left the vehicle and spread out quietly in the heavy, wet foliage keeping to the car tracks to avoid the mines. Our attack was to be two pronged as one side of the installation was a mirror image of the other. The night was moonless and cold. Our breath was muffled by the balaclavas. Nobody spoke: we all knew what to do.

Piet and I moved quietly until we had our assigned sentry in view. We waited motionless and then all of a sudden ... it was too good to be true. At one minute before three o'clock he lit a cigarette. The spurt of flame showed that he was turned away from me facing the direction that Piet planned to take. So the guard became my target. As I stealthily moved toward him I knew that someone else at the other end of the compound would be making the same move at the same time. Seconds later I was crouching behind the sentry box. My heart was pounding, but my breathing was normal and quiet. The attack was impersonal: you have a job to do, you do it and then concentrate on the next task. You move from one planned task to another until the mission has been accomplished, or it has failed.

One point in our favor was the fact that the Germans had designed a secret weapon for us: their own helmets. Unlike most Allied helmets, there was a flap of steel coming down low on the nape of the wearer's neck. If the front of the helmet was grasped suddenly from behind and jerked violently backwards the chin strap would cut into the throat. This tended to stifle a cry and with luck the edge of the rear of the helmet would break the neck.

Five feet away from where I crouched the sentry drew on his cigarette, trying to hide the glow with his cupped hand. I stepped out quickly and jerked his helmet. His head snapped and the cigarette flew from his hand. With my foot around his ankles and a firm grip on his helmet, I drove the knife into his back. As he fell and buckled the knife was almost wrenched from my grip and I had to lean over him and plant my foot close to the blade to draw it out. I rolled him down the slope and into the stream, wedging him against the wooden bridge supports. There was a bubbling sound and then silence.

I gave a short bird call and Piet came towards me. We moved together down the road and took up our rehearsed positions, one on each side where we had been told the patrolling sentry would make his rounds. At six minutes past three he appeared. We were on him before he was aware and with one blow to the neck from Piet he fell to the ground, dead. My strong partner picked him up and laid him in the underbrush. We hid his weapons where we could find them later.

We had to wait for each sentry to complete his circle and as two more came we dispatched them silently. Then we moved towards the inner ring leaving the other sentries in the outer ring to be dealt with by the follow up team. On the other side of the power plant an identical approach had been made. Other men had the task of cutting the power lines that controlled the alarm system. We knew that there was a short time before that would be noticed. We linked up with the others and each of us took a sentry in the inner ring. There was not a single outcry in our fast and ruthless assault. Only one sentry put up any resistance. He slashed the neck of one of our team and would have killed him if we had not come up from behind. Piet broke the German's neck with a quick pull of his helmet. Our wounded companion bandaged himself with the emergency kit that we all carried, but the bleeding continued.

Our two sharpshooters had rifles with silencers and they shot both sentries in the towers with a single shot apiece. The first loud sounds that we heard that night were the bodies of the sentries falling to the ground.

The detonators were ready and the gates were opened with heavy wire cutters. The current was off, so the alarm made no sound. We placed explosives in four pre-determined positions around the power plant. Then we left as silently as we had come, collecting the captured weapons along the way. Piet was carrying our bleeding young partner who was limp. As we came to the wooden bridge we thought our friend was dead, but couldn't see properly in the dark. He was placed gently on the ground near where the sentry lay still in the water. Piet paused to make sure that the young man was dead, and feeling certain that he was, he drew his knife across his throat. We removed his weapons, attached two grenades to his body, moved the pins and rolled his body into the deep water as it was important that he not be identifiable. After seven-seconds we heard the double thump of underwater explosions as we ran to our waiting car. Ten minutes later we heard the first of four massive explosions and saw a huge glare behind us. There was an even greater explosion as the whole installation seemed to fly into space. As the glare faded we started dropping from the vehicle at two minute intervals, hitting the ground and rolling into the dark; a method used to prevent us from being captured all at once.

With thanks to the careful planning, our casualties were very light: one dead, two with minor injuries, and one broken toe. We learned that the installation and everything around it was destroyed. The Germans were understandably furious and our raid set off a series of brutal reprisals. Successful though we had been, it was hard to feel satisfaction when we knew that innocent people were suffering because of what we had done. Just one more incident to add to my regrets after the war.

A report of the destruction of the power plant went directly to Heinrich Himmler, head of the Gestapo. Somehow, later on, my identity was known and I was associated with the raid. Another result of the raid was that my name had been added to the death list compiled by, or for, Obersleutnant Otto Scorzeny.

My third sortie from the house was less successful. We went out after curfew, but the operation was called off. As we were returning, a German patrol car stopped us. They didn't know we were Resistance, but breaking curfew was a serious crime and those who broke curfew were seriously handled. Our papers were given a cursory glance, but it made no difference and we were carried off to the large prison at Scheveningen and tossed into a cell. Not one word was spoken and finally a photographer came to take pictures of us. I was sure that eventually we would be taken to headquarters in Arnhem for inter-rogation. I had no illusions about the methods they would use to get information from me, so I spent a cold and miserable night. We were held in a cell block separate from the rest of the prison and in the morning hustled into a van for transfer, but the Dutch had infor-mation concerning our transfer. A road block had been set up and fortunately the van in which we were locked was not heavily guarded. There was a driver and one armed guard seated beside him. When the van had to slow down for a barrier a burst of small arms fire shot out the tires and another killed the driver and wounded the guard. We captives, sitting in the dark van, looked at each other with hopeful expressions. In a moment, with a great wrenching of metal, the rear door of the van opened and we came stumbling out. Our rescuers whisked us to a waiting car and drove away very quickly. As I looked back there was a great flash and the whole scene exploded.

I was taken to a new house and hidden for several days with another Resistance group. Eventually the leader of that group came to the house and said, "The Nazis have learned that you were involved in the destruction of the power plant and the prison picture of you has been posted in public places all over the country. You are a wanted criminal and should no longer stay in Holland. We will send you down the Comet Line."

I was eager to leave and more than ready to go as my usefulness in Holland had ended and I didn't quarrel with the decision. The way might be long and arduous, but at the end of the road was Arlette.

chapter 6

LA LIGNE COMET, THE Belgian escape route for downed fliers, was started in 1941 by a brave and very determined girl named Andrée de Jongh, called Dédée. It ran from Brussels south through occupied France to the Spanish border, a distance of some 700 miles. It was a shadowy chain of human contacts, guides, and safe houses where fugitives might be sheltered for a few hours or a few days. Most of the men aided in this way were downed fliers, but other escapees also used the Comet Line. Members of air crews picked up by the Resistance before the Nazis could capture them were fortunate, but they could be in danger from the wrath of angry civilians who sometimes considered them murderers of women and children. In Germany some were hanged from lamp posts, and in Holland, Belgium, and France, some were handed over to the Germans instead of the Resistance. After a fugitive was able to avoid capture he still needed good fortune and a strong constitution to reach the Spanish border. He might travel the length of France only to be captured crossing the Pyrénées. Some travelers were more skillful and determined than others and it helped to be resourceful, ruthless, highly motivated, and tough.

My Dutch friends gave me their blessing and a valuable commodity: a bicycle! Before they sent me on my way, however, the leader of the group talked to me very seriously.

" Members of the underground are very concerned about traitors at work in both Holland and Britain. Too many fleeing by way of the Comet Line are being picked up by the authorities as are men and women of the Resistance who were trying to help them. Air drops of ammunition are falling into German hands and SOE agents are being captured and shot as they land. Radio messages to London are being ignored, or perhaps suppressed."

He wanted me to carry a coded message down the Comet Line

and deliver it when I reached England, and not to share it for any reason with the British in friendly Portugal. I was not told what the message meant. All I needed to know was that it was of the utmost importance. I saw the troubled look on the leader's face and I knew he was worried that I wouldn't get through safely. I told him I would do my best.

My first guide was a very silent Dutchman who came at night and waited outside. I never saw his face. I had the coded message in my mind, two compasses hidden in my buttons, and a map hidden in the hollow of my shoe. Going along the dark roads, I followed the Dutchman's light on the back of his bicycle as closely as I could. I knew he would leave me before dawn, with instructions and codes for my next rendezvous the following night. I would be sleeping in the woods during the day, but this didn't trouble me as it was far better than the smells in my dark under-the-floor hideout.

My Dutch friends warned me not to approach farm houses, laborers in the fields, and to stay completely to myself because some of the locals were so afraid of the Germans that I might be turned in without any hesitation. I might have to steal food and there were times when I did. I am sure my Dutch friends had their doubts about my survival, but they badly wanted the message taken to England. I was to say nothing, trust nobody, not even clergy. Always obey my guides.

The plan was to cross the border between Holland and Belgium near the city of Tilburg. Crossing the border turned out to be easy. I walked across with a group of laborers and only once did I have any real trouble. As I was pushing my bicycle along the side track of a small village near midnight, a German sentry stepped out of the shadows and ordered me to identify myself. I approached submissively, but not in the way he expected. I dropped the bicycle when I was close to him and rushed him, zig-zagging the last few feet. He tried to get his rifle up, but it is difficult to aim at a leaping shadow in the dark, especially when you are not prepared for an attack. I rammed him just above his belt buckle and he went over backwards. Before he could cry out I was on top of him with my hands on his throat. He struggled and my desperation gave me strength. His hands clutched at my fingers but he could not move them. I choked him until I was sure he was dead and then dragged him into an opening between two houses. I picked up my bicycle and moved on.

As I recall, the safe house in Brussels was in the Rue Babylon. Several fliers were sheltered there: RAF, USAAF, one or two New Zealanders. We didn't talk much to one another; we were all weary. I didn't trust anyone.

From Brussels I was guided on to Paris, where the refuge was run by two very brave women. Later they were seized by the Gestapo and sent to their deaths in one of the concentration camps. Altogether, more than 700 downed fliers and others were rescued, but the cost was high. At least 20 members of the Resistance were executed by firing squad, including Frederic de Jongh, Dédée's father. Another 130 died from starvation or brutality in the various concentration camps. These heroes and heroines are largely forgotten now, but the free world owes them all an enormous debt.

The Resistance would assign a guide to fugitives to assist them from Paris to the border with Spain. In my case it was a young Belgian woman, about my own age. She was petite, very fit, and had been trained in the British Isles. She had returned to Paris from the south of France to aid more fugitives. Although I was not a flier I was assigned to her and another girl who was shepherding two downed fliers.

We all boarded a crowded train for what seemed an endlessly long ride: almost fourteen hours to Bordeaux. German police patrols came through the train intermittently to check identity cards and papers. I can still remember those cold eyes searching the photos on the forged papers, then the face of the traveller, and back again to the papers. I had dyed my hair, and there are other ways to make yourself look different; you can also change your appearance by your posture and the way you walk. I thought it would be unlikely that I would be recognized as the subject on posts and train stations in Holland, but at times I had a dreaded fear that the Nazis were letting me escape until I could be captured and lead them to a whole section of the Comet Line. My guide knew nothing about me being known to the Nazis as a criminal, but if she had I am sure that she would not have hesitated to take me along. I owe my life to her and remember her with deep affection. We correspond to this day and enjoy occasional reunions.

During the trip the young women chatted in French to each other. Seated opposite me was a young RAF Navigator, shot down some days before. He had been warned not to open his mouth as he spoke no French, and he had been forbidden to walk if any Germans were close by as natives of different countries walk in different ways. The Nazis, police, and others were taught to watch for mannerisms. I was told to speak to him briefly in French whenever the Luftwaffe police came through. I did and could see that he was under increasing strain. We were determined that he not be a threat and we watched him carefully.

Our two courageous shepherdesses brought their fairly silent and tense charges to Bordeaux. From Bordeaux we continued on to Dax. Bicycles were waiting for us in the luggage area of the station and we cycled into the night towards Anglet. With our lights off we kept a wary eye for German patrols. At one junction we heard a patrol coming and the guide, myself and the flier dived into a ditch. We submerged our bicycles in the stinking mud. When we finally climbed out the seats were slippery and it was miserable cycling onwards. I had a flat tire and was able to find a rain barrel to put the tire in and then found the hole as the bubbles came up. With thanks to a small kit hanging from the back of the bike I was able to repair the inner tube and ride on.

We were sticky, and surely smelly, as we met the de Greef family. Madame Elvire was a Belgian woman about thirty-five, small, with red hair: known as Tante Go. Her husband, called l'Oncle, managed to get a job in the Kommandatur as an interpreter. This gave him the opportunity to forge documents using official rubber stamps. The de Greefs had tried to leave Europe when the Germans invaded, but unable to do so they moved into a deserted house in France near the sea. They carried out their activities from there. Communications with London were rare, but finally word came that I was to aid the Resistance in any way that I could and remain where I was until further notice. The orders were disappointing, but I had no other option. The de Greefs put me in touch with a band of Basque Resistance whose mission was to harass the enemy in much the same way as the underground. These fierce men were Communists, but I had no idea of that at the time, nor did I even know what Communism was. They barely tolerated me and a French Canadian, and spoke no English but only Basque which neither of us understood. We lived in the open and sometimes had to steal food. Our clothing soon became inadequate in the cold weather and our shoes wore worn through. It was a miserable existence and fortunately for me it did not last long. In the spring word came that I was to make my way to Portugal and home and the de Greefs helped me reach another guide.

I was taken to Ciboure, a small coastal town close to the Spanish border. Madame Barbara Maguirza, and her sixteen year old son Robert, ran a small bistro on the Place de Fronton. Two of us were hidden there in the small back room adjacent to the bar/cafe which was frequented by German sailors and soldiers. Only a rough curtain separated the rooms and we spent the better part of two days under a table behind a cloth hanging down almost to the floor. The owners, both French Basques, often pulled the curtain aside so we could actually see the enemy. The Maguirzas, as careful as they were to keep us hidden, seemed to accept the risk stoically and expected us to do the same. They were not deeply involved in the Resistance movement, but provided an occasional safe house. Sadly, after the war, Madame Maguirza was accused of collaboration with the enemy, but it was never proven.

After a few days, Robert guided me to another house and on the way I was able to spend a few minutes in a nearby church. With the door just cracked open, Robert acted as lookout as I prayed. How that lifted my spirits and gave me strength to move on! I spent a few nights in the cellar of Madame Cataline Aguirre. She was a thin, small, dynamic woman whose bravery earned her honors after the war. She arranged my contact with Florentino, a stocky, Basque peasant, who spoke hardly any French or Spanish; just Basque, a language of virtually unknown origin.

Florentino was about forty-five and knew the mountain passes intimately. During the Spanish Civil War he had guided many fugitives from Spain into France. Now he was helping downed fliers and others in the reverse direction. Larger than most Basques, he was extremely strong. He agreed to lead me and two others, both airmen, across the border to the Spanish town of Irun.

Through an interpreter he said, "We will travel by night and the going will be cold, difficult, and dangerous. If anyone lags or disobeys orders I will cut your throat."

I had no doubt that he would.

Later, when I was safe In England, a German patrol caught Florentino with a close burst of machine gun fire, shattering his legs. They took him as a prisoner to the hospital in Bayonne. There he lay for days receiving excellent care from the nuns who knew him to be a hero of the Resistance. Suddenly one day, a detachment of Nazi soldiers appeared, led by a menacing Gestapo officer brandishing orders to transfer Florentino to another hospital. This officer treated the wounded Basque so roughly and brutally that the nuns were horrified and protested vehemently. Florentino was almost dragged to a waiting car and driven away. What only Florentino knew was that the sadistic officer was Tante Go's husband, Fernand. They made off with Florentino and the Nazis never did find him.

Most of the mountain passes were still heavy with snow, which meant that patrols might not be watching with great vigilance. There were one or two routes in lower altitudes where, with good fortune and a good guide, a small party might get through.

It was a fearful journey: mostly uphill, splashing through icy streams and stumbling and falling in the dark. We struggled to keep up with our tireless leader. I had a pistol which the de Greefs had provided, but the two airmen were unarmed. When one of them became exhausted trying to cross a raging torrent, Florentino picked him up like a child, held high above his head, and carried him to the other side.

Our final barrier was the fast flowing Bidassoa River which separated France from Spain. Florentino, with the wave of one mighty arm, pointed us across the river in the direction of a farm near Irun which was one of the last stages on the Comet Line. As one of us was speaking to him he melted into the shadows and was gone. Half an hour later wet, cold, and weary we ran straight into a detachment of Spanish police armed with sub-machine guns. We had been warned to avoid them if possible, but not to argue with them. There was no chance to escape. As they surrounded us with guns pointed I threw my gun into the bushes. They herded us and took us towards Irun.

Since Spain was neutral, we were entitled under International Law, to be interned.

Knowing that the Franco regime sympathized with the Nazis I was afraid that we might be handed over to the Gestapo. I had heard that this happened sometimes, no doubt for an exchange of money. I thanked God that evidently the Spanish did not know I was wanted. After what seemed an endless walk, my flier companions and I were placed in Irun jail. The next day, manacled, we were transported to the notorious Miranda del Ebro prison on the Ebro River in Castille. This was a disgusting place consisting of huts surrounded by barbed wire, searchlights, and guards with machine guns. The only light came from Sardine oil lamps. The food was wretched (worse than at school!) and the punishments were severe. The method of execution was by garrote: said to be quick and relatively painless. It did not seem so to me.

Many of the prisoners were men who had fought on the losing side in the Spanish Civil War. The veterans of that war were treated harshly by the Franco regime. The guards were surly, watchful, and tough. I did my best to keep out of their way, keep my mouth shut, and be inconspicuous. I said nothing to my fellow prisoners because I was sure there were informers among them. I convinced myself that British Intelligence would find out that I had been imprisoned and would arrange for my release. Meanwhile I would have to survive in this dreadful place, which I knew had to be the worst Hell-hole on earth. The time would come when I would look back on Miranda del Ebro as a place of enlightenment and benevolence. As I had done all the way down the Comet Line I kept my hopes alive by intense prayer and thoughts of Arlette and of the moment when we could be together again. To some extent this kept at bay the misery that I saw all around, but there were times when I came close to despair. All of us were constantly hungry, and my clothes were reduced almost to rags. The nights were cold and crawling with vermin.

After some weeks British Intelligence did learn that some of us were incarcerated in Mirando. A British Major came up from Madrid to look us over and make sure that we were not impostors. He was a supercilious fellow who looked at us in disgust. I must admit it was hard to blame him. We were filthy, and lousy, with shaved heads and unshaven faces. I was wearing an American battle jacket acquired somehow, my shoes were worn through and my dirt-encrusted pants hung on me from the months of half starvation. When we were declared genuine we were driven to the British Embassy in Madrid where we were deloused and given hot baths and clean clothes. We were fed, but the food was too rich for our stomachs and we were all sick.

The next stage of the journey was Portugal, another neutral country, but much friendlier than Spain. I was given new identity papers as a worker from Southern Ireland, probably because I can imitate a very credible brogue. We were driven at night, in great secrecy and stealth, to Lisbon.

In 1944, Lisbon was a wartime capitol full of bright lights and gaiety. It was also a hot bed of spies and agents of all nationalities. German officers in civilian clothes with monocles and dueling scars sat in the sidewalk cafes seeming overbearing and arrogant. Japan had its spies, too. They kept a close eye on shipping, and when a vessel was sunk off the coast, the Japanese used their fast outboard motors to reach the scene to search for any information or intelligence that might be of use to the Axis.

After the hazards of the Comet Line, Lisbon was an exhilarating experience. There was food, there were good wines, and I was no longer looking over my shoulder, although habits die hard, and I was still wary of every footstep. Most of all I knew my reunion with Arlette was not far away.

I was flown across the Bay of Biscay with a few others and headed for home. It was a hazardous flight due to the presence of German fighters based along the coast of France. It was on a similar flight that the film star Leslie Howard lost his life. (It is believed that he was carrying dispatches for the British government.) When we landed in England some were un-British enough to kneel and kiss the ground. I didn't join in, but could understand the feelings of those who did.

I was in hospital briefly and given the very best attention and care. I was not allowed to contact anyone until I had been debriefed at the Royal Patriotic School in Wandsworth, London. It was Colin Gubbins who presided and received the coded messages from Holland. It was received in silence and I had the feeling that my superiors thought they had better sources of information. I did not expect gushes of thanks, nor did I receive them. I wondered if Winston Churchill had heard of my return and whether I would be summoned to report to him. No word came. I had been sworn not to discuss our meeting with anyone, and I had not.

When I finished my reports I was permitted to telephone my parents. They asked me if I could say where I had been and I made light of it saying I had been overseas, but not in a combat area. I could hear the disappointment in my father's voice and I was saddened by his attitude. I could not tell him anything until years and years later.

All over the British Isles mighty forces were assembling for Operation Overlord, the long awaited invasion of Europe. I felt deeply for those people I had met and for all those who were suffering under the bloody yoke of Hitler. I prayed for a fast and successful victory. London was a bustling hive of activity, but none of this mattered to me at that moment. I needed peace, rest, and a reunion with Arlette. I knew she would be at our flat as soon after work as she could. I had taken the usual three taxis, and I knew she would be doing the same: standard procedure for most in SOE.

At last there was the sound of the key in the lock. I heard the door open. I was home. She was safe. There was complete joy in seeing each other, an emotion surely understood by any in the same situation.

chapter 7

BRIGADIER COLIN GUBBINS, LATER to be Major General Sir Colin Gubbins, was a tough, unflinching, uncompromising soldier capable of being entirely ruthless where his job was concerned. Winston Churchill had chosen him to carry out the mission of Special Operations Executive which was to "set Europe ablaze." We called our leader "Gubby"(not to his face) or sometimes "Gubski" a tribute to his legendary exploits in Poland at the beginning of the war.

I was always uneasy about my secret role as a member of "Z" and when I came back from Portugal I was relieved to be told that I no longer had to report to Claude Dansey. I was quite sure if my connection with "Z" had come to the attention of Colin Gubbins he would have thrown me from the nearest window.

In those days there was great rivalry and suspicion between SOE and MI6 and these two were also frowned upon by the regular line officers who often said their work was useless. "Playing silly buggers," they liked to call it. Some even said they wanted nothing to do with a "gang of hired assassins" as gentlemen did not conduct themselves in such brutal and devious ways. There was spasmodic cooperation of the two with the Free French under Charles de Gaulle and Colin Gubbins and Claude Dansey constantly had to fight for cooperation and support for missions. The RAF provided aircraft, sometimes grudgingly. At one point when requests were ignored for handguns and ammunition for drops to Resistance groups, SOE contacted the police in New York City for help. The police in turn appealed to the Mafia and SOE received a shipment of .32 caliber automatics. The Mafia promised to send ammunition later, and they did.

D-Day came on June 6, 1944. Now British troops were fighting on the Continent. I had never been in combat as a regular soldier and asked Colin Gubbins for reassignment.

Shaking his head he said, "Just be patient. You will get all the combat you need. We have other plans for you. There's an operation in the works. You will be told about it when the time comes."

The operation, Market Garden, called for a massive drop in southern Holland. It was designed to outflank the German armies in Belgium and France with the hope of ending the war before the winter set in. This assault was three months away. In the meantime I was to spend the summer with airborne troops and if I was needed I would make a sortie into France, which I did. I was content with this as it gave me more time to spend with Arlette. I knew if she became pregnant she would not be allowed to continue her highly dangerous missions into France and Belgium and I did my best to make this a reality. When she did become pregnant she was happy to be expecting our baby in November, but insisted that she would return to the field quickly.

" I could have this baby in the bush and be fit for safari in a week," she said, and added with great feeling, "I know that if anything happens to me you will take care of the baby."

My chances of survival were no better than hers, but I didn't say so. There were many young couples like us living from one day to the next and grateful for that. Looking back I know that those few short months in the summer of 1944 that we spent together were some of the happiest of our lives.

Arlette continued working at SOE headquarters in Dorset Square and I went off for specialized training with the airborne troops at Thame Park near Oxford. The paratroopers knew I was not one of them, but they accepted me along with a few others without asking questions. I worked at becoming more proficient with radio, knife, and Sten gun. Sometimes I was able to get to London and be with Arlette for a few days. I could not take her to visit my parents because our marriage and my activities were still a secret. Once we obtained a pass to visit Cornwall, at that time a restricted area. I showed her the rugged and magnificent land where my ancestors were born and the church where they had worshipped and were buried long before the Reformation.

Arlette told me almost nothing of her work in F Section, and I never discussed mine. I was sure that when she made her flights from

England she left from the same airfield at Sandy, probably with the same RAF sergeant adjusting her parachute in the little hut in the corner of the field. I never knew how she was returned to England. Instead of the duties of war we did what young couples usually did; we fed the ducks and walked in Green Park; we danced at the Hammersmith Palais de Danse, a very ordinary place despite its fancy French name, where the large dance floor was crowded with girls and men in the uniforms of many countries.

By now the Buzz Bombs were hammering London. They were faster than most aircraft and only our Typhoon fighters could overtake them. Anti-aircraft fire downed some, and the cables of the barrage balloons snared a few others, but many got through. You could see the fire trail of their primitive, but effective engines against the night sky and as long as you could still hear the stutter of their engines you were in no immediate danger, but when the noise stopped you knew that a thousand pounds of explosive was falling from the sky. The blast effect of these missiles was especially severe and air raid wardens and fire fighters went about their business with tireless dedication. The people of London endured this with the same dogged determination that they had during the Blitz.

As with many others, I thought Operation Market Garden would end the war quickly and decisively. When I was told that our target was to be the area around Arnhem, I expressed surprise that I was to be sent back to where there was a price on my head.

"But have you forgotten that there is a price on my head and I am wanted dead or alive? Along with four or five other agents my photograph is on posters in all police stations in Holland and probably Belgium as well."

I was told in Baker Street, "There won't be any problem as the Arnhem operation cannot fail. We have lost so many agents that have been sent in that you are needed to make contact with the Resistance forces and to act as a liaison with them and the troops of the First Airborne Division. Being in uniform you will not be recognized by the Germans. Besides," I was told, "the Gestapo does not know your real name."

When the forces completed the operation and began their sweep around the Siegfried Line and into Germany, I would be recalled and would be able to return to Britain. This meant that I would return to England and my wife before the baby was born. I was very happy about this and sadly mistaken.

chapter 8

OPERATION MARKET GARDEN HAD been planned as the means to secure the bridges across the Rhine and connect with the Allied Armies of Generals George Patton and Bernard Montgomery and make a successful run to Berlin. As history has shown it was one of the worst debacles of the war in Europe and it proved disastrous to approximately 17,000 Allied troops. The Dutch Army had tried to persuade the powers that be that the attack would not be successful as it was planned. Henri Knap, Arnhem's Chief of Intelligence, warned that there were two Panzer divisions in the area that had moved in on September 4. For some reason the intelligence that reported this was either lost or ignored. The story behind this is one of treason and betrayal.

It was Sunday, September 17, 1944, when we waited beside the large Horsa glider for the massive airborne assault to begin. I was in the uniform of a Captain wearing regular airborne battle kit. I was not loaded down with equipment as the regular troops, but I had a Sten gun, some hand grenades, and two Fairbairn commando knives: one in my belt, another on my right leg. The Sten that I carried was the Mark 11, usually used by resistance groups. It weighed less than eight pounds and could be stripped down into four parts. Firing more than 500 rounds of ammunition every minute, it was a highly effective weapon except when it became overheated and jammed.

The men of the 1st Airborne who were in the glider with me were young, tough, well trained, and eager; and wore their red berets with great pride. I had been issued a red one and another of regulation color. Because my objective was different I might wear one or the other as circumstances demanded. The purpose of the paratroopers was clear and direct: to drop out of the sky, kill as many Germans as possible, cross the Rhine and march to Berlin and end the war by Christmas. My objective was to make contact at two successive rendezvous points. The first was with another member of SOE at the railway bridge in the village of Oosterbeek, not far from Arnhem. The name he was using was Ian Elliott. He was senior to me and I knew very little about him. He would give me information from the Dutch underground and then I would move to the Arnhem-Utrecht crossroads where I would report to Major General Robert Urquhart of the Airborne Division. Then I would return to Oosterbeek with additional orders for Elliott. The time of the planned rendezvous at the crossroads was between 1500 and 1600 hours. My ultimate assignment was to link up with the Dutch underground and assist them in sabotaging enemy troop movements. I was not to engage in combat if it could be avoided. The main objective was to get to the rendezvous on time. The thought was that with the element of surprise in our favor there would be very little resistance.

We took off amid an endless procession of aircraft: fighters, troop carriers, gliders. When the tow line was cut we slanted down over terrain that was familiar to me as the same Dutch country I had parachuted into such a short time ago: tough country for para-troopers and gliders. Looking down I saw several Horsas with their backs broken and bodies scattered around. That morning 10,000 of Britain's finest soldiers arrived from the sky. By the end of the battle about 8,000 would be killed, captured, wounded, or missing. Our glider skidded to a stop and we scrambled out;:weapons ready, red berets vivid in the sunlight. I was the last to leave. My orders to avoid combat became meaningless. German trucks came streaming down the road with soldiers spilling out of them and running into the fields. Many of them were young boys and were followed by SS Troops. I found myself in the middle of a battle of mostly close range combat, often hand to hand. We had been trained for this: hit the ground, roll, fire, jump up and move on. Try to spot the enemy before he sees you. Use your Sten gun sparingly so that it will not overheat or jam. When possible use your knives or even butt with your head. This was my first combat experience. I am sure that others have the same initial anticipatory fear, but once you are in the actual thick of battle there is an exhilaration, a tremendous release of energy and you have no time for fear. The enemy is a killing machine which you must disable. You don't have time to think: you act and react. You are sweating and your throat is dry. I felt very little pain when one of the fallen boy soldiers swung his rifle at my legs just above the ankles. He died instantly from a burst of my Sten and I limped on. There were German soldiers appearing from behind bushes and trees and British soldiers fighting back. There were still and moaning wounded all over and I couldn't see any medics.

I was trying to make my way to Oosterbeek through deep woods that offered me considerable cover. Thanks to my service compass hanging around my neck I was able to move quickly with the stealth I had learned in my guerilla training. About now my ankles had begun to swell from the blow to my shins. I continued on with a sense of urgency for my meeting with Elliott. He had been described to me as tall, dark haired and clean shaven. He would be wearing a British uniform even though he had been among the underground in Holland for some time.

Street fighting was severe in Oosterbeek and I dodged from house to house, garden to garden trying to avoid any confrontation. In the streets the dead were piling up, and already there was an odor beginning to pervade the crisp autumn air.

At the railway bridge there was no sign of Elliott, but after about five minutes I saw a man in uniform coming up from the tracks on my side of the bridge. He carried a Sten gun and kept it trained on me until we could exchange codes then he smiled grimly as we shook hands. Elliott was a big man, about 6'3" all muscle and with thick wiry hair. I thought he spoke with a faint Dutch inflection even though his manner of speech was definitely English public school. We moved away from the main road where the fighting was fiercest and came to a house with a walled garden. Suddenly we saw a flicker of metal in the sunlight beyond the rear wall. We froze and then saw that it was the helmet of a German soldier. Three SS men had mounted a machine gun beyond a second wall that enclosed the vegetable garden. That meant that there were two gardens and two walls between us. The soldiers had removed some stones from the second wall so they could mount their machine gun facing away from the gardens. A British paratrooper appeared on the scene and we all decided to take out the machine gun. Elliott would make a half circle and would come upon them from the far side. I would try to get across the first wall and get close enough to toss a grenade and the paratrooper would stay close to the house and give us covering fire.

I ran quickly to the first wall and vaulted over it landing in soft dirt amid vegetable plants tall enough to conceal me. The Germans did not see me, but suddenly they did see the paratrooper and fired a burst that cut him down near the rear door of the house. To my astonishment the rear door of the house opened and a small boy of about five or six came out. He knelt beside the fallen sergeant, tugging at his shoulder trying to help him. A voice cried frantically from behind him and an elderly man appeared. He ran toward the boy, but was stopped instantly by machine gun fire that cut him down. I kept quite still and heard a German laugh. A moment later I heard the gun firing again, but could not see their target. Before the gun stopped I ran forward, pulled the pin on the grenade, counted to three, and lobbed it at the group on the other side of the wall. Immediately I lobbed another. The first took the machine gun into the air and with it the three SS men, one of whom whose head was parted from his body as it made a bloody circle in the air. I crept quietly to the wall and could see that two of the men were dead and a third wounded. I killed him with my Sten and sat down for a moment to catch my breath. All around me was the smell of explosives and the stink of death. A short distance away lay Elliott who had tried to run close enough to the Germans to kill them with his gun. Unlike me, he had little or no cover and his whole body was riddled with the result of the machine gun burst. I approached him warily, searching everywhere for the possibility of more SS. I gazed at him briefly, then closed his eyes, took his ammunition and moved back through the gap in the wall.

Still taking cover, I went back through the garden where the sergeant lay dead and the little boy was sobbing and clinging to the body of his grandfather. As I made my way towards them I saw that the machine gun fire had unearthed some carrots. They lay there, a vivid orange near the body of the old man. I picked up two to chew on later. I gathered the child in my arms and carried him to the back door of the house and pushed it open. A passage led to the front door where I saw a woman holding her hands over her face in grief and terror. When she saw the boy, she held out her arms and he ran into them. I could not stay as I was already late for my rendezvous at the crossroads, two miles away.

Limping, I headed in that direction through incredible confusion. The Dutch were overjoyed at the prospect of liberation, which many considered imminent. Despite the bloody street fighting, some came from their houses with food, coffee, and Dutch gin which they offered to the Allied troops. Some were decked in orange sashes and all were wild with a delight that was not to last long.

I was making for the main road past the Wolfheze Hotel and joined a platoon led by a Captain Marcheson. By now it was minutes before 1600 hours and I had arrived at the place where I was to meet General Urquhart, but he wasn't there. (I learned later that he had been wounded.)

A Bren gun, which is a light cannon, as opposed to the hand-held Sten gun had been positioned to command the junction, but no one was manning it. The majority of the platoon had crossed to the other side, but I had not joined them when I saw a staff car approaching at high speed. Four German soldiers were in it. When the driver saw me run to the gun he tried to put the Citroen in reverse. I fired a sustained burst and Marcheson's men were also firing from both sides of the road. The Bren and Sten guns found their targets. An officer in the front passenger seat tried to open the door. As he did the burst from the Bren killed him. The driver and the two men in the back died, too. As the car came to a halt, shattered and broken, I looked at my watch. It was exactly two minutes past four.

The officer in the car was Major General Kussin, field commandant of Arnhem. He was returning to his headquarters after a trip to the front to asses the situation. Historians have reported that he was advised not to use that road, but he did anyhow.

Later Kussin's body was pulled out of the car and photographed lying in the road. Thee was some controversy about who had killed him. A paratrooper brought in one of the general's epaulets and claimed credit, but his claim was discredited because he had the time wrong. He had reached the scene quite a bit later. I was not able to make my report until months later.

Over a mile away German mortar began shelling the area around the crossroads. The sound of mortar fire can be frightening and some of Marcheson's men may have been hearing it for the first time. Even though they took cover in the woods they took the full force of the barrage. Some found slit trenches that had been dug by the Germans, but they afforded little protection.

Battle recollections are sometimes murky and confused, and mine are no exception, yet today some are very clear. I remember staring at my hands and then something (maybe part of a falling tree) hit me on the head. My next awareness was of a face peering into mine. I learned later that his name was David Knowles. He said, "Something knocked you out old boy. I'll carry you to those trees over there, otherwise you'll be cut to pieces." My head was swimming and I wondered if I would ever connect with Piet Kruyff, regional resistance officer for Arnhem, or his backup Johannes Steinfort. I expected that they would have further information and be able to tell me what Elliot had been unable to.

Knowles, small and wiry, put me on his shoulders in the fireman's carry, but suddenly spun with a cry and dropped me. He stood, struggled toward me and continued trying to get me to cover. Suddenly two Germans appeared out of the trees. One raised his weapon, but not soon enough. Knowles killed him first and then the second one as he backed for cover. Knowles managed to cut away his sleeve and I found a piece of shrapnel that had entered his upper arm, gone through the muscle and left a larger hole where it had exited. As I was trying to apply a field dressing I saw three more infantrymen approaching. "Play dead," I said to Knowles and threw myself across his legs. The Germans passed us by and when they were bunched together and some yards away I gave them a burst from the Sten gun. They clutched the sky like puppets and fell.

I must have passed out. When I came to Knowles had gone. As I was lying on my back unable to move, a German soldier came past and with two thrusts of his bayonet attempted to attack me. The first thrust aimed at my chest and I managed to roll sideways and took a slice in my right arm. The second thrust came upwards and entered my stomach just below the belt. He must have thought he had given me a mortal blow because he moved on. Behind him came another German soldier who slashed at my throat as he ran by, ripping it open with the very tip of his bayonet, but just missing the jugular vein. I looked down at the wound in my belly and could see my intestines bulging out. I managed to draw my web belt across the wound and clasp it to give support. I passed out again and was not aware of anything until I awoke in pain and in darkness. I had been carried off by Dutch farmers who had come to the battle area when the fighting had subsided.

I was carried to a farm house where my wounds were treated by what, I think, was a medical student, with a rudimentary knowledge of wound care. With three others I was hidden in a shelter made of bales of hay with a space in the middle. From the outside it looked like a solid stack.

I drifted in and out of consciousness for what seemed like a very long time. I had dreams of battle, men dying, Arlette, my mother and father, the English countryside which all seemed a million miles away. The hay was dusty and it made it hard to breathe. German patrols came frequently and stuck their bayonets into the hay without success. Many times I was afraid that one loud sneeze from one of us would be the end of our hideaway. My wounds were beginning to fester and the one in my arm was the most painful.

Eventually it was decided that if my wounds and those of another were not properly tended to we might die. Those brave Dutchmen carried us over war torn roads to the grounds of the Saint Elizabeth's Hospital on the outskirts of Arnhem which by now was in German hands. There had been fierce fighting in the hospital with soldiers shooting back and forth across the beds with patients still in them. I was propped up in a wooden chair with the back legs stuck into the ground and tilted so that I would not fall over. The farmers faded away and I was left with a stick with a white piece of material attached in case a German soldier would find me. I resented the implication of surrender and hid the stick.

Whether it was by a military patrol or hospital staff, somehow I was taken to the hospital where surgery was performed and my wounds were cared for. I had so much faith in the abilities and strengths of our Allied forces that I was sure that they would recapture Arnhem and rescue me in a short time. In the bed next to me was a British 'corporal' who had been wounded in the stomach. Something about his rank did not ring true to me and, I found out later, he was really a Brigadier: John Crocket under whom I served after the war. One morning he told me he was leaving, and tightening his bandages, he calmly walked out of the hospital under the noses of the Germans. He was hidden by three Dutch spinsters until he was well enough to get back to our lines.

One day a Gestapo officer came into the ward. I noticed him talking to one of the nurses. In one hand he carried a piece of paper and in the other a length of rope. He came to me and prodded my sore arm roughly and held up the piece of paper. It was the wanted poster with my picture on it. This was what I had dreaded most.

I stared straight ahead and gave my name rank and serial number: all that is required of a POW. In excellent English he said," There is no use denying who you are, Captain. It will do you no good. So listen you pig..."

He looped the rope around my neck and pulled me violently from bed. My hands were secured in front of me. As I fell to the floor one of the medical officers came forward and made some protestation which was ignored. I was dragged into the hall and down the corridor. I felt like a trapped animal; which is exactly what I was.

chapter 9

THE CORRIDORS OF SAINT Elizabeth's had wide, bare, wood floors. I was dragged to the main entrance and down the curving double stairway. I stumbled trying to keep my balance, half falling, half sliding and trying to hold on to the rope with my tied hands. I had nothing on but a hospital gown and my feet were bare. The sunny autumn weather had gone and the skies were grey and the air was raw and damp. A German staff car was waiting and the rope around my neck was tied to the rear bumper with about two feet of slack. I hung on to the rope and ran to keep up with the car. I am sure I made a pathetic sight to anyone on the street and I am also sure that I was being used as an example of what could happen to those who incurred the wrath of the Germans. Once the car stopped suddenly and I banged into it. My nose was bruised and bloody and I could feel seepage through my bandages.

Gestapo Headquarters was not far from the hospital, near Arnhem on the other side of the road. I seem to recall a black door with a metal grill across it. I was pushed down a flight of stone stairs to the basement and shoved into a cell that might have been a boiler room. The floor was slippery with blood. There was a bundle of rags in the far corner; quickly I realized it was a body. It stayed there for several hours before it was removed. If this was done to frighten me, it worked!

I sat on the cold stone floor and tried to fight off the overwhelming feelings of despair. The Resistance had rescued me once before, but this time I knew that my whereabouts wasn't known to them. I had no contact since being left at the hospital and no one knew where I was.

The door of the cell opened and two men came in. They were young, hard looking, and wore SS uniforms. They glanced at me with contempt and with my hands tied I started to crawl into a corner. One of them kicked me in the groin and both continued kicking until I passed out. A bucket of cold water revived me and I sat in the corner wet, cold and shivering. Blood had matted on my badly swollen face.

Then a strange dialogue took place. They asked me what I felt of the Judische Welterfahr,(the world wide Jewish menace). I replied that I was unaware of it and I knew nothing of the Jews. "But you went to school with a Jew," one said. "His name was Byron Kaufman." I could not imagine how they knew about him and it was a frightening thought. If they knew such a minor detail, they must know a great deal more.

I answered that I knew him and that he was the only non-Christian in school. "You were his friend. Why?"

"I don't know. I just liked him. We were in the same class."

"Your mother has Jewish blood, doesn't she? And that makes you a filthy Jew."

I answered, " If my mother has Jewish blood I am not aware of it and anyway, it's unlikely."

"It will do you no good to lie to us. We will get the truth soon enough."

Suddenly the door slammed and they were gone.

Later that day, as I was ordered, I cleaned up the blood using my left arm as the other one was almost useless. Then I was taken to another room and told to wash in a bucket of cold water. I accidently upset the bucket and was made to mop up the water. While I was on my knees I was beaten over the back with a rubber hose.

I was returned to my cell: miserable, in pain, and despondent. To take my mind off my situation I looked to the only source of light and ventilation: a small barred window leading to a small compartment underneath the sidewalk. The ceiling in the compartment was frosted glass. This glass ceiling was hinged and I thought if I could somehow get through the bars I might have a remote chance of escape. I found a nail protruding from the wall and worked it out and began to pick away at the mortar around one of the bars. It seemed as if I picked for hours, but I know I didn't have the strength for any sustained work. Soon the fingers of my left hand were bleeding and

I dipped them into a bucket of urine in the corner to get some relief. Finally, using all my strength I was able to jiggle one of the central bars. When I heard someone coming down the stone stairs I hid the nail and scraped the mortar into the bucket of urine.

I was squatting in the corner and when the door opened I looked up. Standing over me was a man I recognized from photographs I had seen in Baker Street: Oberstleutnant (Lt. Colonel) Joseph Schreider. He was a short, stocky man, almost bald, with small eyes. He wore a ceremonial dagger and a Luger PO-8 in a holster. He had been a policeman in pre-war Germany; now he was the senior Gestapo officer in Holland. Schreider was in high humor because now he had his hands on a dangerous criminal. He had arrived from headquarters in Scheveningen to view this prize catch.

"So you have turned up in Holland again. This time in British uniform," he said.

I told him, " I was always a British officer," and gave him name, rank, and serial number.

" We are aware of your name and all of your activities." Then he came to the point quickly. "If you give us all the information that we require, you will be treated as a prisoner of war under the Geneva Convention and allowed to go to a camp for officers. If not you will be shot after our interrogators are finished with you. You will suffer so much pain that you will beg us to kill you." He paused, "We know you will break. We know you are weak."

He went on and on boasting that his men had captured all agents in Holland. "We knew every move you made. If you have any sense you will recognize this and come over to our side. Germany is going to win the war. You saw what happened at Arnhem. Didn't that convince you?"

I shook my head and said nothing.

"Let's not waste any more time. Will you give up the names of those you worked with in Holland and those who helped you escape last year through Belgium and France? No? Then we must persuade you to change your mind."

Angrily, he left the cell and the two SS men entered. One was carrying something in his hand and started to hit me over the head with it. I groaned with pain as I was being called a filthy assassin, dirty pig, a degenerate criminal who killed decent Germans from behind. I repeated the Lord's Prayer over and over silently as I tried to wipe the blood out of my eyes. I thought saying the prayer might counteract the evil that I felt all around me. I thought of the cyanide tooth fixed in my mouth and at that point I made up my mind to use it if the pain became unbearable.

Schreider came back and stood over me. My face was so swollen that I had to hold my lids up with two fingers to see him. He stood back and read from a document first in German and then in English. The statement said that I would be tried by court martial under military law for crimes against the Third Reich. If I was found guilty I would be shot. Then, very abruptly, Schreider changed his tune. He told me that if I would cooperate the court martial would be cancelled. "Why won't you give the information we want?"

I knew that they thought me weak; now I would be cussed. I suspected that my fate was sealed anyway. I mumbled, "I have no information and surely if you have captured all the agents from England you have all the information you want." Schreider nodded his head to the SS thugs and left.

Then came another savage beating; the beginning of their 'intensive interrogation'. My arms, legs, hands, kidneys, and testicles took blows and bruising. Thankfully, I lost consciousness again.

Time came and went as I was alternately interrogated and abused. The knowledge that the Gestapo had of British Intelligence and what went on in Baker Street was incredible and astounding. I was sure that someone from within must be supplying the information.

I gave names and places that they already knew or that made no sense. We had been instructed to do this, but it did not fool my tormentors. Their system was frighteningly organized. Schreider would urge me to cooperate and insisted that I give the names he wanted. He assured me I would be sent to a camp where there would be music, women, good food, and all the comforts of home. He stamped his foot and said that I would beg them to kill me before they were through with me. I told him that he had said that before. I felt elated that I had not broken, yet was afraid that I would. I prayed that God would give me the strength to bear whatever I must and hoped that if I couldn't I would not be too weak to break the cyanide filled tooth. I hoped that my family would know that I had been strong and knew deep down that they never would, and most likely, would never know even the smallest part of what had become of me.

At times the underground rooms would resound with screams and groans. It has been suggested that it was only a trick the Germans had used: recordings to terrify prisoners and destroy their morale. I don't think that was the case. There was plenty of pain and suffering and a fake recording was not necessary. I think I must relay some of what was done. I describe these horrors not to suggest that I was exceptional for I know that others suffered much more and never broke. Odette Churchill was a prime example: Her fingernails were penetrated with wooden sticks that were ignited and allowed to burn the bleeding flesh. She is one of those honored after the war and there were countless others. The ordinary citizen who might look scornfully at spying and others who work undercover without any recognition, have no idea of the debt owed by us all to these unsung heroes.

I was strapped to a board with a wet sack thrown over me and beaten. When I was sick the soldiers laughed. After each session there were always the same questions. I was beaten on the bottom of my feet. There was the fake drowning. (Today we know it as waterboarding.) I was put through this only once and suffered temporary deafness as a result. The irony of this procedure is that there was a doctor in attendance to make sure that all the water was expelled from my lungs and that I was back to normal ... whatever that was.

As the October days went by I lost track of time. Now and then when I had the strength I worked at the mortar around one of the bars in my window. Gradually it loosened, but I had little hope of accomplishing an escape; I had no clothing to protect me against the increasing cold and my badly beaten feet would not carry me very far or very fast.

More than once I had considered breaking the tooth, as death sometimes seemed preferable to any more punishment. If I had crushed that tooth and found it harmless I think the betrayal would have broken me completely. I never tried to use the cyanide. I think there were two reasons. The first was the dim hope that I would see my wife and new child someday. The second was an attitude against suicide that had been implanted in me as a child. I was taught that anyone who took his life might be denied burial in consecrated ground. The decision for life or death was in God's hands and this conviction was impressed upon me from an early age. At Arnhem, and later when conditions became even worse, I never tried to take my own life; yet I came perilously close to it.

I will never know if Schreider's men could have broken me because their approach changed. Perhaps they still thought that I could be 'turned'. One day I was surprised that, with the little strength that I had left, I was able to wrench free the middle bar in the window just wide enough for me to crawl through. Even though my hands were still manacled I was able to get through, push the hinged glass ceiling of the little compartment open, and crawl onto the sidewalk. As I did so, much to my surprise (and his, too) along came Oberstleutnant Schreider walking along the street with a roll of papers under his arm. I tried to stand up and he pushed me to the ground; not hard to do. A pair of NCOs coming out of the building dragged me inside. I looked up at them and said, " Well, I had a bloody good try."

One of them drew back his boot to kick me and Schreider stopped him. In German he said, "The Captain must not be injured because he has questions to answer in an hour." I was taken down the stone steps to the room where I had spilled the water and I was allowed to wash in a better way than before and given my uniform. I put on my khaki shirt which had been washed and the rest of my uniform which had been cleaned. The sight of my battle dress gave me a lift and I thought, "At least they haven't taken that from me."

The trial (if you can call it that) took place at 6 p.m. It was a farce because my death sentence had already been signed by General Christiansen, Commander of the German forces in Holland, and also by Heinrich Himmler and Heinrich Mueller.

I was led into a harshly lit room with windows overlooking the Neder Rhine. I stood in a crude sort of witness box with two German soldiers on either side of me. I was weak and dizzy and supported myself by leaning on the lectern in front of me. I cannot remember exactly what happened, but charges were brought against me for espionage and murder. My name, rank, and serial number were read as well as the code name I had used with the Dutch Resistance. I was asked if I had anything to say in my defense, but I said nothing as

I knew it was useless. In twelve minutes I was sentenced to death against the Third Reich and told I would be executed at five the next morning.

Back in my cell I tried to think back on my short years on earth: how my parents and grandparents had loved and cared for me, my siblings, the friends from school. I seemed to hear their voices all clustered together at home. I was deeply saddened that I would never see Arlette again. I had been raised an Anglican and I tried to make peace with God. I prayed that He would help me to die with dignity. Over and over I prayed that my wife would survive the war and marry again and I recalled how she had often said that our love would survive even death. Sitting there on the stone floor I could feel her close to me giving me courage and strength.

Before dawn the door was opened and I was dragged up the stairs and out to the rear of the building where the grass sloped down to the river. It was dark and frosty. Suddenly, headlights blazed from four trucks parked together. I was made to shuffle forward with my hands manacled behind me and a chain going to my feet. I was reciting the twenty-third psalm over and over to myself. Placed against the wall I leaned back to conceal the fact that I was shaking. I hoped it would be quick. An SS officer came forward with a blindfold, but I shook my head that I did not want it. He shrugged his shoulders and walked away.

My fingers groped the wall behind me grasping for support. I heard the click of rifles and a moment later the order to fire. The volley filled the air and the wall behind me shuddered and I stood there dazed. The shots had deliberately gone over my head. No bullet had touched me.

I was led away to my cell and became very sick in a corner.

For the next four mornings I was told to prepare to die and the same routine was duplicated: the truck lights illuminated the wall, the flames of the rifles flashed, and the wall shuddered behind me. Each time the terror seemed to increase. On the fifth morning with my back to the wall I think I shouted out some incoherent defiance: I had nothing to lose. When the shots rang out, I lost control of my legs and fell in a heap.

Later, Schreider came to my cell and said, "Execution is too good for you. You will be sent to a camp designated for criminals just like you."

I was too sick and dazed to care. So often Schreider had changed his mind that I thought I would just wait to see what would happen next.

The next morning I was taken out again and I thought I would be facing the firing squad one more time. Instead, a prison van was waiting. My uniform had been taken from me and the rags I wore gave little protection from the wind and cold.

Other prisoners were crammed into the van. Each of us had an armed guard as we had been classified as dangerous criminals. We were all so battered that we hardly threatened danger to anyone. My feet were so swollen, black, blue, and other colors of the rainbow that the wooden clogs that I had been given made it very painful to walk.

We were blindfolded and driven for what seemed hours. Then abruptly it was decided that the van was too crowded and we were shoved out and made to walk the rest of the way, perhaps about three hundred yards. A train stood there on a siding. It had a number of cattle cars; open on top and with slatted sides. An appalling smell came from the cars, and a low murmuring that sounded like a continual moan. As I stupidly stared at it all, I realized that the cars were filled with humans. I thought, "They will never get us on that train. There is no room."

But they made room.

chapter 10

THE TRAIN HAD BEEN waiting for us. Guards were standing all along the platform. Two at a time we were thrown into the cars as new chains were attached to us. The chains went over a bar that ran the length of the train with each end attached to a prisoner. We had to coordinate the lowering and raising of our hands with the person on the other end of the chain. It was not possible to sit or lie down. We could only hang there upright, wedged in with others, who fouled themselves and their neighbors because they could not move at all. Even when the train moved and the wind blew through the slats the stench was nauseating. This was an incredible journey through and to the depths of Hell. Everyone stared blankly, except for a slight flicker of resentment when another body was crammed in. As the train picked up speed I was remembering the troop train that I had helped dynamite the year before. I remembered that we had heard that two of the cars had Jews on their way to the camps. Now I wondered, as I did for many years after, if those poor souls may not have been more fortunate than we were. Day after day the train rumbled along. The cold wind went right through me: my hands and feet were always numb. Our train was a low priority cargo, so often we waited on sidings for other trains to pass. Whenever the train stopped the stench became unbearable. I tried to motion the people nearby to kick their excrement out through the slats. Some did, but many were too weak to try, or just didn't care.

Hanging from my chain, I tried to sleep, but it was not possible. I thought of my wife who at least was safe at home in London. I concentrated on God and wondered how He could permit such cruelty to humans who had done nothing to deserve it. All around me were moans, and cries. When someone died the guards would cut the chains and toss the body from the train. I was near the side of the car and could see the grey landscape and occasionally a body fly by. It looked almost like a scarecrow or bag of rags being discarded. Sometimes their arms would wave as if in a final goodbye. Although I felt such pity for these poor souls, I also felt a guilty relief because there was a little more room for the rest of us.

Once a day the guards would throw us scraps of food, offal mostly. We would stretch out our hands to try to catch it before it was trampled into the filth on the floor. I cannot recall being given any water. I lost my clogs when I was thrown onto the train, but later I was able to recover a pair of heavy socks from a man who died beside me. I tore a jacket from another dead person and gave it to a small woman. Only her eyes said thank you. She could only put half of it on because of the chain on the other arm. Later I took a pair of trousers from another body and tied them around my neck for some warmth. It was necessary to salvage these things quickly before their owners were thrown overboard.

I have tried for years to forget much of this long nightmare, but some things stick vividly in my mind. One is of a small child clinging to her dead mother's neck until the little girl died, too. I recall also a woman who must have been beautiful, murmuring something in a foreign language which seemed to be filled with wisdom and intensity. I was so emotionally frail myself that I wept and saw my tears drop onto her chains. Yet throughout it all the smell and the crowding and the jarring of humanity when the trains were coupled or uncoupled is what I remember the most. As people died there was more room, but also it was colder because we lacked the warmth of other bodies. When it rained it was a blessing because some of the filth was washed from us and the car. But drying in the cold wind had its bad effects, too. I tried to count the days and nights. I think there were ten.

At last, in the predawn hours of a cold autumn, the train came to a screeching halt on a siding surrounded by a barbed wire fence. I saw SS and other soldiers waiting for the train to stop. We were unchained and I recall even now what a relief it was to be able to lower both arms at the same time.

We were marched off across rough and stony ground with shouts and curses urging us along. Somewhere I could hear dogs barking. Most of us could barely stand, let alone walk; but there was a spark of defiance left. I remember saying in French, "We must be strong and keep our heads up and march with courage and not let the bastards see how weak and ill we are." I don't know if anyone understood. It did not matter because I was really talking to myself.

We had arrived in Buchenwald.

I have often wondered what the German soldiers thought as those trains discharged their cargo: stumbling, emaciated, filthy, stinking, starved, half mad, degraded, and repulsive. It must have made it easier for those guards to regard them as animals. They could whip, hang, rape, torture, and amuse themselves with abandon. The prisoners were things whose feelings were of no importance.

Hitler believed that the Aryan was the master race and all others should be eliminated. This included Jews, Catholics, gypsies, homosexuals, old people, disabled and of course many criminals like me. This dehumanized the thinking of those carrying out this mass erasure of people and made them immune from feelings related to torture, pain, and execution. As we were marched away from the cargo train in the pre-dawn I had no Idea of what was ahead, but I knew that we had come to a place of pure evil. I could sense it, not physically, but psychically.

A square building stood in front of us and we stopped before an iron gate surmounted by a wooden tower. There was an inscription in German overhead: My Fatherland Right or Wrong.

We were herded into a compound with many low buildings and for the first time I saw the prison garb: dirty white suits and berets with vertical blue stripes. A group of men stood there who had earned some status as prisoners and who would hold a degree of authority over the rest of us. They were called Kapos. They seemed to curry favor with the SS by treating the rest of us with the utmost brutality so that discipline and order were maintained. The prisoners had to be cowed into submission and the Kapos knew how to do it.

We were taken into a long room, stripped of our clothing and made to lie on the cold, tile floor. After a long wait we were allowed to take showers with cold water and poor soap. To be rid of the filth was an enormous relief and I dried my self with my dirty shirt. We were moved to another room with bright lights and electric clippers hanging from the ceiling. All of our body hair was shaved off except for a thin tuft from forehead to the back of our necks. Our genitals were painted with a white disinfectant which stung for several days after. We looked like shorn animals.

Prison clothing was issued, the same blue striped material, and mine was too small. When I asked for a larger one I was thrown to the ground by a Kapo and kicked. We had wooden clogs that made walking difficult and clumsy. We were issued tapes, with our name and number, to sew into our jackets and trousers. There was no tattoo on my arm. I was told later that because of the large influx of prisoners at that stage of the war the practice had ceased ... at least in Buchenwald. We were probably going to die soon anyway.

Each prisoner wore a specially colored badge to designate his category: purple for Jehovah's Witnesses, red for political, pink for homosexual, etc. The Jews wore a special yellow star along with the other color. My badge was green for criminal.

By now it was daylight and the scene before us was frightening. Walking around were skeletons with bloody wounds, running sores, every form of sickness. We heard the screams of women being flogged, sometimes to death.

Wild rumors flashed among us. I remember a Captain Perkins of Special Forces warning us sternly: "This may be the worst concentration camp in Germany. Do not admit that you were an officer, or that you held any position of authority. Do not trust any of the Kapos: They will betray you for a cigarette, or for no reason at all."

Prisoners were organized into Kommandos(squads) and most were assigned to filthy or back-breaking work: cleaning latrines, hauling wood, dragging stone in the quarry. I still had no feeling in my hands or feet. Our only food was a cold watery soup which had no nourishment. Our sleeping quarters had three tiers of wooden bunks with two men to a bunk. There was a meager amount of straw and one blanket for the two to share. We had to turn over at the same time to keep warm and covered. During the day we were not allowed into this filthy place, but at night thin voices moaned and cried in a dozen languages.

By late October of 1944, when I arrived in camp, the life span of an average prisoner was less than sixty days. Of the approximate forty-two Special Operations personnel there, only seven or eight of us survived. Every morning the hollow eyed emaciated prisoners had to form ranks for Appell (roll call). This was an ordeal that lasted sometimes four or five hours.

While we stood shivering in the cold, hundreds and hundreds of names were called out. The answer was 'ad sum' a Latin phrase: I am here. Strange that a dead language was used by half dead people. It was considered a good substitute for the many various languages that were represented. Most orders were barked in German. When an officer strode past "Mutzen Auf" (hats off); when he passed "Mutzen Ab"(hats on).

Every day prisoners died of starvation, were worked to death, or were killed by the guards. Some chose suicide by walking into restricted areas where they knew they would be shot; others walked into the electrified fences that surrounded the camp.

The administration of Buchenwald was run by prisoners who were Communists. Supervision was constant as the SS were everywhere. As the fighting and disciplined men had already gone to the front, what remained was nothing that the German army could brag about. These thugs would kill for any or no reason. They had dogs trained to rip out a man's throat or tear off his genitals, leaving him to die, or begging to be killed. Other men and women were hung from gallows or trees on the compound. A favorite method was to tie the prisoners hands behind him and hoist him up by his wrists. Eventually the shoulders would dislocate and the arms would straighten out. I swore that if I ever returned home I would let the world know all of this so that it might never happen again.

The women in the camp were fair game and at the mercy of the Kapos and SS. All that an SS had to do was point to a woman and say, "you ... now!" and she would have to follow him into a wash room or some private place. Refusal meant death. Women were degraded in many ways: sometimes made to run naked from one place to another while the SS laughed. Sometimes women would come to the hospital and offer themselves for some medicine for their child. Once I found a woman lying on the ground and it was clear that she was dying. I was too weak myself to carry her inside so I held her hand until she died. I covered her face with her skirt, but that left the lower part of her body exposed. Somehow this was a symbol of all the inhumanity which surrounded and enveloped us. There was a brothel in the camp, called the Sonderhaus, where some of the girls were prisoners from the women's camp at Ravensbrück, who found this their only means of survival.

There was a pack of children that had been allowed to run wild. They turned vicious and would stone prisoners, sometimes even to death. Eventually they became such a menace that the SS had to remove them. God knows to where.

We were always hungry with a dull gnawing ache that never went away. Lack of food can affect your body and your mind and after a while it is not possible to think clearly. There was a garbage can that sometimes had scraps of food. We fought for this, hurling weaker people aside to get at the filthy remains. After one of these episodes I was so repulsed that I never did it again.

Strangely, there was a military band that played loud martial music, partly for the SS and partly to drown out the screams of those being tortured for some supposed wrong behavior. The band was dressed in the uniform of the Royal Yugoslav Guard, but wore wooden shoes.

There was an underground bunker where a madman tortured and killed people. There was a large tree in the compound which was known as Goethe's tree which was accompanied by a superstition that as long as the tree was standing Germany would not fall. I heard that the tree was damaged in September when an allied air raid unloaded some bombs that hit Buchenwald. Their target had been the Gustloff munitions factory nearby. In that raid four hundred people and eighty guards died in Buchenwald. Every prisoner who passed the tree hoped that this was foretold the coming downfall of the Third Reich.

Soon after my arrival I got into trouble the SS and was punished for fighting with another prisoner. I was drenched with cold water and, with a sack around my head, pushed naked into a cage that was five feet high and three feet across. The cage was near the main entrance to the camp and I was there for about four days and drenched with water while the guards laughed. When I was let out I could not stand and I collapsed.

I came to in a hospital bed wondering if I was dead and was in another dimension, but I didn't remember dying! The hospital was called Revier, and the doctor, a friend of Himmler, was not a qualified physician, but was called Herr Doktor Ding Schuler. Terrible experiments were conducted on inmates, mostly Jews. They were injected with typhus and other disgusting germs and then studied with acute interest while they died. They were used also to study the effects of experimental vaccines and when surgeries were performed it was usually without anesthetic as supplies had been depleted by the time I arrived.

The German mind found nothing odd or contradictory in restoring a prisoner to health so that he could die. The Kapo of the hospital was named Dietch. He had been a prisoner for a long time and he spoke on my behalf to the doctor in charge. He said that I might be useful as an orderly if I gained a little strength.

Part of my duties involved carrying severed limbs outside where they could be collected for disposal. By the end of the day I was usually covered in blood. Buchenwald had no gas chamber, but there was a crematorium where I was sent frequently to deposit bodies. The sights that I saw there are indescribable: people hanging with hooks coming through their mouths; others strung up by piano wire. I heard the strangled sobs and cries and began to wretch violently. Some of our Special Forces men died this way and I heard stories of their bravery as they marched in step knowing they were going to die but not giving the SS satisfaction.

Under such circumstances it was not surprising that a high percentage of prisoners in Buchenwald became demented if they were there for any length of time. As the weeks passed I had trouble separating reality from this Hell and was not sure if I was in the real world any more. I retained enough sanity to realize that I must continue to appear to have some usefulness. Another prisoner and I, a Polish Jew named Janek, had been given large tongs that we used to grab the bodies by the ears to drag them from the hospital.

My head, arm, and stomach wounds had still not healed and I was worried that they might get worse and I would be too weak to carry limbs or bodies. This job was what was allowing me to stay alive. Even in this depraved place it was important for me to keep clean and as an orderly I had access to warm water, but seldom soap.

When there was access to soap it had been made from the fat, boiled down, from Jews who had died. There were mocking markings on the soap to tell you so. Each time I used it, I said a prayer for those who had died: a ritual that Janek and I performed together.

One day Janek was not there and I knew that if he had become too weak to carry out his duties the same fate awaited me. I asked what had become of him and the guard answered, "Oh, we hung the Jewish pig." But that was not true. Years later we met in Tiberius. He was an old man with white hair and his blue eyes filled with tears when he recognized me. For moments I didn't know who he was. We talked of meeting again, but I was not emotionally able to.

There were many nationalities in the camp: Poles, Russians, Hungarians, Spaniards, French, Canadians, Danes, and a few American fliers. I was told that the whole Danish police force had been arrested and sent to Buchenwald. There was a Russian soldier in the camp who had been there much longer than I. He was very strong, aggressive, and violent. You could see the hate and madness in his eyes. He would attack another prisoner for no reason; sometimes he ran with the pack of children. They egged on this pale youth and encouraged him to assault other prisoners, even killing them for amusement. The guards never restrained him, for his homicidal rages amused them and killing another inmate was just one less for them to deal with.

As I said, Buchenwald did not have gas chambers, but the bodies were cremated after death. I was standing outside the hospital one early morning watching the smoke from the furnace as it curled from the chimney and the association of smoke with death and horror became so connected that it became part of the blackness for years. Near the end of march I had been hit on the head with a large stick. I don't know for what reason, nor by whom. I had a concussion and was dazed for several days as the attack opened the wound in my head causing it to bleed profusely.

As spring approached, if I had been thinking clearly, I would have realized, that the end was nearing for the hated Nazi regime: As Germany collapsed so did organization in Buchenwald; it slipped into chaos. The latrines overflowed and the well which held the drinking water had dead bodies floating in it. Prisoners continued to drink from it because they were too weak to haul the large bodies out. The

SS made a pile of corpses and set fire to them attempting to obliterate as much evidence of atrocities as they could, but in their haste they left a smoldering pile. The pitiful rations we had were depleted. Men died in their bunks from starvation or fell down in the compound and lay like a bundle of rags until they were added to the rows outside the crematorium.

Suddenly everything stopped and that was almost as terrifying as what had gone before because we were sure something terrible would happen.

Then, on a cool, sunny day in April 1945 the rest of the guards disappeared. The SS and their boots and whips were gone and nothing was left but a pile of corpses and shambling human skeletons wandering around with dazed looks unable to comprehend that their ordeal might be ending. I was having a hard time separating reality from hallucination. I heard the sound of gunfire and the rumble of approaching tanks. Then I heard shouting in a language that seemed strange, but familiar. I thought that I must hide and I did so behind another pile of corpses left for burning. I hoped that I would be confused with the dead. Lying there with my grisly camouflage I saw a tank come through the main gate and stop. I knew that the large white star on the side was not anything like the swastika. My clouded mind thought this might be some kind of trick. As one of the tank crew climbed down I can still remember the look of horror on his face. Allied Intelligence may have known about Buchenwald and its horrors, but this American G.I. did not. The soldiers came upon the whole scene without warning and the conditions they saw made them outraged and angry which I was to discover soon enough.

As a soldier approached, something made me realize that he was a friend and I rose from the pile of dead and tried to wave to him. As I thanked God for these saviors I held out my hands and ran toward him weeping for joy.

Later I was told that I didn't run; I did the only thing I could do: I crawled.

Three long years before I had been an innocent schoolboy.

chapter 11

THE AMERICANS DID NOT believe me when I told them I was a British officer. I was babbling in French, German, and some English gibberish. Something in the back of my mind, due to intense indoctrination, kept me from mentioning my connection to SOE. The more the soldiers saw of the hideous secrets they had stumbled on, the angrier they became. Soon they learned that I had been an orderly in Ding Shuler's infamous hospital and the full vent of their anger turned on me. I remember the flushed face of the Major who had been assigned to me. Tears ran down his face as he looked at where the depraved experiments had taken place.

"Damn you, boy. If we find you are some kind of Nazi, we're going to blast you to blazes. I can promise you that."

I was weak, confused, and giving strange answers. I had no tattoo on my arm and this added to the suspicions of the Americans. Why didn't I have a tattoo like some of the others? Didn't this mean I was part of the machine? I kept repeating the denials and they kept shaking their heads. If I really was a British soldier, what was the name of my commanding officer? I tried to remember, but couldn't. There was so much that I had forgotten.

Soon I was locked in the same guardroom as before. An army doctor gave me drugs to quiet me and encourage sleep. I was a mess: I weighed eighty-five pounds, my bones protruded, my hair was falling out, and I was feverish.

I vaguely remember seeing General Patton, who looked at me steadily and demanded that I prove my identity. I asked him how I could prove anything. I suggested that he contact a General Gubski in London who would certainly vouch for me. He growled that he had damn well better.

Within days a message came from London that Captain Keith

Armstrong had died by firing squad in Holland the previous year. The Dutch underground had been given this information and even claimed to have seen my bullet ridden body. This made my story more suspect than ever and the Americans even angrier, if that was possible. I begged them to have London send information about my family so that they could question me about that. They agreed to do this and back came a number of questions: What was the name of the hunting dog that we had when I was a boy? What were the names of my paternal grandparents? What was my mother's maiden name? I struggled to answer … particularly the last one. I tried to concentrate and I could not think at all. The men shouted at me that I better hurry, I must know my mother's name. The medical officer kindly suggested that I be given a little time. I struggled to pull facts from the back of my clouded mind. They sat me down and put a blanket around me and I could feel the warmth surging through my body.

The Americans waited and I tried hard to picture my mother, my grandfather, and how he was addressed by others. I struggled and struggled and then it came to me. "Her name was Saint Aubyn," I said, and started to sob. Then other answers came to me and everything changed. The Americans crowded around with kind words and sympathy. They had more questions and when I managed to pull myself together I said, "I cannot answer any more questions as I am under oath. I have signed the Official Secrets Act."

"What in Hell is that?" I heard someone ask.

From that moment a cloud of secrecy and care surrounded me. From my window I could see German citizens who had been brought from town to help clear the terrible mess. Their faces were horror stricken and sullen. Later I heard that the Burgermeister was so appalled that he went home and shot his wife, children, and himself. True? I can't say, but possible. In spite of the efforts of the Americans, the camp was still Hell on earth. Many died in spite of the liberation: some just did not have any strength left; others died from choking on their food. I was allowed only liquids for some time. I wondered why I was surrounded with so much security and why I seemed so important. I did not know then that orders had come from on high that I was not to be questioned. I was to be transported to England and I was to be kept alive. I still was not fit to travel and I couldn't stand. I watched outside my window as two G.I.s built a wooden bed for me and I was given two army blankets. Two medical orderlies had been assigned to me.

The days that followed were vague, but I was aware of being transported overland through war torn Europe, still under tight security. Traveling with me was a nurse of the VAD (Voluntary Air Detachment), a Captain of the Royal Army Medical Corps., and two Military Police. They had all been flown from England to Germany to collect me. I could not understand this. Why was a broken down, half mad young man so important?

In England I was in Millbank Hospital, not far from the houses of Parliament and overlooking the Thames. I was still confused and very nervous. I jumped at every little noise, and colors had an intense brilliance. I remember that weeks later, when I was allowed a short, accompanied trip from the hospital, the sight of the London buses noisily charging at me practically paralyzed me with fear.

Gradually, the mist began to rise, but I still had terrible nightmares of Buchenwald and would waken dripping in perspiration. It was during a sleepless night that I remembered that I was married. Where in God's name was Arlette? I wanted to see her right away. I rang for the night sister and she firmly told me that I must ask someone in the morning. After a week of frustration and evasive answers I could contain myself no longer. In a rage, I broke my bedside locker and the window in my room. I was gently and firmly restrained and moved to a locked room where orderlies looked after me. All together there were probably ten people who tended me. They were all patient and kind when I ranted and cursed. Without their care I might have gone completely mad.

Now and then officers from SOE would visit me. They always asked the same questions. "Did you give any information to the Gestapo? What did you tell them? Did you ever pass along the information we gave you?" This puzzled me because I had been debriefed after returning from Holland last year. The SOE officers told me that I might have to appear as a witness for the Crown in some forthcoming investigation involving N Section. I could not understand why. After some days I was removed to a military hospital in the Midlands which had a wing for service personnel who had broken down under strain: former POWs, fighter pilots, and other members of SOE. I had a room to myself and was visited every day by a woman doctor who never gave me her last name, I simply called her Dr. Anne. She seemed to have an amazing knowledge of SOE affairs and asked many questions. Often she would say, "You are lying to me because there is no official record of that." I would hear that refrain so often for so many years. At the time I was not aware that all records pertaining to me ... everything ... had been put into deep files. It was she who told me that my wife was quite safe and happy, but she had been ill, and that we would meet again when I was better. I was beginning to doubt everything. I was improving, but could not see my family? Did my parents know that I was alive? Why was Arlette kept from me? And not even allowed a phone call?

Claude Dansey, who had originally recruited me for Z came to see me. So did Ivor Dobson, the head of N Section. Both were kind and considerate, praising me for my work in the war and urging me to rest and recover. When I was well enough I could see my wife and family. In the interim, it was important for SOE that I regain my health before I could return to the outside world. It was all said very smoothly and plausibly and with a kind message from Colin Gubbins. There was something puzzling in the way they looked at me, as if some final decision about my future had yet to be made.

Slowly I began to recover: my weight was up to 115 pounds, my hair was beginning to grow back, and I was losing the flat footed shuffle and began to walk again with steps that had some life in them. I was benefitting from the training to use my undamaged left arm and it was at this time that I began to paint, a pastime that I still enjoy.

To this day I have no idea how the thought began to form that the hollow tooth in my jaw was not, and never had been, lethal. Perhaps it was Dr. Anne saying, "Well, you were tougher than we thought, weren't you?" That alone would not have been a sufficient clue. Perhaps she had let something slip that I have forgotten. In any event I became convinced that I had been used and betrayed by my own people and by Winston Churchill, too. When Claude Dansey came to see me again I burst out with bitter accusations to which he listened with an expressionless face, neither confirming nor denying anything.

Soon after that I was taken on an outing. The usual sedative injection was not given and I seemed to have more energy, strength, and a clearer mind. I was driven to my old headquarters in Dorset Square accompanied by two nurses. The area was quieter, almost deserted, as the war in Europe was over. As we passed down a short corridor we were met by a man whose name I could not remember, but whose face I knew.

He said, "Well, hello Keith. You're looking well and fit." I knew I was not. "A bit thin, but all in good time"

Still wearing my forage cap I saluted and he gave me a twisted smile that was familiar. He reached for my hand and said, "If you don't remember, I am Colin Gubbins, and you used to work for me." A Lt. Colonel joined us and I was told that I was to meet Winston Churchill within the hour. A wave of bitterness arose within me and I mumbled that I had no desire to meet again the man who had betrayed me. I was told gently and firmly that the Prime Minister would discuss this at lunch. I was expected and I would go!

The ride to 10 Downing Street was identical to the one I made almost two years before. Churchill seemed unchanged: a bit older, a bit worn perhaps. I was filled with a mixture of awe and fury. Here was the man who had guided Britain through its darkest hours and also the man who had sent me into occupied Holland hoping I would be captured, break under torture, and reveal false information to the enemy. I tried to keep myself under control, but I am sure that the anger showed in my eyes.

Physically and mentally I was not ready for a confrontation, but now that I was here perhaps it was a good time to tell someone in authority of the betrayal that I suspected from within. I had repeatedly been warned not to speak of these things, but I stubbornly planned to ignore the warnings.

With the Lt.Colonel, I followed Churchill into his study and we talked quietly until Mrs. Churchill walked in. We were introduced to her again and then she and the Colonel left.

Churchill said, "Well, I suppose you would like to tell me your story." When I made no reply, he added, "If you feel you can I would be most interested." He hesitated, almost as if embarrassed, then said, "Perhaps you would rather wait until after luncheon."

"Sir," I said, "I am told that I have been under a strain and I have difficulty recalling some events. All I recall is that I was sent by you into Holland with certain information. I conveyed this to Orde Dienst. Then I was unable to return except by escaping down the Comet Line. It was during the battle of Arnhem that I was captured by the Gestapo and everything went very wrong. I believe that I am one of only a handful of survivors of more than fifty agents sent into Holland ... I believe ... "

Churchill held up his hand: "I know of your heavy losses in Dutch Section."

"Sir," I burst out, unable to control myself any longer,"why in God's name was it necessary for you to use me as you did? Why did you think I was so weak that I would break under interrogation?"

Churchill stared at me and was silent for a moment as if weighing his words. "It was a calculated assessment," he said at last. "You had not come up to standard in some of your training and so you were singled out with certain others in a plan to deceive German intelligence ... and to save lives."

I responded like an angry and sullen child.

"Well, Sir. Bad luck. It didn't work!"

"I know that and I apologize to you," He seemed uncomfortable and I could see the strain on his face, "but that's all behind you now and I believe Mrs. Churchill has luncheon ready for us."

It was a fine luncheon, but I toyed with my food. Mrs. Churchill was charming and gracious. She tried to put me at ease and said, "My father was in the Army, you know." Churchill asked questions of my family and of my early years. What struck me was the affection between the two of them. He called her 'darling' quite often, (And I was to hear him address his son Randolph the same in years to come). Churchill said that Randolph and his wife would like to hear my story and I must come to their country home for a weekend to meet them. I did visit Chequers a few times and later became firm friends with Randolph's second wife, June.

Winston Churchill asked me what I intended to do with myself in the post war world.

I replied, too quickly, " I will do anything as long as government secrets are not involved. I don't want to continue in the shadowy world of espionage. I have had enough to last me a lifetime." He smiled indulgently and did not press the point.

After lunch we returned to his study where he lit one of his enormous cigars. Then I started telling him certain events regarding Dutch Section and other facts that were under the Official Secrets Act. I have never discussed these since. Strictly speaking, I was violating the OSA, and in listening to me so was he, but I was not telling him anything that he did not already know.

After a while he asked if it would help if we talked about something else. "Have you read of my experiences in the Boer War?" He told me that like me he had been on the run and at times had been lonely and discouraged. He always felt that he had a star to follow. Spellbound, I listened to him and some of my bitterness and hostility faded. As others, I had had a rotten war, but that was over now and I had to pull myself together. Churchill talked of his faith and the strength he derived from it and I began to feel that maybe God had brought me into contact with this great man for reasons of his own.

Soon it was time to go and the Colonel was waiting in the hallway. The P.M said, "I'll be in touch with you," and with a gesture of his small hand he repeated the invitation to come to the country to visit.

I thanked him for the luncheon. A question just came out that I had tried to suppress and had been told not to bring up. "Sir ... what about my wife? They will not let me see her."

He looked away and then at his cigar. "I will speak to General Gubbins about that."

I realized that it was very extraordinary for such a great man to be concerned with a young man like me. One evening, years later, while dining with (now Sir) Colin Gubbins, he told me that when it had been established that I was alive and in Buchenwald, Churchill had given the order that I be brought home safely and returned to good health. I like to feel that as ruthless as he could be, something in him was repulsed by using young Englishmen as pawns in the game with the Nazis: handing them over to be tortured and killed.

I was exhausted when the Colonel escorted me to the car and exhilarated at the same time. I was taken back to the hospital.

Not long after my meeting with Churchill, Colin Gubbins came and talked to me very seriously and very quietly. He told me that shortly after our son was born in November, Arlette had made a sortie into occupied France and had not returned, but there was still hope that she was alive somewhere. Europe was in chaos and many people were still unaccounted for. Our son was being cared for by his Belgian grandparents and perhaps I could see him later when my health had improved. He apologized for keeping these facts from me, but the doctors thought it better. He was truly sorry for the deception (I remember how genuine he seemed) but it had been judged necessary.

He continued, "I know you want to return to civilian life, but the department prefers that you go through a needed period of rehabilitation and then continue to serve. Britain faces many dangers in the months and years to come and young men like you are needed." He added, "In my opinion that is what your wife would wish." There was a note of finality in his voice as if it had all been decided for me.

"Much has gone wrong in Dutch Section and this is an issue of grave sensitivity and secrecy. Whatever you know about it, and that is a great deal, you must keep to yourself. This is your duty," he said with that half smile that I knew, "and you should not question it." He gave me a pat on the shoulder and said, "Think it over my boy. I know you'll make the right decision." Then he was gone.

As I discovered there were plans to use me as a witness in case the department ever came under investigation for the disasters in Dutch Section. This could be another reason why I was treated so kindly and carefully. Eventually my birth certificate was changed to make me older and more credible as a witness to what had occurred during a longer stay in Holland.

The visit from General Gubbins had shaken me. My wife might be alive somewhere, but she might not. Our son was safe. He had been named Stephen as we planned. For the moment I was to have no contact with him or his grandparents. My hopes of returning to civilian life were suddenly dim. Gubbins had implied that the service wanted to keep me because I could be of great value to them. I knew that the real reason was that by keeping me in the service they could control my life and the knowledge that I had. They were perfectly capable of disposing of me if I became a risk and I was sure this had been discussed. The visit left me in a very agitated state and contributed to the delay of my return to stability.

When I was finally discharged from the hospital, I was given a fistful of crisp five pound notes and told to go off to Shropshire to continue my convalescence. I was granted indefinite leave and stayed in a pleasant hotel run by a retired Indian Army Colonel and his wife. They had been told about me and made those late summer days in the old hotel very pleasant and relaxing. Still my mind was focused on finding Arlette, and it was here that I made up my mind to search for her myself.

Casually, (or so it seemed) I met a Major in the Royal Army Service Corps. He was most interesting and told me of his life: a time in pre-war India, skirmishes on the Northwest Frontier, and a period in Egypt when he served in the Camel Corps of the Egyptian Army. He seemed to be content to spend hours with me and I enjoyed his straight-forward manner and his hearty laugh. He was like a friendly uncle and he always advised me, in an offhand way, to make peace time service my career. I finally realized that he had been assigned to keep an eye on me and to steer me towards re-enlistment. I didn't resent him because I knew he was just doing his job. We remained good friends and for years I had many happy visits to him and his wife in their home in Guernsey.

That English summer was calm and beautiful. One night I went to the local cinema to see a light comedy. Pathé news was shown with some of the first accounts of the discovery of the concentration camps and there before me was Buchenwald with all of its horrors. I recognized some of the guards who had been rounded up and forced to carry away the remaining corpses for burial. I stared and then rushed into the street where I became violently sick. Somehow I returned to the hotel and I felt as if my healed mind had been ripped open.

When I returned to London, somewhat resigned to the fact that I would remain in the service, I was given some simple paper work to handle. My office was a gloomy little hole in the basement of Northumberland House. I still had a very short attention span and could not sit for very long as my hip bones had hardly any cushion.

The Germans are a very methodical people and during the war they kept detailed records of everything accompanied by very clear photographs when necessary. My assignment was to sift through a stack of photographs of displaced persons, refugees and inmates of concentration camps to see if I could identify any of them. What a job to give me! Even though it became tiresome and depressing I kept at it hoping that soon I would be given more interesting and challenging work.

One afternoon I was sifting through captured documents and picked up a picture from Ravensbrück concentration camp. It showed a young woman, naked, seated on the edge of a grave which she had probably been forced to dig herself. One leg was folded under her. In one minute bullets would crash through her body, but her look was pure defiance. I stared at the photograph and an icy fist drove into my heart and there was a dreadful roaring in my head.

It was Arlette.

chapter 12

FOR A LONG TIME I believed that the photograph of Arlette sitting on the edge of her grave did not come across my desk by chance. I thought the administration in the Foreign Office arranged for me to "discover" it. I believe it was their objective to observe my reaction to this shock. If it turned me into a fanatical killer, full of murderous hatred, they could take advantage of this in the cold war that lay ahead. If it broke me completely, and either drove me to insanity or suicide they would be rid of a person who knew too much of the treachery in Dutch Section and who might become an acute embarrassment. Either way they had nothing to lose.

One reason I felt that I may have been right was their very quick reaction. They knew I was still very emotionally shaky from the Buchenwald experience. They thought I would be overwhelmed, which I was. They thought I might turn to alcohol to blunt my pain and they were ready for that, too. When I fled from Northumberland House and headed for the nearest pub, I was followed and taken to an apartment that was kept available in London. I was treated with understanding and given the drink that I so desperately wanted. Perhaps sedatives were added. I don't know. All I recall is that the time passed in a blur of despair. I would not be allowed to see the photograph again I was told: it was too painful, too traumatic.

Was it possible that I had mistaken the identity of the girl? Also, the Germans had made me face a firing squad and I had survived. Perhaps the same kind of torture had been used in Ravensbrück? Every effort would be made to ascertain the truth and when it was available I would be the first to know. In the meantime why didn't I go home to my family? They could be told nothing of my wartime experiences of course, but my being in familiar surroundings with people who cared about me would aid in my healing. I should come to London occasionally and report, but the main thing was to regain my strength and get over this nasty shock. What splendid psychology! I should not worry about money. They would supply it. I was not to give up hope for my wife, either, but of course, for the present I could not mention her to anyone

I listened to these words and something in me wanted to believe Arlette was still alive, and I clutched at that possibility, however faint. I also vowed that if authority could not find a trace of her, when I was well enough, I would search myself. With or without permission I would not rest until I found her or until I had avenged her death.

I went back to my family and it was difficult for us all. I was thin, moody, and emotional, sometimes seized by trembling and depression. I hesitated to smile because it was lopsided due to the wound to my throat and my mother was puzzled by my somber expression. I should still have been in hospital. I was not able to discuss what I had done in the war and my father thought I had been a desk soldier. (Some so called desk jobs were extremely important even though they did not have the glamor of combat.) He showed his disappointment in various ways.

In spite of all that my parents did for me they had no understanding of unconditional love. Then, and later, when I needed their support, they were apt to believe untruths and gossip rather than to have faith in me.

In addition there were too many people who were resentful of those who were perceived not to have carried their share of the burden. To some it seemed wrong that I should be home on leave while others were still fighting the war in the Pacific. Why wasn't I at least part of the occupation force in Germany? In our village the talk went around and around. The resentment surfaced in a few extraordinary ways. Most of the time I kept to myself wandering around old haunts, walking down old lanes. I rode for miles through the countryside on my horse and in the market trap and I found some peace from the madness I had known.

Now and then I would take the train to London to report in and it was on one of those journeys that some trouble occurred. A man my age, a serving Navy commando, had picked up some of the negative gossip about me. He began to hound me with it in the railway carriage and I found it difficult to explain to him why he was wrong and his angry words became more strident. I stayed in my seat among the silent glaring looks of the other passengers. My accuser said that he knew I was a coward and challenged me to a fight. He had his proof when I refused.

Finally I moved to the buffet car and ordered some tea. My assailant followed me, so I left the train at the next stop. I am sure that all who were there thought they could see a yellow stripe right up my back.

I waited for another train and was still miserable and choked up. Standing near me was a young Army officer who spoke kindly and asked if there was anything he could do. He was a doctor still in the service, waiting to be demobilized. Then this acquaintance of five minutes took me to a nearby hotel and we shared tea and hot scones. We never met again, but I have always remembered him and been grateful. Surely the love of God shone from him.

One morning there were three letters for me. I stuffed them in my pocket and walked down to the local hotel. It was shortly after opening time and the pub was already busy. The owner greeted me and bought a round of drinks for a few of us. Soon my mother arrived with a few friends. She was the life of any party, and her laughter filled the room.

Sitting in a corner I decided to open my letters. The first was from my grandmother, asking me to visit her. The second was a larger one which I opened with a pencil from a nearby table. Inside was a piece of thin paper and inside that were two grubby chicken feathers. I stared in bewilderment thinking this was some kind of joke. Then the meaning hit me. It was so absurd ... like something out of Beau Geste. I was tempted to laugh, but said nothing to anyone. Later I told my good friend, the Vicar, who exploded in anger at the anonymous sender. "What a sanctimonious idiot, sitting in judgment. I hear half the gossip around here and I'll find out who did this, but I think I know."

I told him not to bother, but the next morning there were two more white feathers and a note that read: "We don't want your kind around here."

It was hard for me to cope with small things in those days and this was very upsetting. I called London and told my Brigadier what had happened. He replied in a clipped precise voice, "You have no problem my dear chap. You know what you've done ... and I know what you've done, so just forget it. Come to London and we'll talk if you like."

So I carefully wrapped my feathers (I saved them for many years) and took them with me to London. The Brigadier took me to lunch and told me that such incidents seemed important at the moment, but when I was finally rehabilitated I would be amused by it all. Somehow I never was! Criticism can sting, and unjust criticism most of all.

The Foreign Office had no news of Arlette, or so they claimed. They were intimating that I should get on with my life: forget I had been married, forget about my son. Make a new life. I pretended to listen, but was determined to follow my inner voice:

Find out what happened to Arlette!

chapter 13

IN THE DAYS AFTER the war it was possible for a British officer to go to almost any RAF station and, if he knew a pilot, catch a ride across the Channel without fuss or red tape.

I telephoned a French officer in the Sûreté in Paris, who had frequent contact with SOE. in the past, and said that I would like to come and see him. I took a train to Peterborough and on to the Royal Air base at Wittering. I went to the main gate and asked for my friend Squadron Leader Giles. I found him and he readily agreed to fly me to Paris the next day as he often carried mail back and forth. I took 500 cigarettes with me because I knew that you could sell them for the equivalent of ten shillings ($2 a pack). I also took soap and chocolate, good for bargaining. In France I exchanged 100 cigarettes for a Leica camera and both of us were satisfied with the exchange.

Paris, like London, was recovering from the war and young girls and men in a host of uniforms were everywhere. When the French at the Sûreté learned that I had been a prisoner in Buchenwald and that my wife had been sent to Ravensbrück, they were extremely helpful. In fact they knew much more about her than my informants in London; or at least they were willing to share more with me.

They told me that she had been a clandestine radio operator reporting to London on the activities of the Resistance. These operators were trained to keep sending their messages even if they were surprised by Germans in detector vans. The Germans were excellent at monitoring such secret transmissions and they could quickly pinpoint the location of the agent. When they closed in on Arlette, she sent out her code to the Bletchley coding station, alerting them of her predicament. She fought and injured a German soldier with her gun, but was overpowered and handed over to the Gestapo who sent her to Ravensbrück. The French knew about this from reports that had come into their hands from the Resistance. The French thought it was likely that she had been executed, but were not certain.

If they were not sure, there was a slender thread of hope and I set about finding out myself.

It was not easy, but I obtained passes from the French allowing me to travel to the recently liberated areas of Europe. As a British Major in uniform I was able to move about quite freely. I went to Basel where I was told records from Ravensbrück were held. I had been advised to contact Air Commodore Freddie West VC, who was the Air Attaché there. He was a retired WW1 fighter ace who had lost a leg in combat and had been quite a hero to us at school. He had recently retired and I came away with nothing. Then I went to a place called Arolsen, not far from Kassel, where the Germans had kept incredibly detailed records of the camps. There were endless files and twenty- eight million index cards and cross referencing of hundreds of individual cases, many of them Jewish. The place was the scene of frenzied activity. A large staff of legal experts and linguists had been assembled to deal with the flood of inquiries: ten thousand a month I was told. I was allowed to search the files in those endless three foot wide corridors, lit by an occasional single bulb with no shade. Alphabetically, I found the very place where Arlette's file should have been, but it was not there. I could see the clean space on the dusty shelf where the file had been. I was at a loss to know if the SS had destroyed it or whether my own people had decided to get rid of it in their attempt to obliterate all traces of my record, including my marriage. Later, I would find the records in St. Paul's Church had disappeared, as well as all reference to her in SOE.

In Arolsen I went from one place to another in a desperate attempt to find some trace of Arlette, but I found nothing. Later, in London, I was reprimanded for going ahead on my own. Any information they had they would be glad to give me, they said, when they felt I was ready to receive it. In the meantime,"You must try to forget that she has ever existed. You have agreed to put the past behind you when you agreed to re-employment, and now ... you must honor that pledge." I was not ready to forget my wife: not now, not ever.

On one of those unauthorized searches in Europe I heard of a wonderful woman in Holland who had been an inmate in Ravensbrück and who might have some knowledge of what had happened to my wife. Her name was Cornelia ten Boom: more famously known as 'Corrie'. She lived in the Netherlands and in the early part of the war her parents were arrested for helping and hiding Jews. Her father died in prison. Corrie and her sister, Betsy, were sent to Ravensbrück, where Betsy died, and Corrie barely survived. Now she was in Bloemendaal, where she organized a kind of hostel to help returning prisoners of war and victims of the Holocaust. When I wrote to her, she agreed to come to Haarlem and we met at the house where she had spent her childhood. The house was called the Beje. Corrie's father had been a watchmaker and the shop was still there. The shop window was on the left as you went in and ahead was another door which led into the work room and beyond that was a staircase. It passed two floors on its way to the top and I had to pause a few times because I still had not regained full strength in my legs. At the top was a secret room where people had been hidden from the Nazis.

At first sight Miss ten Boom impressed me with her dignity and strength. An aura of goodness seemed to envelope her. She was in her fifties, a typical sturdy Dutch woman who still showed some of the ravages of her imprisonment. (Her release was due to a clerical error by the Nazis.) She had agreed to see me at the request of a friend in Orde Dienst.

"You come highly recommended," she said, "and you speak some Dutch." I told her that my Dutch was very limited and I knew only what I needed to get by when I was working with the Resistance. Raising her hands she said, "That must have been suicide."

I described Arlette and asked if she remembered her. "You mean the tall Belgian girl. I think she came from the Congo and came to the camp near the end of the war. Yes, I remember her well."

She looked at me steadily as she talked, with her eyes never wavering from mine. At one point she paused and said, "I can see that you are worried that I will omit some details to spare you, but believe me. I will tell you all I know."

At first Arlette had been placed in the barracks with the ten Boom sisters. These units designed for 400 prisoners by this time held 1400, and they were alive with fleas. While she was there, my wife told Corrie she knew it was inevitable that she would die. Once she joined them in prayer and reading the forbidden bible that they had hidden from the Nazis. They were able to converse in Dutch and Flemish. Then this brave girl was moved to the punishment block. One morning Corrie heard the heavy tread of an execution squad. The only prisoner, carrying a spade, believed to be my wife, was pushed and kicked to the spot where she was to die. There she may have been forced to dig a narrow grave and then marched back. This was a favorite procedure, so she could contemplate her fate. The death warrant would have been read to her and the following morning she would be returned to the grave, stripped naked and forced to sit on the edge of the grave, staring defiantly at her captors until a burst of fire ended her life. I heard from another source that this prisoner had bloody wounds on her back, probably from whips. I have no idea how she found this out. Miss ten Boom emphasized that she had not been in the punishment block for long so her suffering was short, but, I knew only too well that it only takes an hour to inflict the most terrible agonies.

I payed close attention to everything that was said so that one day I could tell our son of his mother's courage. When I considered Arlette's death, a white hot anger burned within me and I was filled with an implacable desire for revenge. The senior people in London had assured me they would do everything to track down her killers and bring them to justice. I had little faith in such promises. I knew there was only one person with the motivation, tenacity, and ferocity to carry out such a mission.

That was Keith Armstrong.

My strength had not fully returned, but I knew what I could and could not do. Walking away, I felt my energy rise to a clear, icy focus. I would track down at least one of her killers and kill him myself. I swore this oath: that I would avenge my wife's death even if it cost me my life, and if that happened so much the better: we would be together again. I returned to London and reported to my Brigadier. I was told again that the person or persons who killed my wife would be tried as war criminals if they could be found. I did not press the matter. I knew I would arouse their suspicions if I did and instead I feigned a degree of shock and confusion and asked for additional sick leave. Medical permission for leave was granted. "Come back when you are able." Like before I was given money from a special fund. What I had was a small fortune for those days and it was not deducted from my pay. I said that I would probably go to Scotland for a rest.

Instead, I returned to Paris. I had heard of an SS prisoner held under close arrest in the Santé prison who was accused of killing many women and children in Ravensbrück. My policeman friend in the Sûreté suggested that I see this man as he might have some knowledge of SS units assigned to the camp. My French friend said he might talk if I told this German I would offer a word on his behalf. The idea of saying anything whatever on behalf of the SS or Gestapo sickened me, but I was ready to agree to almost anything if I could pick up the trail of the killers.

I said nothing of my intentions; only that I was deeply concerned in seeing these men legally stand trial for their war crimes. I wondered if this man in prison could have been one of the executioners; I hoped not, because then the law would deal with him and I would not have that satisfaction.

My Sûreté friend, who spoke good German, went with me to the prison, a bleak place where too many patriotic Frenchmen and others had died at the hands of the enemy. I had a horror of prisons that continues to this day and I had to fight nausea when the doors clanked shut behind me. When we walked into his cell the man was seated at a simple wooden table. He stood rigidly to attention as we entered, knocking over his chair, with his gaze fixed above and beyond us. I had a desire to smash his face with the fallen chair and I almost picked it up. We sat down and questioned him mostly through my friend. It did not take long to establish that he had been transferred to another camp, Neuengamme, before Arlette was killed. That ruled him out, but we were able to extract the names of the two executioners who might have been on duty until the final weeks of the war and before the camp officials fled.

My friend and I left the cell and he thought I looked ill and suggested that I stay with him for a few days. I did, and early in March of 1946 I went searching for the two men we thought we were able to pin to the time of Arlette's death.

The last known address of the first man was in Neumünster,

north of Hamburg. I had my passes, a jeep, and an interpreter/driver loaned to me in the ancient and beautiful city of Celle. It was a windy and cloudless day when we arrived in Neumünster. I found the house where the man had lived and saw a woman and children living in bleak conditions. The war had hit them, too. Her husband was still on the run, the wife told me, and she believed that he was dead. I asked if she had an official report from the Wermacht or the SS. She had not because the systems had broken down in the final days of the war. She said that her husband had been home on leave for seven days and then had been assigned to the last diminishing and beaten armies of the Third Reich. Somehow I felt he might not be my man, but I kept him in mind.

The other man was at Luchow, close to the old frontier of East and West Germany. This small village is in beautiful wooded country about 85 kilometers from Celle and 100 from Hanover. We drove through these wooded roads and lanes and saw the evidence everywhere of the devastation and heartbreak of war. The people were fighting for survival and yet my mind was locked on a single objective as we approached Luchow. I had an overwhelming sense that I was on the right track. As the jeep picked up speed on the bumpy road, I told my driver that I was going to walk and because there were British soldiers here and there I was not conspicuous. I was on leave. I had my passes. I guess if my authority had been questioned news of my whereabouts might have traveled to London, but London didn't know the Nazi I sought was from this area and I didn't think they were keeping very close track of me.

It was easy to find the small semi-detached house; not in good condition and ancient. I waited about forty feet away for only a short time before I saw what appeared to be the man's wife. There were four children in makeshift clothing and one without shoes.

I walked on and made myself known to the Town Major, a jovial Englishman in his mid thirties. I told him I was on leave and just touring around. He accepted this without question and invited me to his small, beautiful house which the Germans commandeered from a local nobleman. The house was adequate for the Major and his two servants, both Germans who were eager for work. He had one batman, a tall lanky man, straight as a ramrod who ended every sentence with 'Saah!' I was offered a spare bedroom. The Major had only occupied his house for a few weeks since the German Major General, who had been living there, made a hasty retreat. Evidently, he left all of his belongings and was seen in the back seat of a staff car only half dressed and speeding away.

My interpreter found other quarters in the village and I went to see if all was right with him. He was entertaining some of the British soldiers with a mouth organ.

British soldiers were forbidden to fraternize with German women: it was a serious offense. However, without my knowledge, my Major friend had invited two very attractive women for dinner. Wanting to impress me, they talked more than they should have and I learned a good deal more about the village and its returning soldiers.

All of my thoughts centered on revenge. I was like a machine and in some way I wondered how I could ever be a part of the governments plan for me. Just as any machine, push too hard and it develops metal fatigue and cracks.

On the Major's phone, I reversed a call to my friend in Paris to see if he had any further information for me. Yes, there was positive information that the man I was seeking had served as a corporal in the SS and had been at Ravensbrück. That was enough for me: even if he had not been the one who murdered my wife, he had taken part in the murders of some of the 90,000. I made plans to watch him carefully. He worked as a wood cutter, felling trees for the stoves or fireplaces of the British. Not much wood was needed then, but he was stacking up for the winter.

We had one cold night while I was staying with the town Major (his name was Arthur) and I offered to arrange for wood for the fireplace. The next morning I walked to the clearing where the man was working and arranged for wood to be brought to the house.

That evening, when it was dark, I returned. I watched for a while and I saw the man's wife and children cross the road to another house. In my left hand I carried a small German automatic (a Mauser HSc) which I had covered with some old rags so that it was not visible. I moved slowly to the rear door of the house and went in. The man was standing in the kitchen with a mug of hot coffee in his hand. Without any warning I fired at very close range. The mug flew across the room, the man jerked backwards, and I knew that he was finished as the bullet from the deadly, accurate, small weapon had taken away part of his face. I threw the rags into the fire and turned to leave. As I did his wife walked in. For half a second we stared at each other. I knew I had no choice, unless I moved quickly I could be hanged for murder. I knew she was stunned, paralyzed for a moment. In another moment she would scream. I couldn't give her time for that.

As silently as I had come, I returned to the Major's house and went up to my room. When he called up the stairs to ask if I wanted a drink, I answered, "Splendid idea, thank you." I finally felt some calm and a sense of relief. I had kept my oath, and bloody as it was, I felt no remorse. I could thank my SOE training for that.

Soon Arthur was informed that there had been a shooting in the village and the Military Police would be investigating. A day or so later, the official report was that the man, a former member of the SS and his wife had been killed by a person or persons unknown. The case was not closed, of course, but was shelved due to the turmoil in Europe. I counted on the fact that no one would think that a British officer could have been involved.

I could not accept Arthur's hospitality any longer and told him I would be moving on. He waved a friendly farewell and on a clear morning my driver and I drove to Celle.

For too long, my purpose in life had been killing and I was more than sick of it, but at that moment I didn't care. I had avenged my wife's murder. Still, I knew that nothing would bring her back.

Within a week I returned to London. Our people kept in close touch with Military Intelligence and they had access to reports such as the one filed in Luchow. My Colonel had put two and two together and called me in. He was furious.

"What an absolute bloody fool you have been. What the hell possessed you? What got into that stupid brain of yours? How the Hell are we going to cope with this one?"

But they did cope with it. It was hushed up. I was kept out of it. After all how could it have happened when I was in Scotland on sick leave? Backed by authority it had never happened.

Arthur never knew, and when I met him again years later he only mentioned the incident briefly and said, "Damn good riddance." He retired as a Lt. General. I went to his daughter's wedding some years ago for he and I served together at British Rhine HQ in 1965.

Killing the SS corporal had somehow stilled the ferocity in me. That terrible scene of Arlette's last brave moments is burned into my mind. I had met violence with violence and yet the aching sense of loss remained. Occasionally I returned to places where we had been together, seeking a closeness that I knew was gone forever. Certainly in this life.

At Wanborough Manor, where we had done part of our training there was an old wooden stile, which crossed a fence in a secluded area close to the ancient manor house. We used to meet there some-times when we could steal time from our duties, which was not often. Brief as they were those meetings had a sort of desperate intensity which were unforgettable. At the stile we promised that nothing would separate us permanently. She was buried far away in a nameless grave that I would never be able to find, but in some way I wanted her to know that I had tracked down one of her killers. I returned to Wanborough Manor and the stile. Not much had changed. The fields were green although during the war they were plowed for planting. At the moment I arrived, the rooks cawed overhead, the sky was blue, and I stood there with my hat in my hand and placed one hand on the stile. As I walked away I turned to look back and in my thoughts I could see her sitting on the stile in her FANY uniform, her hair neat under her cap, her feet tucked under her, with the same look of love as she waved me a last adieu: not goodbye.

It was surely wishful thinking for a brief second. It seemed as though she was there and in a sense it has always reassured me of a life beyond. After a few minutes in the ancient chapel, I walked up the leafy lane I had known so well, up the hill to the Hog's back, a long ridge and now a busy main road. As I climbed I felt God was there and I felt great peace as I took the train back to London.

chapter 14

THE SUMMER OF 1946 was an intense and difficult one for me. In my 'rehabilitation' I was told repeatedly that it was necessary to blot out all traces of my recent past: marriage, military record, everything, so that if a hostile power ever attempted to check on me they would run up against a stone wall. Everything from my past went into deep files. These precautions, my superiors told me, might save my life one day.

The cover biography had me listed as the son of Anglo Indian parents, born a year later than I really was and therefor too young to have been involved in any of the Intelligence work of the war. Post war many British subjects living in India during the Raj had a difficult time verifying their births. Records were not kept well and sometimes the only proof of birth was a scrap of paper torn from an exercise book and signed by a Minister or Parson. My "father" was a veteran of WWI with vast investments in tea plantations. My "mother" was of Russian background born in India.

So that I could become more acquainted with the atmosphere and surroundings I was sent to Calcutta. From there I traveled overland in a Puff and Billy steam engine to Darjeeling where I was to have lived while attending Saint Paul's School. It was a few day's journey that took me through some of the most beautiful country that I have seen: rugged mountains, streams, and tea plantations on the slopes as we climbed to over six thousand feet. When it was necessary to stretch my legs it was possible to walk along the slow moving train. However this was not advisable at night as the train might leave you behind on the tracks with a slit throat and/or an empty purse.

I spent a few delightful weeks in Darjeeling to acquaint myself with the school. This was a fine hill station of great rugged beauty where the air was rare. In the early morning the mist might cover everything, but as the sun rose, Mt Everest stood huge and clear from some viewpoints. Besides climbing in the hills in my spare time, I learned everything possible of St. Paul's School. Who was the Headmaster? Who were the head boys? I learned enough of the language to converse with servants. An amusing incident occurred some years later in London. Someone mentioned to one of the guests in my club that he should talk to me as we had attended the same school in Darjeeling. This man was a delightful Indian who had been Head Boy during my supposed stay at school. To my surprise, he was very pleased to see me and he said he remembered me well! This conversation helped to convince my local friends of my years in India. The charade continued.

As I look back now, it is clear to me that after I was released from hospital in 1945, my mentors in SOE brought me along very slowly and cautiously, at first giving me tasks that required little or no skill at all; just token participation. Yet, some of those tasks had a highly charged emotional element. Perhaps they were testing me to see how much my battered nervous system could stand. In 1945 and 1946 the answer was: not much.

For example, at one point I was assigned to the London Cage. This was an interrogation center for former German officers, at 8 Kensington Palace Gardens. It was under the command of Lieutenant Colonel A.P. Scotland, an extraordinary man who had served as a Major General on Hitler's staff. He had served in the German army for many years, but during all this time had been working for British Intelligence, supplying information to our side. At the end of the war, he simply walked across the lines and demanded to be taken to General Headquarters. When his story was confirmed he was flown across the Channel.

During my assignment at the Cage I was on a court martial for eight German soldiers who had callously killed a German Sergeant Major on the day peace was declared. These men had been confined in a camp in the Scottish Highlands for Germans in the 'black' category, so called because they were fanatical and dangerous Nazis. The Sergeant Major, who was one of them, had simply said that he was glad that the war was over so he could get back to his wife. For that remark they murdered him and hung his body in the bathroom of the camp. They were brought to London for trial.

The president of the court was Colonel R.H.A. Kellie. The prosecutor was Major Richard Hilliard. Two British officers acted as counsels for the defense. Hearing the testimony were two Lt. Colonels and three Majors of whom I was one, and the youngest.

Five of the Nazis were removed to Pentonville Prison, where they were hanged. They had expected to face a firing squad at worst, not the ignominious gallows. I felt no pity for them. My only feeling was that the war was not really over: the killing, violence, and overlay of horror continued.

In those days the highly sensitive question of treason or betrayal inside Dutch Section was like an invisible cloud hanging over everything. We agents were programmed never to talk of any aspect of our work, but with some fifty of fifty-three agents captured or killed by the Nazis, with innumerable radio distress signals unanswered or ignored, it was obvious that there was a great deal to be concealed.

Recent books have made it clear that there was then, and has ever since been, an extraordinary tendency within MI5 and MI6, even when the guilt of an individual was almost certain, to say, "Oh, tsk, tsk! Too bad! But let's not have any beastly publicity. Let's just retire the blighter and get him out of the way." In this climate some of those who were investigated were cleared; some were simply allowed to fade away. Very few were found guilty.

Naturally, the Netherlands government was involved and it was said that a Royal Dutch Commission was going to probe into the situation. Those higher up in Dutch Section who had something to hide were busy preparing a defense that included false statements and misleading testimony from people like myself. Even my birth certificate, on record in Somerset House, was altered to make me older than I was making me capable of being in the service at certain times. (To this day, I have to stop and think when asked for my birth date. It has been changed several times.) I was very carefully briefed on the role I would play if called to appear before the commission, and I was prepared to carry it out if necessary. Some dim reminder of the Ninth Commandment forbidding false witness troubled me and I was relieved when the inquiry was dropped. Perhaps because too many people in England and Holland were afraid of what might be revealed.

Although I have never revealed any of them, my inadvertent discovery of some details of the betrayal in N Section has haunted me to this day and caused grief for me and fear for the safety of those close to me.

One of the players in this drama was a Dutchman named Christiaan Lindemanns, a giant of a man, former wrestler, whose nick name was King Kong. A known double agent, he was regarded by some on the Allied side as a hero for his work in leading bold Resistance attacks in the early part of the war. He also worked for the Germans. There was evidence that in 1944, when his brother Hendrik was arrested by the Gestapo, Lindemanns bought his brother's freedom by passing along the information about Operation Market Garden, which included the ill-fated air drop at Arnhem.

There was an Allied investigator named Oreste Pinto with one of the finest minds I have ever known and with an amazing recall for details. He became convinced that Christiaan Lindemanns was the traitor who enabled the Nazis to move two Panzer divisions into the Arnhem area in time to turn the Allied assault into a disaster. One clue that attracted Pinto's attention was that in many Resistance attacks on the enemy, in spite of his great size that would have made him a very conspicuous target, he always seemed to escape unscathed.

Lindemanns was finally arrested and brought to England for further interrogation. He was so huge that no handcuffs could be found to fit him so he had to be bound with strong ropes. Pinto extracted a confession that covered over more than twenty pages. I saw an English translation. It left no doubt ... in Pinto's mind, at least ... that Lindemanns was the traitor of Arnhem. He was returned to Holland in poor health from an old gun shot wound where he was confined in Scheveningen Prison, a place I remembered all too well. So far he had not been brought to trial, but now one was scheduled.

A young nurse worked in the hospital ward of the prison. The official story was that she fell in love with Lindemanns and helped him organize an escape. With the help of another prisoner ... aptly known as the 'singing rat' ... they sawed through the bars of a window in the cell, and Lindemanns tried to slide down an improvised rope to the ground. He was too weak, however, and was recaptured almost immediately. Then, still according to the official version, he persuaded the girl to join him in a suicide pact. Supposedly, both swallowed a lethal dose of poison. They were discovered, and the nurse amazingly survived. Whether Lindemanns was murdered, I don't know. I am sure that there were many who were relieved to hear of his death! What I do know is that after the war the nurse and the "singing rat" held highly placed positions.

My assignment was to go to Holland with Oreste Pinto and write a report on Lindemanns' death. Again, the mission may have been a test of my reactions. It was certainly a grim assignment. The Dutchman's huge body was still stretched out, face down, in his cell: in this bleak place where so many Allied agents and patriotic Dutchmen had been tortured and killed by the Nazis. My stomach was churning and I could feel the walls closing in on me. With Pinto I completed the report, but the demons of Buchenwald were still with me as I was to learn before the summer was over.

At a social gathering, I met a man named William Nicol Gray, a tough former Lt. Colonel of Royal Marines, who had recently been appointed Inspector General of the Palestine Police. When he learned something of my background he suggested that I join him in Palestine as he could use my experience with guerilla warfare. Palestine had been liberated from the Ottoman Empire by General Allenby in 1917 and declared a British Mandate. Now there was a desire to evict the British and make Palestine a home for the Jewish people. Guerilla groups, led by Menachim Begin among others, were killing British men women and children. My superiors in Baker Street thought the experience would be valuable and as usual I could report any useful information back to them. I agreed and truly hoped that this might be a way to escape from my commitment (bondage, really). After the war SOE ceased to exist and those of us who were kept employed now worked for MI6, a department of the Foreign Office. They were wrong about my ability to handle the assignment; I was wrong about being able to escape my commitment.

As they were trying to find a homeland in Palestine, many Jews were turned away and sent to internment camps in Cyprus. This policy led to some painful incidents. I recall one where a gaunt couple ... he released recently from Belsen and she from Ravensbrück ... threw themselves from a ship that had been denied access, and tried to swim ashore. When they reached the beach they were handled roughly by the soldiers, who were already tense from recent bombings. The whole episode distressed me, reviving painful memories, and I began to show signs of stress. When it became evident that I was not handling the assignment well, I was sent to Malta, where ten days rest at the home of Mabel Strickland did wonders for me. She was a member of an old Maltese family, at least twenty years my senior, friendly, charming, and a generous hostess. Although I was still haunted by the horrors of Buchenwald, I was able to lose myself in reading the history of Malta. I became enthralled by the stories of the Apostle Paul whose ship was wrecked there. He was able, with his dynamic teaching, to convert the island to Christianity. His preaching has captured me ever since. I enjoyed roaming the ancient ruins, too.

Back in London it was agreed that it had been a mistake to allow me to go to the Middle East. "A bit too soon, old chap. Not to worry!" They urged me to go home and rest a bit, saying they would have another assignment for me in due course.

So I did go home, but my stay there was not satisfactory, either. I was restless and moody, and my parents were at a loss to understand me. Once I became embroiled in a fight with some farmers who were trying to pull a badger out of its hole with tongs. Those tongs reminded me of the ones I had been forced to use to drag corpses from the hospital in the camp. In my fury, I roughed them up quite badly and they were lucky I didn't kill them. There were complaints, of course, and it took my father's best efforts to get me off. He could not reconcile the weak image he had of me with this recent incident.

One night I went out with two of the young men of the village and got very drunk at a pub owned by a friend of my mother. I passed out and was put to bed in the pub, spending the whole night there. My mother was convinced that the pub owner had seduced me (evidently she had none too high an opinion of her old chum). The lady had not seduced me at all. For one thing she did not try; and for another, I was not a likely prospect for any sort of amorous activity in those days. My father was heard to say despairingly, "My God, what will the boy do next?"

He would have been astonished if he had known what the faceless wonders had in store for me. So would I.

After my release from hospital in the summer of 1945, when I was able to concentrate for any length of time, I wrote an Intelligence report of my activities in Arnhem for my superiors in SOE. This included the episode where I had destroyed a German Staff car with a burst from the un-manned Bren gun I had found mounted on a tripod at the crossroads. When I wrote the report I had no knowledge of the occupants of the car; only that I had killed a high ranking German officer. I reported that British troops were also firing at the car with Sten guns. Anyone who saw photographs of the car would know that such massive damage could have been caused only by concentrated Bren gun fire.

On January 28, 1947, with only a few days notice, and in full dress provided by my superiors, I presented my self at Buckingham Palace to receive the Military Cross from King George VI. The citation, I was told, would refer to the Bren gun episode.

I was reluctant to go because I felt such a ceremony would give me a high visibility and would tend to interfere with the cloak of anonymity that the 'firm' was weaving around me. It was an order. I had no choice.

I have a vivid memory of the throne room at the Palace. Several other persons were receiving "special list" decorations. This meant that there would be no official announcement. Later such decorations were given by mail and this may have been the last time that they were given personally by the King. Odette Churchill, already decorated for her heroic resistance to Nazi torture was there. Field Marshal Lord Wavell was there and I remember his heavy brown brogues worn instead of regulation shoes. Later he presented me with a small, inscribed, silver tray as a memento of the occasion: a rather extraordinary gesture from a Field Marshal to a very young soldier whom he had never met. I still have and treasure it.

His Majesty appeared, almost magically, through a concealed door that opened from behind the dais. He was a slender man, not very tall, but with a great presence. He had read the citations in advance and so was able to say something appropriate to each recipient as he pinned on the medals. He spoke with a slight stammer, and asked me about the Arnhem episode which I described briefly. "How amazing," he said. "You must come to tea and tell my family about it." Come to tea? I was speechless, and thought he was just being kind. Later I was commanded to come to tea at Windsor Castle where I did meet the Royal family. I wished that my own family could have known of this invitation, but of course, they couldn't know of the Military Cross or the invitation to tea, as I was still under restrictions of covert operations.

Another decoration bestowed that day was a posthumous George Cross, the civilian equivalent of the Victoria Cross. It was awarded to Violette Szabo, another member of SOE, who died in Ravensbrück. There to receive the award were her parents and small daughter, Tania. The King told her that the medal was for her mother and to take good care of it. When someone later spoke to Tania about the medal, she said. "It's for Mummy; I'm going to keep it for her until she gets home." I happened to look at the Field Marshal and I saw tears in that stern warriors eyes. There were some in mine as well.

Later, with some of the others who had been decorated, I went to the Ritz Hotel for a kind of celebratory luncheon. We had champagne and many toasts. Each of us was prepared to foot his share of the bill, but when the time came, there was no bill. It had been taken care of, we were told. We all thought, and I am sure that we were correct, that His Majesty had paid the bill.

I wondered about the award given to me on that wintry morning. I was pleased to receive it as it corroborated my part in the Nazi officer's death, but I was never sure who had initiated it. Perhaps it was part of the firm's campaign to make me more accepting of reemployment. Perhaps ... and this seems more likely ... it was a move by the Prime Minister to compensate for the betrayal that I had suffered at his hands. Later, during one of my visits to Chartwell, Sir Winston told me that he had spoken to the King about me, but did not go into detail. The gift from Lord Wavell made me think that powerful influences were behind the award, but I will never know. My chief at the Foreign Office told me that the medal would be kept in a safe place to be kept and handed to my family in the event of my demise. And so, that and other medals, along with the Croix de Guerre, three from Belgium and the two from France, went into deep files where they remained for years along with other papers relating to my activities.

Today, if anyone tried to corroborate these awards, they would run up against the stone wall of silence that the firm erected around me with such thoroughness and efficiency. Not only the awards would not be corroborated, but my entire years of service as well. For me to claim a high decoration that has not been awarded would be the worst kind of deception and dishonor imaginable.

I was compensated with praise and decorations, but not all of us were so fortunate. During my stay in the hospital, I was on an outing chaperoned by an Army nurse and we were standing in the lobby of the Piccadilly Hotel. An old man shuffled up to us and I heard my code name from training days, Vapor, being called out. What seemed to be an old man held out his hands to me and I saw that all of his fingers and thumbs were missing. He only seemed like an old man because his feet were so badly twisted and crippled that he could hardly walk. There were tears in his eyes and then in mine when I realized who he was: a friend who had trained with me at Camp X in Canada. I had heard that he was dead, and he heard the same of me.

Oblivious to the crowd in the lobby we embraced with great emotion. Slowly during the next few hours his story unfolded. He was a quiet man and had found his training hard. When it was decided that he had not passed the course well, he was not told. (The story was beginning to sound familiar.) He was parachuted into France with information that was incorrect, designed to confuse the Germans when extracted from him by torture. When the torture became unbearable, he tried to use the cyanide tooth, but of course it didn't work. To his eternal credit he steadfastly refused to reveal anything. Now he was bitter and crippled and alone. The 'firm' had done nothing for him and refused to acknowledge his existence.

I was so incensed that I went to my superiors and demanded that some action be taken. "If no action is taken," I said, "I will try to have this injustice brought up in he House of Commons." It was at this time that Irene Ward (later Dame) began assisting former members of SOE with similar circumstances.

I was told,"Mind your own business. There are reasons best known to us that the case should not be discussed. You signed the Official Secrets Act. The matter is closed."

It was far from closed as far as I was concerned. I placed my friend and myself in a taxi, and over his protests, went to #10 Downing

NO CLOAK NO DAGGER

Street, where Winston Churchill was still in office. I told the keepers at the door that I had no appointment, but I would wait until I had seen the Prime Minister. After a long wait and three civil servants who tried to dissuade me, Winston Churchill came into the hall. I asked if I might speak to him alone and we went into his study. I explained with considerable force and feeling what had happened to my friend. He said that if my facts were correct "something would be done" and he looked me in the eye and stuck out his chin. I knew then that he would help. Then we went out into the hall and he took my friend by the wrists and said,"I would like to shake your hands." My friend was overcome.

After we had some refreshment, a taxi was ordered and Mrs. Churchill showed us to the door. As we left, a policeman on duty opened the door of the cab for us and said, "Well, Sir, whatever you came for it must 'ave been important!" To me it was. It was the beginning of my fight against injustice.

My friend received the Military Cross and a substantial pension. He should have had greater compensation for his fearful damage. He should have been given the George or Victoria Cross, but I was happy for him. A year or so later, somewhat rehabilitated, he sailed for South America and never returned. I had carefully written letters from him occasionally. He had settled down and was teaching mathematics in a local school. A brave man indeed, one to whom we owe so much; and we forget too soon.

It was at this time that my in-laws returned to Belgium taking my son with them. The firm allowed me to see him once before they left. The de Roche family still didn't know what had happened to Arlette and I was not allowed to tell them. I was glad that my little boy was going with them for I knew they loved him and he would get good care and in a way he was some small compensation for all they had lost. It would be years before my superiors would allow me to see my son again.

chapter 15

BACK HOME AFTER MY return from Palestine I was supposed to rest and gain my emotional equilibrium. My mother and father greeted me in a lukewarm way. Had I really been looking for a job? Was I ever going to amount to anything? Yet there was a concern beneath their annoyance and my father was able to get me a job with a contractor that he knew through business.

I was glad for the chance to be away for a while. I knew the firm would keep an eye on me, and when it suited them I might be called back to work. I was in no hurry for this to happen and in the meantime I was to appear the same as many other young men and women struggling to rehabilitate.

My job was not too demanding and my co-workers were kind and interesting to talk to. I had access to a swimming pool and would go in every morning to do laps and in the winter of 1946-47 many a morning I had to break through the ice. My friends thought I was mad, but I had every intention of staying tough and keeping my body in shape. I tried to appear like other young men and I made an occasional date, but my heart was far away and the memory of Arlette was strong. One night the San Carlos Opera of Naples presented a performance of 'La Boheme'. I was so deeply moved by Mimi's wraithlike demeanor as she was dying that I left when the curtain fell. I walked into the night and there under the stars I vowed that I would never marry again; I meant it with all my heart.

Now and then I would see my family who lived not too far away. When money due me from service arrived in the mail, without my knowledge, my father kept it from me leaving me with very little funds.

Gradually, I became increasingly restless in the job and asked to be excused as I knew that I could easily be replaced.

When the request was granted, I went straight to London, feeling a sense of relief and freedom, but also very poor. My father controlled the purse strings at one end and at the other, the 'firm' was holding my pay in a "special fund."

To stay alive I got a job as a dishwasher and clearer at Lyons Corner House, the big cafeteria restaurant in the center of London. Although my hands were wrinkled and cut from the washing up, I had the advantage of stuffing left over food in my pockets when I was clearing the tables. Sometimes I saw people I knew. They were astonished to find me clearing tables, but I told them I was just getting back on my feet. The news soon reached home.

Occasionally I would sleep in Green Park which came alive with prostitutes and other people of the night. Sometimes I had conversations with 'ladies of the evening', and one called Joan, was a pretty girl about my age. She felt sorry for me and took me home to her luxury flat off Knightsbridge. Rationing was still in force, but her two large refrigerators were stocked with all the food that one could not easily buy. I found her a kind and compassionate girl who often sold herself, only to officers and preferably Americans, who had the most money! She said she was ready for a holiday and having me there would make it possible. She went shopping and when I was not at work I stayed in her place, read, and appreciated the quiet and solitude of that flat high above the noisy street below. Soon I realized that Joan had to be about her business and I had to leave.

When I could afford it, I frequented the Royal Overseas League, a pleasant club just off St. James Street. In those days it was a great center for service people. Occasionally I had invitations to the country, to stay with families who offered their hospitality to servicemen and women. I stayed with three families for long weekends and they could not imagine how grateful I was for these respites.

One day the firm let me know I was to meet a bank clerk who would be my contact. I went to Cox and Kings Bank to cash a small check and without looking up, a man next to me continued writing, with his lips barely moving, and told me to report to a certain house in the suburbs.

The next day I went to Potter's Bar on the outskirts of London. I was met there by a distinguished, well spoken man, who had the mannerisms of an officer. He took me to a pleasantly furnished flat nearby. "Well, young man," he said rather pompously, "here we are again." (we had never met before) "Seems to me it's time you went back to work. Must have enjoyed the rest ... eh, what?" I thought, 'you idiot' and nearly told him so, but quickly his manner changed to one of complete authority. "In a short time we expect to have a job for you. We want to see how you handle it," he paused and looked at me hard, "but first ... a little refresher course. You'll enjoy it, I'm sure."

I was given instructions to a 'safe house' in the country, an establishment for rehabilitation and advanced training. "You may wonder why you came here first," he said, "but, I need to see if you're fit and sound. Seems to me, aaah ... you look well enough, though a few bags under the eyes ... been living it up?" said the idiot with a wolfish smile. I think he was trying to provoke me to see how I would react. "May I offer you a drink?" I shook my head thinking what I really wanted was a good meal. "Offer you a sandwich?" That sounded much better.

"I suppose you've nowhere to sleep tonight?" he went on. "Better stay here then. Put you up on the sofa with a sleeping bag ... nothing like Joan, though ..." and he laughed heartily to himself. I did not move a muscle but I realized then that everything I did was known to my employers.

The next morning was bright and sunny and my host towered above me with a cup of strong tea. "Wakey, wakey," he said and as he stood there I realized that he was a homosexual. In those days the threat of blackmail and the possibility of an agent being compromised was so great that homosexuality among us was taboo and I wondered why the firm had employed him. I dressed before I touched the tea as I was eager to get away. Had he been sent to test me? After all, the department knew that I was lonely and not interested in women. I will never know because I made a hasty exit. Before I left he proffered two white fivers.

"If they came from the firm, I'll take them."

With some annoyance he said, "Well, yes, they did."

I walked off onto the bright warm morning and never looked back as I ran for the red double-decker bus.

I had four days until I had to report to the house in the country. I was rich. I had two fivers, which in those days could buy a great deal. I settled myself in a modest hotel costing ten shillings a night, and I had a few drinks and a good dinner that evening.

The next day I called a girl I had met at the Royal Overseas League and asked her to lunch. She was vivacious and beautiful, and had been a WAAF officer. Being with her made me realize what I was missing and I wished to God that I was sitting there with Arlette. The girl was curious about what my plans were for the future. She said that she knew how difficult it was to get settled, but "don't leave it too long." After lunch, as she walked away, I watched her disappear into the crowd and nearly went after her to tell her how badly I needed a friend, but I didn't think she would understand.

I still had two days before I had to report, so on impulse I took the train to my old school and walked down the hill to the Junior House in hopes of seeing my old Housemaster, Clive Mainwaring. There he was in shorts and long socks, puttering in the large garden with smoke billowing from his pipe.

"My dear Keith," was his spontaneous greeting, and before I knew it we were in his cozy sitting room, drinking tea, and reminiscing. I looked through the window at the playing fields where not so long ago, but really a lifetime ago, I had been just a young boy playing cricket. This man was one of the bright spots in my school days. He was a fine athlete and a scholar who taught Latin and French. He gave so much to young people and especially to me, a young boy who lost school time from illness.

When it was time to leave I walked up the hill through the ancient market town, across the bridge and on to the railway station where I took a train to London.

Two days later I took a train to Sussex, where in a sudden rain shower I was met by a tall, gaunt man in a battered felt hat and a too small army trench coat draped over his shoulders. He approached me with a smile, offered his hand and then took my small suitcase from me. "I'll pop that in the back of my car," he said and continued,"no need for identification ... I studied a photo of you." He squeezed his way into the driver's seat of an ancient Morris car, patted the wheel, and said,"Jolly fine ol' horse." So often the British take such pride in these old cars and this one was highly polished and glistened in the

rain. "Me name's Goshens, Major, 52nd Punjabis ... Indian Army y'
know. So you've come to join our band of rogues, eh what? Might as
well put you in the picture right away. Don't ask questions ... suppose
you know all that sort of stuff? You'll be told a great deal; all of us are
given new surnames for this sort of 'jolly' y' understand? Colonel's a
fine fellow, but bloody stickler for discipline." He puffed away on his
cigarette as we drove along.

We had been driving for about half an hour when, suddenly he
made a turn to the right almost as if it was unexpected. It was quiet
on the lane as we drove under leafy trees, but within seconds two
men in civilian clothes stepped from the bushes and stood firmly in
the middle of the road. They viewed me carefully and without a word
waved us on beyond the iron gates. Not a sign of anyone as we walked
through the massive front doors of the old Jacobean house. The smell
of an old house mingled with the aroma of cooking from the below-
stairs kitchens.

"Now then ol' fruit, we're home at last. Welcome. It may be the
last kind word you get... heah?" I followed him up a wide staircase
and down a hall to a room with two beds. "There's yuh cupboard,
have a wash, and come down to the library for a spot of tea, and meet
the fellows."

After unpacking I went down and entered a room marked 'library'
where ten men and two women sat drinking tea. Each looked up
with interest and as I was introduced I found that my name was
to be Lindlay. I was introduced to the commanding officer, Colonel
Anstruther (so called), a tough soldier who gave me a sharp, apprais-
ing look. It was a motley crowd: all had been given officer status. I
learned that one had been a very successful safe cracker before the
war. He had been taken from prison for his expertise, dropped into
enemy territory, was decorated and went back to prison later for a
similar offense. I was impressed by a Sergeant Major, short, barrel
chested, hard as nails who had been a prewar soldier in India on the
Northwest Frontier in the days of the Raj. He had merry eyes and a
keen sense of humor. The two women said little, but it was obvious
that they were completely capable of taking care of themselves.

Starting at dawn the next morning we were thrown into hard
training and often worked more than ten hours a day. First came

intensive written tests. At school, tests were always hard for me, but surprisingly I found now that I could do very well. Perhaps the flat speakers placed under our pillows at night somehow penetrated our brains as we slept. Often we were wakened with flashlights glaring into our faces for sudden harsh questioning. I was being programmed to give false testimony in the inquiry into Dutch section and every detail had to be letter perfect.

We had several days of training in guerilla warfare in the surrounding woods, often in the rain, and always at night. This was old hat to me and I could do quite well in these exercises: dealing with trip wires, booby traps, and loud speakers set up to confuse us. These exercises were miniature war games and we were expected to play rough if necessary. One day the Sergeant Major and I decided to 'capture' the Colonel's command post ... with him in it. We did this by watching the way the rabbits avoided the electrically charged wires around the hut. That helped us locate the wires and with rubber handled clippers we cut the wires, marched the startled and furious Colonel back to the main house, where he finally calmed down and poured us a drink.

Much less amusing were the sessions in the very realistic cells designed to teach us how to handle ourselves if we were ever captured and tortured by the enemy. (The enemy now were the Communists.) I had already experienced what the Gestapo and later the SS guards in Buchenwald could do so I had very little patience with it. We were left alone, in a bare cell, naked, with nothing but a single blanket. At times we were chained by our wrists with feet barely touching the ground and "interrogated" by "jailers" who might spit in your face, punch you in the stomach or groin, all the while keeping up a torrent of foul mouthed abuse. One interrogator I privately named 'the thug' because he seemed to take particular delight in the roughest of abuse. I don't know where they recruited these people; some spoke with foreign accents, some did not. In any case they thoroughly enjoyed their 'work'. The solitude, cold, beatings, and the darkness gave one plenty of time to build up anger and resentment. Certainly this was true of me. When the thug finally opened the door one night and told me to get dressed for dinner, I kicked him hard with my bare foot and left him writhing on the stone floor.

The house and the surrounding wooded grounds had very tight security with armed sentries, electrified fences, and guard dogs, not only to keep intruders out, but to keep us in.

One night at dinner Colonel 'Anstruther' said to me, "I have an idea ... you're very good at this guerilla stuff, Lindlay. Why don't you see if you can get out of this place. D'you think it's possible? How about you and the Sergeant Major having a try?"

I said, "Will I get some kind of reward if I do? Or will I be shut up in some bloody cell if I don't?"

Almost gleefully he said,"Well ... we'll have to punish you a bit if you try, and then fail, which I am sure you will. Might as well be honest about that, ... eh, what?"

"If you insist, Sir, I'll bloody well take you on, but it will cost you fifty pounds, if you lose. What do you say to that?"

"Damn cheek," he glowered. "Thirty-five."

"Now it's gone up to seventy-five. Or not at all." The Sergeant Major who had been watching us all this time from behind the Colonel's back, grinned, and made the thumbs up gesture.

"Well, all right. You have three days," Anstruther said rather sourly.

"No time limits, Sir. We've made the bet. You can't change the rules."

We left it at that, and after three days the Colonel wanted to know if we were going to make a move. I told him I was thinking about it, but it seemed a silly idea and anyway if we lost I had no money to honor the debt, as he knew. This was said to make him think we had abandoned the idea, but we certainly hadn't. Nights spent in the soaking rain had made the Sergeant Major and me well acquainted with every inch of the grounds. We knew the movement of the guards: when they came on duty and when they were relieved. The biggest problem were the dogs, fierce Alsations, trained to bite a man's right arm, and fortunately not his throat. We made ourselves arm guards, wrapping long strips of tape around bits of cloth: crude, but, we hoped effective. We had our knives and I felt confidant with this splendid soldier beside me. As usual, it was raining on the night we chose. The 'thug' happened to be on duty near the entrance in the small hut surrounded by trees. We knew there would be trip wires, too. As we silently approached the hut, an Alsation came at me out of the shadows and threw me to the ground, its teeth buried in my padded arm. Seconds later, the knife from my left hand was in its throat. The Sergeant Major had done the same with a second dog. A third dog got a handful of pepper in its eyes. (I had been collecting it from the dining table and pouring it into an envelope in my lap. I left some in the shaker so as not to arouse suspicion.) Pepper can be very effective if thrown at close range and if there is no wind. It distracted the third dog long enough for the knife in my left hand to do its work.

The noise alerted the 'thug' who came out of the hut like a bullet. When we closed in, I must say, he put up one fierce struggle, striving to get to a trip wire that would have set off the alarm. He laid my partner's cheek open with a blow from his fist, and I caught an elbow in the mouth before we hammered him to the ground and put him to sleep with a not so gentle tap of the foot. We put him back in the hut and sat him at his desk, hunched over, as if he was simply dozing.

The gate was wired and so was the fence, so we ripped a long plank from the roof of the hut, leaned it against the gate, scrambled over. We knew this would trip an alarm elsewhere, but we were outside now and didn't care. In short order, Colonel Anstruther came running along with three guards. One of them went into the hut and called out that one security officer was injured. "Christ!" said the colonel and disappeared into the hut. He came out, saw us on the far side of the gate, and said, "You've gone too far with all this Lindlay. I hold you responsible to the injury to my man."

"Balls!" I said and walked through the open gate. I felt the whole thing was bloody silly, but if they had wanted us to prove something, we had proved it.

Back at the house we were reprimanded quite severely, especially for killing the dogs. "Those animals were valuable," he said. "You went too bloody far."

"Well, Sir, you know how often we've been told to eliminate anything or anybody who gets in our way." (I was not happy about having to kill the dogs, but it couldn't be prevented.)

The medical officer was not available that weekend so I put some whisky on the Sergeant Major's cut and my own bruised mouth, drank some of it, and went up to my room to clean up. The Indian Army Major, my room companion, turned on the light. "Bloody hell, ol' boy," he said. "You ARE a mess!"

"So's that bastard who pushed us around," I told him grimly.

The next few days were busy, but finally the Colonel came to the mess and said, "Lindlay, you and the Sergeant Major were not bad; quite a good show, I must admit."

"Thank you, Sir, and I would not mind having the seventy-five pounds."

He paid up without a murmur, probably from the fund of ready cash that always seemed to exist in these places. I thanked him and gave the Sergeant Major half.

Now I had ten days of easy living, relaxed moments, hours spent talking to a doctor or sometimes two at a time. Suddenly everyone seemed to be on my side. I was told to forget the difficulties, the bad dreams, the flickering memories. They offered to help me with hypnosis and drugs. I was concerned about what I might say under those circumstances and called London to get the firm's reaction. They said I had nothing to fear and to cooperate fully. I did, with a few reservations, and soon the war seemed hazy and far away, the loss of Arlette seemed bearable, and I felt better able to deal with life. In retrospect, much of the training I had in that place was brutal and unnecessary, but the mental conditioning was effective and when I left I felt in good order and in reasonable shape. Little did I realize that it was to the firm's benefit that I had placed some of the war behind me. At the time I was a willing participant to the programming and the later deceptions.

I was given fifty pounds for expenses, which added to the sum I won, made me feel rich. I was told to go to Brighton for a week of relaxation then return to London where at the proper time I would be contacted.

Soon after, at the Overseas League a small quiet man carrying a rolled up umbrella and wearing a bowler hat, spoke to me politely. "I say, would you join me for tea?" As we drank tea and ate little sandwiches, he said with a smile, "We thought you did rather well in the country. Sorry there were so many tests an' all that, but we really needed to test you for another job, d'you see? In the mean time your account at Cox and Kings no longer exists." This was when I was told that any money earned would be held for me, gaining interest, until retirement or for my family should I meet with an untimely demise. Incredibly these many years later I am still trying to recover that money and much more. "And now," the little man said, "it's about time you went back to some serious work. Don't you agree? Here's what you must do ..."

chapter 16

IN THE DAYS AFTER Germany's collapse, young agents in British Intelligence, like myself, were constantly told that a new world had to be created from the ashes of war, and Europe had to be rebuilt quickly to withstand the Communist threat looming in the East, and we were fortunate and privileged to have a hidden, but crucial part in this noble cause.

Europe was in turmoil. The war was over, yet on the Continent a fierce and secret struggle was taking place between the Americans, British, French on the one hand and the Soviet Union on the other. The struggle for each side was to acquire the best brains, the best scientists, the best technicians, the best rocket engineers: in short anyone who had worked for the third Reich. In this brutal competition kidnappings were common and sometimes people died. Many Nazis were still in hiding. Some remained in Germany while others fled to South America where there were friendly governments: particularly in Argentina.

In the world of Intelligence, former German Abwher officers were sought by the West for knowledge they had of Soviet subversives and spy networks. Especially prized were those who had worked for Admiral Wilhelm Canaris, Hitler's Chief of Intelligence. Even if some of those were war criminals much could be, and often was, overlooked if they cooperated. They were simply 'denazified'. The Soviets had the same objective, of course, and they often used the families of such people as hostages to compel submission and obedience. Either you worked for them or you died or were sent into slave labor, where you might die anyway.

In 1946 when SOE was disbanded, some of us were integrated into MI6. Now the main adversary was no longer Nazi Germany; it was the Soviet Union. In the USA the OSS had been dissolved and replaced by the CIA. To aid in the manhunt in Germany and behind the Iron Curtain the CIA had set up one of Hitler's brightest officers, Major General Reinhardt Gehlen, as head of a highly secret organization known as ORG. ORG had almost unlimited quantities of American money, and not surprisingly, a fair number of its personnel were former Nazis. These men were ruthless, disciplined, and it was thought their hatred of the Jews could easily be turned into a hatred of the Soviets. It did not take much turning. All of this was rationalized on the belief that the Soviets were now the enemy and every effort had to be made to contain them. In this event, as in all Intelligence work, the end was believed to justify the means.

Gehlen was a thin, balding man who usually wore dark glasses. He had a clear, keen brain and an unswerving loyalty, not to Hitler or the Nazis, but to his native land. He was willing to work for the U.S, but his ultimate goal was to build an organization that would hasten the rebuilding of Germany. In later years I came to know him well and I think he knew more about me than anyone outside of British Intelligence. He always treated me correctly and sometimes even with kindness, but he would not have hesitated to have me killed if the need arose. Years later Gehlen broke away from the US.

The 'job' the department had in mind for me was a part of the ultra secret Gehlen operation being carried out in central Europe, but I knew nothing about it at first.

Soon after my encounter with the man in the bowler hat, I went to an address I had memorized near Russell Square, an unobtrusive house with dirty lace curtains. A large woman answered the door wiping her hands on her apron. "We're full up," she announced, which was what I was expecting her to say.

I gave her the required answer, "I came to see the room and I telephoned last week." She stepped back without another word and swung the door wide open.

Inside I was told that I could stay the night and someone would be by the next morning. The bed was lumpy and the sheets smelled of someone else, so I used my face towel to cover the pillow. The room rattled all night as the traffic passed outside, yet my newly acquired confidence and well being persisted and I looked forward to the next day with anticipation.

The large woman provided a good breakfast with sausages: a treat as there was still strict rationing. Then I sat by the small, black, cast iron fireplace, warming my hands and waiting for the visitor. He arrived shortly, a nondescript little man who sat with his raincoat on. Quietly he said, "This room is rather small."

I replied, "It's fine enough for a brief visit."

Now he was relaxed and sure of me so he told me to make my way alone to Horse Guards Parade. "Across the Parade Ground you will find gardens. Walk to the pond, sit on the first bench ... and wait. Be there exactly at noon." This may seem unnecessary to the reader, but it was all part of obedience, discipline, training, and security.

He left me as quickly as he had come and I took leave of the large lady. I caught a bus to the Strand and walked past the Savoy Hotel where Claude Dansey had recruited me for 'Z' section. It seemed a century ago. Then I walked past Northumberland House and across Horse Guards Parade to the green bench where I was to wait. Soon a stranger sat down at the other end of he bench. With a sigh and a pause he said, looking intently at the water,"Well, you arrived safely."

I replied, "Yes, I enjoyed the walk." Again, both prearranged signals. Undercover of his newspaper he passed me a welcome sum of money and told me to take a train to a house in the country.

"You'll be there a few days," he said. "Good luck to you," and with a cough he walked away.

I took the train as I was instructed and from the station in Dorking took a taxi to the address I had memorized. It was another bleak looking country house, set back from the road and surrounded by trees. There were three men at the door and one showed me to a room: austere, but comfortable. On my bed was a note (to be flushed down the loo) informing me my name for this exercise would be Jack Wellbeloved, rather a whimsy and it made me smile. Well-beloved by whom? I wondered.

There were eight men at dinner, the three who had met me and four others who were all to be part of this operation. I was told, "You will have three days of briefings and some testing to make sure you are fit. You will have joint command with a 'Major Leeds'." He was a young man who spoke English with a slight Polish accent and who was also fluent in German.

Leeds and I were told separately that our objective was to bring back two former Nazis who were being held in Poland, both war criminals, both very dangerous. We were not told why they were wanted, but the Soviets were after them also, and might cause problems for us. When all was ready, a five man team would go to Northern Holland and wait at Groningen for further orders.

The next morning we were up early. The running clothes laid out in my room were warm and they fit well enough. A young man appeared who had a no nonsense manner. We were told to address him simply as 'Sir'. He took us out and worked us hard remarking at one point that I was rather out of condition, which I wasn't. Later that day, with a smile, he challenged me to put him on the ground by any means I might chose. I did instantly, before he had all the words out of his mouth, knocking the breath out of him. This is not difficult if you move twice as rapidly as your adversary expects and you use your head. I hooked my foot behind my opponent's ankle and hurled myself forward, lowering my head and driving it into his throat with all my strength. The head is a deadly weapon, if it is hard enough, and mine was. Despite the ferocity of the encounter there were no ill feelings. Our trainer remained friendly but he did not ask me to fight again.

The five of us traveled separately to Holland and met in Groningen. We were supplied with two Jeeps, each with a military policeman and each with a kind of cradle in the rear, designed to hold our prisoners when we finally had them.

After a long drive we came to a steep bluff overlooking a beach where the remains of barbed wire and sea defenses had been torn aside. A very clever device had been constructed to conceal a cave where we hid the Jeeps. The entrance was covered and the tire tracks were obliterated. Our drivers would meet us there when we returned. The five of us were paddled off shore to a gunboat flying the Danish flag. The cabins assigned to us were excellent. I shared one with Leeds and on the second morning at sea I noticed his back crisscrossed with deep ugly scars. I heard later that he had been a 'guest' of the Gestapo in Yugoslavia. He had fought with the unfortunate General Mihailovitch, who was executed by Tito with the support, if not the actual consent, of the British government.

Although the Baltic was freezing cold, I managed to spend short sessions on deck enjoying the clean, crisp air, and watching the stars. The captain spoke good English and although we touched on a few subjects we never talked about this mission, although he said that this was not the first time he had been on such an assignment. He felt strongly about the many war criminals, who were, as he put it, "being let off the bloody hook." On the third night at sea the captain announced a "man overboard" drill. This was a hazardous exercise and I wondered if some unlucky participant might be lost forever. We were issued life jackets that were equipped with a flashing red light that was activated with contact with water. In a waterproof compartment those jackets also contained a small German automatic pistol with a silencer, making me wonder if we were going to sail close enough to shore for us to swim to a beach. This was just a precaution, the Captain told us, in case our vessel was sunk by a mine or surprised by a hostile patrol.

Our youngest officer, 'Captain Young', was the first to go, dressed only in some warm outfit used by the RAF. Half a minute later the captain gave the "man overboard" signal. As the vessel slowed, our inflated dinghies slapped the water and four of us leaped in after them, swimming fast to scramble aboard and reach for the paddles. Forbidden to use lights of any kind, we had to assess the current and find our companion before he died of exposure. We paddled furiously and within three minutes we saw the underwater glow of light. We were not allowed to call out, but Leeds gave the cry of a seagull, which was answered faintly. Quickly, we had the man aboard and back to the ship where rope ladders were hanging over the side. Warm coffee and a snort of cognac was more than welcome for us all.

During the next few nights this drill was repeated and I learned just how cold the Baltic Sea could be. I was picked up quickly, but one of our men was caught in a strong current and it took a little longer to find him, very worried and half frozen. In all, a dangerous exercise.

At the rendezvous point we lay to rest in the darkness: no lights, no engines, no talking coughing, or smoking. Finally in the blackness we heard the faint sound of rowing and a small boat suddenly appeared. As expected, we were met by the small craft near the Polish city of Utska. Without words, but using hand signals to identify themselves, the men came along side. Leeds and I had handguns trained on them. He spoke quietly, in Polish, to the stocky man who seemed to be in charge. The 'bodies' were successfully identified from photos and they were signed for and the transporting began. The two prisoners were hauled up to our deck by winch and we got a good look at them even in the dark. They were both well over 200 pounds and were manacled hand and foot with a chain around their waists connecting both. Their mouths were taped with thin strips of sticky bandage. These highly dangerous followers of Hitler had been brought this far at great risk of being intercepted by Polish, in other words, Soviet authorities.

After the winch was lowered, the two Nazis were lifted and taken below to a specially built container in the hold. This steel cage was seven feet high and three feet wide, and I remember thinking that it was far more roomy and comfortable than the one I had been in during that week of punishment at Buchenwald.

Both men were unshaven and smelly and their bodies and faces were bruised as if they had been given a hard time. They must have been drugged because their eyes had a vacant look in the dim light of the hold. The men were pushed inside and the spring locks closed with very little sound. The Pole who had brought them reached inside and unlocked their chains and pulled them free. They rubbed their wrists saying nothing, but looking surly and angry. I wondered why they were of such enormous importance to the powers on this side of the Iron Curtain. Leeds and I checked the prisoners constantly even when it was not our watch. We had a sensitive intercom from the hold which relayed every sound. Fortunately the intercom did not pick up the foul smell. On my orders the portholes were kept screwed shut to insure silence as our boat moved swiftly towards our embarkation point.

The prisoners, whom I mentally named Hans and Fritz, were not allowed to wash, so the cage was hosed down every day. Their food was pushed through a slot in the door of the cage. One morning, Fritz picked up the tray and hurled the food back through the bars and it landed all over the cook. We turned the hose on Fritz knocking him to his knees with a powerful jet of icy water. He cursed us furiously in German and I caught a reference to Der Tag, evidently when he hoped to have the pleasure of killing all of us.

Twice messages came by code for us to change our course and timing. Evidently our activities had become known to the Soviets and efforts were underway to intercept us and recover the prisoners. If such an effort was made, our captain had orders to kill them immediately, weight the bodies, and drop them overboard. There were no undue incidents and soon we reached our starting point.

The Jeeps and the two drivers were waiting for us on the beach. The prisoners were drugged again, taken ashore, and lashed in the steel cradles on the rear of the vehicles where they could look forward to an uncomfortable ride. We set off overland: Leeds and me in one Jeep with our MP driver; the other Jeep following close behind. We travelled mostly at night, constantly alert for danger. Automatic pistols with silencers were in holsters clipped between our legs to the framework of the vehicles. We were heading for Bad Segeberg in the British zone of West Germany near the East German border. We knew that some of our people were creating a diversion elsewhere and we hoped this would throw the Soviets off our trail, but we were wrong. They waited until we were almost to our destination then, without warning, they hit us. It was in the misty pre-dawn and as usual we were moving cautiously, at a relatively slow speed, along a secondary road with dense woods on either side. We had our head lights off and our wind shield open to give us as much visibility as possible. I was sitting next to our MP driver and as we came around a curve, somewhere ahead I heard the dull thud of a silencer, followed immediately by the wet slap of a bullet striking human flesh. The Jeep veered wildly as our driver's head snapped back from the bullet to his forehead. He never knew what hit him. Behind me I heard Leeds curse in Polish. I grabbed the wheel, pushed the driver hard onto the road, and wrenched the vehicle into the heavy underbrush where it came to a sudden stop. Our second Jeep came to a halt just behind us.

No matter how hardened you may think you are, it is still shocking to have a man beside you take a bullet to the face. It has happened to me twice: this was the first time. When your training has been good your reflexes take over and Leeds and I jumped out with pistols ready.

I hand signaled the three officers to circle forward and take the enemy from behind. We motioned to the remaining driver to stay where he was and guard the vehicles. Leeds and I began to move forward, crouching low, about thirty feet apart. I saw that Leeds had pulled up his trouser leg to have ready access to his knife, and I did the same. Ahead two more shots thudded and I heard a muffled cry as Leeds fell forward and I was sure he had been hit as a death rattle came from his throat. A razor sharp wire with saw teeth had cut his shins to the bone, a sign that our adversaries knew exactly what they were doing.

I was sure Leeds was dead and I kept very still and sniffed the air; the wind was in my face. I smelled them first and I heard two men approaching very stealthily, one behind the other. They paused within six feet of Leeds' body, but they didn't see him. I raised my automatic, but before I could fire, Leeds sprang from a crouching position. His head struck one of the shadowy figures in the midsection, knocking him flat, winded and stunned. Seconds later the other man fell from a bullet that hit him squarely in the wind pipe. There was a choking gurgle as his life's blood spurted forth. I saw Leeds' knife flash in the semi darkness and there was a sighing sob from the first man as he too died.

Leeds came towards me, his shoes covered in his own blood. "Well done," I muttered and turned back to the jeep for bandages. Grunts came from one of the prisoners whom I had almost forgotten.

From somewhere ahead came a splattering of shots and a few moments later our men returned, having dealt successfully with the remainder of the Communists. "Got all three of the bastards," Young muttered.

"These may be forward troops," I said. "We had better move on quickly."

We wedged our driver's body in the rear of the cage in the Jeep. There was no time for any burial, nor could we allow him to be found. We continued our journey, arms at the ready, and about two miles further on we came to a road block. We were ready to blast our way through or around it, but a voice in English called out, "Steady there. We're friends." A tall young Major whose accent was unmistakably from Southern Ireland came forward.

Behind them in the growing light stood a large unmarked police van. It had been prepared with steel rings on the padded floor and walls to receive our prisoners. The senior policeman told me that the men we killed had been tracking us for a long time. "They were a specially trained squad. You were lucky."

Although I certainly had been no hero in this encounter, not even firing a shot, his remarks nettled me somewhat. "Not lucky at all," I told him. "We were trained to do that ... and better."

At police headquarters our prisoners were placed in cells and Leeds had medical attention: stitches for his legs which were badly torn.

The next morning we all were transported in an army ambulance: the two prisoners, a medical officer, the rest of our crew. We had a long ride and allowed the still chained prisoners time to stretch their legs. We waited until we found isolated stretches of road as we wanted no more trouble, and there was none. We arrived at the Hook of Holland and were met by a landing craft. The bow dropped and we drove aboard. Leeds and I were able to relax and join the crew for some good food.

The prisoners were chained again in a steel cell, but halfway across the North Sea, Hans became very seasick and was placed in a comfortable cabin requisitioned from a crew member. I watched him lying there, half doped, his hands chained, his enormous feet sticking out beyond the end of the bunk and I wondered again why the Allies would employ such a person. He must, I thought, have some special qualifications.

Hans opened his eyes, stared at me, and then addressed me for the first time. "Haben sie ein zigarette ... bitte?" There was a pack lying on a table nearby and I lit one and passed it to him. He took it without thanks and as he did, his chained bare right foot shot out and kicked me squarely in the crotch. I flew across the cabin as if a tank had hit me and I crashed into the door. Fortunately, ever since my mistreatment by the Gestapo, I wore a protective device when on assignment, and this saved me from serious injury. Hans lay there rocking with laughter as I staggered out and onto the deck into the arms of our young officer. I was violently sick. My man was furious and quite ready to beat our Nazi insensible, but I told him to get the doctor to sedate him more until we reached the Tilbury docks. In the morning we were all driven to London where the prisoners were put into cells.

About a year later I was sent to the Gehlen organization's headquarters in Pullach, Germany. At a formal reception I was introduced to a number of guests and one was a tall German, immaculately dressed, with typical Prussian arrogance. As we shook hands, he bowed slightly, clicked his heels together and as I looked into those stark blue eyes I had a shock: it was 'Hans'. He didn't recognize me, or if he did, he gave no sign. I felt an uncontrollable urge to plant my foot where he had done and it was with a real effort that I didn't. It was ironic that this man who had served his Fuhrer so well was now serving us, but there were many like him and it was not my place to question how or why. I informed London, but heard no more.

After returning to London, I filed a report on behalf of Leeds and myself which took me the better part of a day. I was informed that I would not be needed for such violent assignments, at least not for a while. I was told to find a civilian job that would give me freedom to move around and keep my ear to the ground. Eventually I did become a roving photographer. The pay was poor and the hours long. I was supposed to make friends with a certain set of returning young warriors who congregated at hotels and local pubs and to keep my ears open for bits of conversation that might indicate Communist leanings or other subversive trends. I was to appear as a somewhat impoverished bachelor and it did not require great acting ability to appear so.

In the summer of 1947, something did occur to brighten my day: a command, not an invitation, but a Royal command to present myself at Windsor Castle.

chapter 17

KING GEORGE VI HAD not forgotten our brief conversation at Buckingham Palace. My superiors in Downing Street informed me by telephone that I was to come to London to prepare, or rather be prepared, for a visit to Windsor Castle where I would have tea alone with Their Majesties. Amazed and puzzled, I replied, "I don't have enough money for a railway ticket."

"Borrow it," they said unfeelingly. So I did, thinking how strange that the semi pauper that I had become was facing an honor such as this: an honor that could not be refused. Also I found it ironic having agreed to make myself as inconspicuous as possible, that now I was required to meet the Royal Family. I knew there would be no publicity, no splendidly written command. Even so, I would have to come partly into the open to approach royalty. It seemed a negation of all that had been planned for me.

I took the train to London and out of habit changed busses two or three times to reach a 'safe' apartment owned by the Foreign Office near Sloane Square. It was sparsely furnished, but very comfortable and presided over by a silent, elderly woman who apparently did the cooking and cleaning and who watched my every move for a while before sniffing and finally retiring to the kitchen.

I had been told to expect a visitor. About an hour later the doorbell rang, and a tall, handsome man in his mid sixties entered with his hand outstretched, and apologized for being late. When I asked him to identify himself he smiled tolerantly and handed me a small, folded identity card where a photograph was inset with his name: Brigadier General James Fortescue O'Neill. The rank of Brigadier General had been discontinued earlier and replaced by Brigadier so I knew he must be a veteran of WWI. He said, "I suppose you know the form ... meeting royalty and all that? You know how to address His Majesty?"

I said that I did. "Ah, yes, you were at the Palace recently. Jolly good show." He went on to tell me what I should wear. I would find proper clothing in the bedroom that would fit me. Also I should not worry unduly about what to say to His Majesty or the Queen. "Of course," he said with a cough and a slight wave of his hand, "we would like to know exactly what you do say!"

He told me that I would be driven to Windsor Castle by a member of the Metropolitan Police. "Splendid fellow. You'll meet him this evening. Name's Trouncer. He'll stay the night here with us and drive you there tomorrow."

We met Trouncer for dinner that evening at a modest restaurant in Knightsbridge, and sat in a quiet corner where we could see everyone (a common practice that I prefer even today) and the general paid for a fine dinner. Trouncer was a strong featured man nearing retirement. He had served on the Northwest Frontier and astonished me when he casually said he had served under my uncle in the Sappers, (Royal Engineers). "A fine officer," he said. "Very sad to hear he was killed. On the road to Damascus, I believe." I remember thinking, "These damn people know everything about me." Some years later I was to think the same thing under less pleasant circumstances about the Soviet Secret Police.

After dinner we returned to the flat where the General told me what I could and could not say to the King. "Do not make any representation to him, y' know you are restricted by the Official Secrets Act." I knew this was not the King's request, but what my people wanted. The general coached me a little more on etiquette. I recall even practicing walking backwards, although this was hardly a state occasion; I never walked any way but forward.

The next day just after three o'clock a car was waiting. General O'Neill left us and wished me luck. "God speed m' dear fellow," and he moved off without looking back. We never met again but such men remain firmly in my memory as the very essence of the once great British Empire.

The drive to Windsor took about an hour and I sat beside Trouncer in my well tailored grey suit wondering why the King remembered me at all. Finally the Castle loomed magnificently against the sky, as it had for many centuries. We stopped at the King Henry VIII gate and a policeman stepped out from a doorway on the left. He saluted and said, "Please go through, Sir. You are expected." Trouncer said he would be ready whenever my visit ended and I could find him in the small guardroom. I made my way to the house of the Governor of the Military Knights, a house I was to know well in later years. I was met by a secretary who walked me up hill towards the apartments of the Royal family. I waited in a large room with magnificent furniture, mirrors in gilt frames, and fine paintings.

Shortly I was presented again to His Majesty and this time also to the Queen. Queen Elizabeth was wearing a blue dress with a single strand of pearls. His Majesty wore a business suit.

I made the discovery then, as have many others, that these people regarded by most at the time as demi-gods, are just plain human beings with warmth, good manners, and true concern for their subjects. They did their best to make me feel at ease as we drank tea, spoke of my family, especially one member they had met years before when he was the senior medical officer at the Royal Hospital Chelsea. The King must have been briefed because he mentioned a number of people we both knew. He made special mention of my former chief, Sir Colin Gubbins. After tea, he turned the subject to my war experiences. The King said, "I would be most interested to hear of Special Operations, if ...you feel you can talk about it?" I had been told beforehand what I could say but I was also assured that he would not repeat any of it. So I expressed my true feelings that too many had suffered horribly and died under terrible conditions without being recognized. I told him, out of the Queen's hearing of my friend who had lost all his fingers and toes.

"We feel," the King said, and I didn't know if he was using the royal 'we' or simply meant to include his wife, "we feel very deeply about this." His slight stutter became more pronounced. "When I spoke to Sir Winston I was horrified about what he told me of your case. We owe a debt of honor to men such as yourself." It was impossible to doubt his sincerity at this point.

We went on to talk about the Battle of Arnhem. I had already explained to him that the incident at Arnhem was mainly coincidence. "Ah," he said, "but you had the presence of mind to deal with the situation." He said it was his father, King GeorgeV, who had instituted the Military Cross. "It was given for a specific act of gallantry above and beyond the call of duty and I was happy to award it to you." Now it had more value to me. The King continued talking to me in a friendly way and I felt more at ease.

Their Majesties last words to me were that they hoped I would visit again, and of course I said I would be honored. The doors opened signifying it was time to leave. Trouncer was waiting for me in the guardroom and we left the Castle, driving again through the King Henry VIII gate. I felt so emotional, filled with great love and respect for the rulers of our land. I wished that Arlette could have been with me. Perhaps in a way she was.

It was back to reality in London, where I removed the borrowed clothes, made myself tea, toast and eggs left for me by the sniffing lady along with a note. That morning I had a call instructing me to wait in the flat for some money to cover my out of pocket expenses. There had not been many, but I was glad to comply and soon I had ten pounds sterling in my pocket. Ten pounds went a long way in those days and I made my way to the Overseas League, happy to spend a portion on a good lunch in the downstairs dining room.

I was introduced to a stunning girl named Joanna; a tall, elegant, honey colored blond. I was attracted to her and it seemed to be mutual. She had been in Royal Air Force signals at Bletchley, where the very hush-hush code breaking work known as Ultra had been carried out. She didn't tell me, and I didn't tell her I knew. In fact I told her almost nothing about myself.

We started seeing more of each other. For the first time since Arlette's death I was attracted to a woman. She told me that she had had a brief love affair with a pilot during the war, but spoke no more about it. The memory seemed painful to her and I wondered if he had been killed. We enjoyed each other's company. We spent time driving in her little red sports car to various places in the country and even once got a lift to Scotland on an RAF plane (totally illegal) where we stayed at Glamis Castle with Tim Bowes- Lyon, sixteenth Earl of Strathmore, his sister Lady Nancy Blair and her husband John.

Although I was immensely attracted to Joanna, there had been strenuous indoctrination where it was constantly emphasized that marriage was not for me, because I was married to the firm. I knew it would take an act of defiance of which I was not capable at the time to ignore or overrule this edict. After much agonizing and hesitation, I told Joanna that we should not see each other any more. It was not easy for either of us, but I was gradually able to put her out of my mind and eventually she was happily married.

Months had now passed since I had seen my in-laws or my son, and I sent a strongly worded demand that I be allowed to do so. The firm did not like this request, but perhaps they thought I would be driven to outright rebellion unless it was granted. Finally, I was told that I could go to Brussels for one brief visit; that I could say nothing about myself or my work; that I could tell the family what I knew about their daughter's death; and that I could see my son this once. In their opinion it would be better if his grandparents returned to the Congo, where Stephen would be more out of harm's way in case the new enemy discovered he was my child and tried to harm him or take him hostage.

With all these restrictions ringing in my ears I made my way to my in-law's home. David had an excellent nurse and constant affection from his grandparents. When I saw him I was startled by his resemblance to Arlette. For the first time I realized how much I was giving up. The probability that he would never know his own father devastated me, but now I was so irrevocably in the grip of the firm that there seemed to be nothing I could do.

I waited until after dinner to tell her parents about Arlette's death. They took it with more calmness and fortitude than I had expected. "We were sure she was dead," they said, "although there always was the tiny chance that she had been swept up by the Soviets, or lost her memory, or had survived in some manner." Now they knew that she had died bravely for her country, which is what she had been prepared to do. They could accept that because their Catholic faith made them confident they would be reunited with her someday. Soon after, as a tribute to Arlette and to somehow assuage my loneliness, I converted to Catholicism and practiced that faith for sixteen years.

I was not sure whether it was wise, but I told them about killing one of Arlette's executioners. Her mother looked at me with eyes so like Arlette's and murmured, "Did you have to do that?"

I said quietly, "Yes, I did."

Arlette's father stood up and went to the window with his back to us. "Well, then," he said, "our daughter is avenged." We talked no more about it.

Before I left the next day, they assured me that Stephen would always be loved and protected. They thought he would have better schooling in Europe than in the Congo, and this he did, eventually going to University in Heidelberg. They sensed that I was unable to talk about myself and they asked no questions.

The visit left me reassured about Stephen's welfare, but profoundly saddened, and as 1947 drew to a close the cumulative strain of the past few years caught up with me: the visit to Belgium, the Baltic assignment, the horrors of Arnhem and Buchenwald, the never ending need for secrecy and deception, the growing feeling of being trapped, all seemed an insupportable burden. The old nightmares returned and my mind started to become clouded.

The firm should have noticed and taken action, but it was my own father who became worried and arranged for a stay in a hospital specializing in combat fatigue cases: very comforting and also very expensive. I stayed for about eight weeks. At first I was very confused and talked to the doctors who, not knowing anything of my past, were amazed at what they considered my extraordinary 'lies'. They told my father about them further confirming his opinion that I was irresponsible.

In some way, word of my condition reached the firm, and General Colin Gubbins (now Sir Colin) came more than once to see me. On the first visit he cautioned me strongly against "talking out of turn" and on his last visit, just before I was to be released, he told me with even greater emphasis that unless I kept my mouth shut the consequences could be dire. "You know too much, Keith," he said, "and that puts you at risk with certain people."

Colin said no more, but by now my mind was no longer clouded, and his message struck home with considerable force. When he left I sat for a long time, thinking. I knew that Colin Gubbins had come to see me because he was genuinely concerned about my welfare, but I knew he had also come to make sure I had not talked to anyone about my role, past or present, in the firm ... or said anything that might be an infringement of the Official Secrets Act.

I had not, but the intensity with which he had warned me to keep my "mouth shut forever" made me realize that the knowledge I had acquired over the years as a member of 'Z', as a member of N Section, and as an agent in Holland and France during the war would indeed cause a mighty uproar if it became known. It was not the complete story ... I doubt that will ever be revealed in my lifetime ... but it was enough knowledge to be highly dangerous to certain people in the firm. The purpose of the visit was to put the fear of God in me: It worked!

I want to say here quite clearly and firmly that I knew the Foreign Office to be composed, for the most part, of honorable, loyal, patriotic people. What I feared was a little core of men, well entrenched and with a great deal of power, who had good reason to be wary of the truth where Dutch Section was concerned and whose long-held and deep-seated secret concept of what the face of Europe ultimately should become would be imperiled if that truth came out.

As long as they were convinced that the Official Secrets Act would guarantee my continued silence, these people probably would take no action against me, but what if somehow they became convinced that this barrier was not sufficient? In that case, from their point of view, there was only one remedy: get rid of me altogether. If such a decision was made, it would be carried our ruthlessly, as it had been with others, one way or another. There would be no chance of my revealing anything, because my mouth would be closed forever.

Sitting there in my hospital room I could see that there was no use in deceiving myself. From now on my life would be in constant jeopardy, not just from the enemies of Britain, but also from some of my own countrymen. Even if I had no intention whatsoever of violating the OSA (and I had not) that would make little difference to those empowered to make life or death decisions if it was decided that the risk existed. Past services rendered by me (or anyone else) would make no difference; the order would still go out. A cold-blooded form of betrayal, certainly, but I had known betrayal before.

I had been confused by Gestapo torture, by the horrors of Buchenwald and to some extent by "rehabilitation" at the hands of my fellow countrymen. I had been programmed to tell lies to a royal commission and then reprogrammed to forget I had ever had such instructions. I was tortured by the loss of my wife and our son, but now I was capable of thinking clearly.

There was only one way to protect myself, and that was to make certain that if I met with sudden death or what seemed to be suicide, that would trigger precisely the events that were feared. I could arrange things so that my death under those circumstances would automatically release the information they were so eager to conceal. The documented facts could be assembled and planted with great secrecy and care in safe places around the world known only to me. The arrangements for their release also could be worked out quietly and in foolproof detail. Once they were in place and the firm learned of this plan, as they certainly would in time, there would be nothing they could do about it. They might punish me in one way or another. They might refuse me advancement or give me assignments so dangerous that I might not survive. They might damage me financially, blacken my reputation, or even try to drive me to suicide, but they could not kill me outright without grave repercussions to themselves.

It would be a standoff.

For the past sixty years, that is exactly what it has been.

chapter 18

ON MY RELEASE FROM hospital, I reluctantly went to live at home, gradually resuming my employment as a photographer. To my family I still seemed secretive, somewhat unstable, and unreliable: incapable of adjusting to post war life. They were baffled when I disappeared for days at a time, always with the excuse of looking for work. During these absences I made visits abroad for the department, mainly as a courier to various connections on the Continent.

Before each journey I was called to London where I spent half a day or so being carefully briefed on my assignment and cover. Usually I was a middle class businessman with false papers and connections. The Department always made sure that my clothing, ties, and accent fitted the cover perfectly. Sometimes I might have a different hairstyle or color, or alter the contour of my face with pads. The messages that I carried were usually on microfilm and concealed internally. For the most part I travelled without difficulty.

There was one uncomfortable, but minor mishap when I posed as a Canadian doctor in one of the remote villages of the Midlands. A man I knew well at home happened into a gathering where I was and asked someone what I was doing there. When told, he said loudly, "He's not a Canadian and he's not a doctor." This caused some consternation among those I was deceiving. When asked to explain I maintained stonily that it was a case of mistaken identity. It was a nasty shock to have my cover blown so abruptly and unexpectedly. I reported to London immediately and I knew they would have to take some action and they did. Someone very discreetly called on my acquaintance and I don't know what was said, but when we met again he backed away hastily saying, "I don't know what you are up to and, by God, I don't want to know."

A good example of what sort of reaction can result from being threatened under the Official Secrets Act.

The Department could be heartless and ruthless, and at times solicitous. I expressed to a friend how I missed having female companionship. I was badly misunderstood because much to my surprise I was assured that something could be arranged. They had no difficulty finding patriotic women willing to do their duty for King and Country. I was amused that the Foreign Office, which could be so indignant of moral lapses when it suited them, perhaps could find nothing wrong with acting as procurer for their agents.

In the spring of 1949, I went to a holiday camp that needed seasonal photographers. I assured the management that I was very competent with a Leica camera and was willing to work hard. I was given a chance and went to work with gusto; the department in London approved. I was told to keep fit so I worked out during any spare time. We were a team of photographers and were furiously competitive, getting up and out early to catch the campers as they streamed out of their cabins. It cost half a crown for three postcard sized pictures. The subjects had to be caught early in their stay or they would have been snapped enough by others.

The bars and lounges were packed in the evenings and in an attempt to attract more sales, I often sang with the orchestra: Irish or Scottish love songs or even arias from Italian operas. I enjoyed the work, being busy, and was finally beginning to feel normal. My parents were happy and said, "Keith has finally found himself." Visits home were welcome and enjoyable.

One warm Saturday in May I was near the swimming pool looking for prospects and saw the owner of a pair of attractive legs lying in the sun with a newspaper covering her face. I went up and asked the legs if I might take a picture. "Can't afford it," said the newspaper in a muffled voice. Eagerly I said that I would do it for nothing. Then I found myself looking into the big brown eyes of a lovely dark haired girl who looked familiar.

"You have asked me before," she said with mild exasperation. "I work here too, you know." Her name was Audrey Bigelow. She and a friend had come from their home near Edinburgh to earn some

money and have a little vacation at the same time. She was English and
Scots. Staring at her I realized how very pretty she was. I asked her to
meet me when she had some time off. Within a week we were seeing
each other frequently. After all the misery that I had been through,
meeting Audrey was like a breath of fresh air. She was decent, self-
possessed and I found her intriguing.

Soon I knew that this was the girl with whom I wanted to share
my life. I was aware that even if she could be persuaded I was going
to have a problem with the Department. I was forbidden to marry
anyone. Even if I defied this command I would not be able to tell
Audrey of my work with the government, or my first marriage, now
so well concealed. She would have to be kept in the dark, perhaps for
as long as our marriage lasted. The thought of such obvious deceptions worried me, but I was in love and was able to place those worries
in the back of my mind.

I had a rival of sorts for her affections. There was a young man
on holiday who asked her to marry him. I asked her about him one
afternoon and she answered,"I don't want to marry him."

"Would you perhaps marry me?" I inquired, and with this exces-
sively eloquent proposal the future course of our lives was set. I felt
so much for this lovely girl and I wanted to marry her for all the right
reasons, but there was another consideration in my mind. Perhaps if I
had a wife the hold the Department had on me might be weakened.
They might demand less of me; expect less. Perhaps I might be spared
some of the seemingly suicidal and complicated missions that they
might have in mind for me.

I did not tell London of my plans. When we decided to have
an engagement party for some close friends it was a true gesture of
defiance on my part. I had not said a word to London. They heard
about it, of course, and summoned me to London.

They gave me a hard time: "Marriage is not for you. You are
married to the Department. Forget this bloody, silly nonsense and
you can look forward to better pay, not in the distant future, but
soon. There are plenty of attractive young women in the world: one
just doesn't have to marry them! Go away and think about it. Do
you realize that you are jeopardizing a promising career?" There were
stern looks and, "We feel, on reflection, you'll see the light."

I did go away and consider it carefully, but my mind was made up. I had lost one woman I had loved deeply: I was not going to abandon this one even knowing the power of the department. That following January Audrey and I were married in a Catholic ceremony. My family came and on the surface all was well, but Audrey's mother was not anticipating that this daughter would marry and not be there to look after her in her old age. Her approval was hard to come by; it never did come!

When the department discovered the news of our wedding, they exploded. They said, "We intend that you continue employment, marriage or no marriage. If she suffers it will be your fault. If you have to lie to her that will be your bad luck. From now on you will obey orders implicitly or there will be dire consequences."

Audrey knew nothing of this, of course, and the early days of our marriage were happy. For a short period I continued my photography work, but soon the department let me know that I was to take a job with a company near London. A senior member of the board knew that I had been planted. Each day I would set off for work and take a train for London. At times I would pretend to do work at the company, but I was receiving further indoctrination in psychology and combat retraining: all very intensive. Each day I would return by train in time to meet my new wife from her job at the telephone exchange. She had no knowledge of the double life I was leading; nor would she for a long time.

After I had been with the company for some months I was ordered to look for an advertisement in a certain newspaper for work in Hampshire. There it was: "photographer wanted for roving photography. Good pay,"etc. I was told that if I applied for the job, I would get it, and I did. The department's reason seemed to be simple (but nothing ever really was). If I lived within reach of Portsmouth and I was needed for courier work in that area I would be closer. Eastbourne was a pleasant seaside town in the picturesque south of England. Housing after the war was at a premium and we hunted for rooms and found an apartment above a tailor's shop.

The work was much the same as it had been: daylight hours spent photographing people along the sea fronts, evenings stalking them in hotel lounges and bars. Weddings paid best, but the competition

for booking them was keen. I tried booking Hunt or Military balls at
the Majestic Hotel and later at the Queen's Hotel where my contact
lived. It had a busy night club and I began spending much of my
time there. This often kept me out late at night, which was hard on a
young wife, but she accepted it and helped me with paper work and
sorting photographs.

Eventually I became tired of working on commission and decided
to freelance. The department approved as it meant more free time
for courier work which was taking me to towns in the area more
frequently. I was told to keep an eye on shipping and report conversations I heard which might have some bearing on the activities of a
foreign power.

My cover as a free lance photographer seemed infallible as I could
always say that I had been covering a wedding or some other late
work. During this time only once was there any real melodrama. A
meeting was to take place in a wooded area and as I approached I saw
a man sitting with his back to a tree. He did not move and when I
came nearer I saw that his face was blackened and contorted: his eyes
bulged and his tongue protruded. No one was in sight. I didn't touch
him nor summon the police. I called my contact and reported what
I had found and he relayed the information to London. Word came
back immediately: I was to forget the incident as it was none of my
concern. The scene stayed with me for weeks. Who killed the man
and why was he killed? I had to remember that I was just a small cog
in the vast machine. Perhaps he was no longer useful; perhaps he had
accepted some offer; perhaps someone was afraid that he would talk.
The players on both sides were considered expendable.

Looking back I often wonder why I didn't break with the department and walk away and try to rebuild a life for Audrey and me
without them. There were several reasons and I can identify four.

The first was patriotic, or something close to that. I had been
indoctrinated with the idea that I was part of a small, but select group
of people in whose hands lay the fate of the British Empire and indeed
of the whole Western world. One did not discard such an assignment
lightly. One owed it to oneself, to King and Country to keep faith.
Honor demanded it. Duty required it. Sacrifices had to be born and
good soldiers would bear them. (So they said.)

Another reason was financial. I was receiving no pay from the government directly, but money was being held for me with a high rate of interest, and those funds, tax free, would be available to my family if anything happened to me or when the time came for me to retire. (Or so I was led to believe.)

The third reason, If I'm to be honest, was that the life of an undercover agent, even a minor one, was bound to be more exciting and stimulating than the life of a free lance photographer struggling to support a wife and children in a resort town. When I went to London I left my other life completely behind. On one assignment in London I met a friend from the country whom I knew when I worked there. His name was Bonar Colleano, an actor who had had many film and stage roles. At the time he was playing opposite Vivien Leigh in A Streetcar Named Desire. He introduced me to her backstage after one performance. She was warm and cordial and we remained friends for a long time. Neither Bonar nor Vivien ever knew that I had a wife, and Audrey knew nothing of such friendships in my other life.

A fourth reason that kept me tied to the firm was that most basic of all emotions: fear. On one of his visits to me in hospital, Colin Gubbins let me know that when I turned up in Buchenwald in the spring of 1945 there was great consternation in Dutch Section(N) among certain individuals who had considered me dead. Now that I was alive it was thought that I had certain information about the tragic loss of agents in Holland and the success of Nazi counterintelligence in anticipating our moves. Therefore I was a distinct threat to those who had something to hide. Some of these people wanted me eliminated and thus silenced forever. Others thought that I might be helpful in constructing a defense in case of an investigation, which at that point seemed likely. Still others argued ... Sir Colin among them, I am sure ... that if I could be persuaded to accept recruitment I would then be under the control of the firm and not likely to cause any trouble. Indeed with intensive training I might prove to be a useful agent in the inevitable conflict with the Soviets. This was the view that finally prevailed, but not by much. It was close, Sir Colin implied, and therefore I had to be doubly careful to display unswerving loyalty and always maintain rigid security.

I had displayed disloyalty of a sort by marrying against the firm's wishes. I knew very well that this was a black mark on my record. But perhaps I was not as firmly under the firm's thumb as they thought. They were not aware that I had planted documental evidence beyond their reach to be released upon my sudden or suspicious death. I was not yet ready to reveal my plans; I was saving them as a last resort. Until then I would have to run the risk that a negative decision might be made about me.

It was quite a ride from the Queen's Hotel to my home. At first I rode a motorcycle, but in time I bought a car: a small seven horse-power Austin, twenty years old that cost me thirty pounds sterling. I kept it waxed and fine tuned and it would run like a dream. After our daughter Anne was born the four of us...Anne, her brother Nigel, Audrey and I would drive into the countryside in this museum piece, have tea, and give Audrey a respite from what, for her, was a pinched and monotonous existence. I still remember those excursions with fondness.

Now and then, as I drove home at night, young policemen eager to get credit would stop me for a nonfunctioning tail light or some other minor infraction. "Why are you out so late?", they would ask. I told them the truth, but increasingly they seemed to regard me with suspicion. One night, driving fast and most likely half asleep, I tried to avoid an oncoming car, drove up onto the slope and the car flipped on its side. I wasn't hurt, but was fined for reckless driving. After that I seemed to be on a blacklist at police headquarters. I was considered a suspicious and erratic character. I was even questioned about some jewel robberies in the area. I was able to prove my whereabouts at the time, but still detectives searched my house without a warrant and frightened Audrey.

A chief inspector named Sewell had a particular dislike for me. I am convinced now that he was told by the firm to harass me as they had their reasons for wanting me to establish a pattern of irrespon-sibility. Sewell's men began to give me a hard time whenever they could. On more than one occasion confrontations became violent. Then I had the option of accepting beatings from the officers, or using my unarmed combat skills, which I was not permitted to do. Each incident added to my reputation as an irresponsible and unde-sirable person. Audrey accepted these episodes stoically with the same strength as when our income was very limited and our post war living conditions were not very good. Her reproachful silences became more frequent, and it became apparent that small cracks were beginning in our marriage.

My contact, Hamish Fergusson, was an attractive man who had been in N Section of SOE. When we met for the first time in the club, I was simply a local photographer who, supposedly, enjoyed a good time and occasionally seemed to drink too much. Once the link was established we became good friends. He was intelligent, highly strung, and impulsive. He had a full time job as director of a small factory giving him a good income. He had a wife, Janet, and four small children and something else: a girl friend. She was an attractive, hard-edged blond named Jane, who claimed to be in love with him. We knew she was grasping and selfish and 'Jamie' as we called him, was often paying her debts. I felt sympathy for his wife who was aware of his affair and joined me in various attempts to end it. What troubled me most was knowing that the affair was extremely dangerous for Jamie if the department learned of it, which they almost certainly would in time.

Observing Jamie as he seemed to become more infatuated I saw what obsession may do to a man. No arguments would sway him. I knew he was under great pressure and he began to drink, and this was even more alarming because his reliability would come into question. If the Department decided that he was becoming a serious security risk they were very capable of taking action. His wife knew it too, because she also had worked for the firm and knew what the consequences of Jamie's actions could be. During those days I began to admire Janet immensely for her dignity, poise, and loyalty to her husband in an almost impossible situation. She and I began what was to become a lifelong friendship.

Since Jamie seemed incapable of ending the affair, I decided to take action myself, thinking I could beg, cajole, persuade Jane to end it. One night I went to her flat and talked myself blue in the face to no avail. She scoffed at the idea that her relationship with Jamie could put him in danger; and I could not tell her why.

The drama continued and finally the firm became aware of the affair. I am sure that Jamie was warned to stop and there probably was some ultimatum. All I know is that the end came suddenly and violently and the events surrounding it were extraordinary.

Jamie had not only been my contact, but had become a good friend. In London I had been told in unmistakable terms that the affair and heavy drinking were not going to be tolerated any longer. I argued so strenuously on his behalf that I was told to go away for a short rest and "find a new perspective on life." I went to Cornwall with a friend and even though the change was necessary I felt guilty about leaving the family, but I had my orders. After a few days, I had word from the firm that there was an assignment for me in Norwich and my friend, Charles Boddington, suggested I stay at the home he had there. The department's contact in East Anglia said that I was to stay until I had specific orders to return. Audrey and Janet knew how to reach me and early one morning I had a telephone call saying that Jamie had died that morning in hospital. The previous evening he had visited his brother for a drink in the officers' ward- room. As he left there had been a sudden swell and he slipped between the dock and the gangway, hit his head and fell into the water. It was 'death by misadventure'.

We will never know the real circumstances of Jamie's death, but I had a conversation later in London when someone said, " Your friend simply would not stay in line. Damn sorry about that, but I suggest that you consider this carefully." Was this a threat or warning? Had they sent me away so that I was out of the way when Jamie died? I will never know, but it certainly gave me cause to think twice about the possibility of walking away from this whole business. The department had a very original plan for me and in less than a year I found out what it was.

chapter 19

IN SEPTEMBER 1956 I was arrested by the local police and charged with stealing six pence. The authorities had all the evidence they needed as I had come from a store with marked coins in my pocket that I had picked up according to instructions. Of course, my 'friendly' local police were not surprised that this suspicious character who they were always stopping late at night was finally found with the 'goods' on him. During my sentencing I remember hearing the magistrate express his disgust that someone with my background and education would stoop so low. After what seemed like an interminable tongue lashing I was sentenced. He had no way of knowing that the whole operation had been planned by the firm and of course, neither did Audrey.

My superiors in London wanted it on public record that I was in jail serving a six month sentence. If I was in prison then I could not be carrying out a special mission for the Foreign Office. It was in the local newspaper and soon my family knew of my disgrace, too.

When I was first told about this extraordinary plan I was aghast. "What about my wife and children? What will happen to them if I am branded a criminal and sent off to prison?"

" Well, we warned you not to marry, remember? We said it would be a mistake and that you would have to lie to your wife if necessary and now it's necessary. This mission is far more important than anything in your private life. Your family will live through it ... and so will you, we hope."

Furiously, I said that I could not do that to Audrey and the children.

Their reply was that I could and I would. "Just put them out of your mind until this mission is over. We know you can do it. We've taught you how. Dissociate yourself from everything except the job at hand and focus on nothing else."

Reluctantly, I realized that they were right, gritted my teeth and asked, "What is the assignment?"

"You will be briefed when the time is right," they said. "Don't look so glum. It's only petty larceny. You'll get a light sentence."

Only petty larceny, but here I was, staring at my inky fingers, sitting in a jail cell where I had been brought in handcuffs. It is hard to imagine how incredibly stressful it is for the average person to be charged with a crime. The arrest is humiliating; your reputation is destroyed, your family is shunned and you are forced to imagine a life without freedom. I thought about my superiors and that there may have been an extra bonus to this arrest. They knew that I was good at my job, but if I ever decided to throw over the traces they had me: I would have a record and who would ever believe that it was an offense instigated by the firm? All the denials would fall on doubting ears ... and they have!

My thoughts turned to my uncomplaining wife. She had been a stalwart companion in spite of my often erratic behavior. Now she would be branded as the wife of a convicted thief, left to support herself and two small children. There was no help forthcoming from either of our families. She tried to believe my protestations of innocence, but I could tell that she was dubious.

When I was brought to the jail I saw no other prisoners. This cell was isolated from the rest. I had been incarcerated for just a short time when I heard footsteps and a key turned in the lock and a man who said that he was the governor stood there with a friendly smile on his face. "Well, Sir. You are free ... in a way. In half an hour a car will arrive to take you to wherever you are going. Not my job to ask questions. Perhaps you will come along with me and wash up a bit, have a drink in my quarters."

I thanked him and we walked along the bleak and empty halls. "Had to put you in the punishment cells," he murmured,"to keep you away from the others seeing you."

In the governors quarters I washed and changed into clean clothes that were provided for me. A buzzer sounded and the governor said, "Ah, they have arrived." He held out his hand and said, "The best of luck."

It was raining when I stepped out of a side entrance of the prison and the car was so close that it almost touched the wall. A hand reached out with an identity card showing that the owner was a Superintendent of the Special Branch from Scotland Yard. " I have been sent down from London to get you, Sir. Please settle yourself in the back and we'll be getting along."

As I climbed in and closed the door a man turned from the front seat and I gave an exclamation of delight. "Maurice!" It was such a relief to see a friendly face. "What are you doing here?" It was Maurice Oldfield, whom I had known in the Foreign Office. Later, as Sir Maurice, he would head MI6.

He squinted at me through his ever present haze of cigarette smoke. His round face smiled at me and he said, "Just wanted to make sure everything went as planned. Bad time for you, I know, and of course, Hell for your family. It's all rather complex, but we've got to fool those bloody Russkies, and this seemed the only way. It's important, I assure you. You'll learn soon enough." He puffed at his cigarette and turned back around in his seat.

We drove for about fifty miles, stopping for food and continuing on through the night to London.

Maurice led me to a small apartment overlooking a park. "Your room's down the hall, Keith. Everything you need is there: toothbrush, towels, razor, pajamas. Get a good night's sleep because you will be busy tomorrow. I'll be here if you need me."

After making my way to the bedroom, I automatically locked the door and checked to see if there was an alarm on the windows. I was emotionally and physically exhausted and after showering I sank into bed. As I fell asleep my thoughts were of Audrey and the children so far away in another world. I also could see the look of glee on the Inspector Sewell's face as he said, " Well, we finally caught you, didn't we." Some years later I felt some small comfort in the fact that he was sent to prison for conspiracy and bribery.

The next morning was sunny and bright and when I came out of the bedroom, Maurice was sitting with a cigarette dangling from his lips and a telephone gripped on his shoulder. The ash was falling on his rumpled clothes; no surprise because he was never the picture of sartorial splendor. "They're ready for us. You'll be briefed at eleven o'clock. Have some breakfast. It's in the kitchen."

Maurice chain smoked impatiently and when the car was late he scolded the driver. We drove to Carlton Gardens where I was hustled into a familiar house. Three men were sitting at a long table. One who seemed to be the senior man said, "Sit down."

They came right to the point. The Foreign Office was concerned about the situation in Hungary where a student uprising against the Communist government had been anticipated. If it did occur and showed signs of succeeding, the Red Army might move to suppress it. Consequently information of Soviet troop deployment and military capabilities was crucial. Some information was already obtained and was being held in Budapest. My assignment was to get into the city posing as a businessman, learn all that I could, also receive intelligence from our embassy and get it back to London. I would enter from Austria and return the same way. Contacts would be provided in Vienna to guide and assist me. I was shown the photographs of two men who I would meet in Budapest who would give me microfilm of the utmost importance. I was to make an extreme effort to leave Hungary safely. If by chance I was arrested by the Communist authorities, I was to destroy the film and, as a last resort, myself. I was not to be taken alive. "Not much chance of that," I was told cheerfully. "The whole setup has been planned so carefully that no one will suspect you." At least if I didn't succeed I had assurance that my family would be taken care of. It seemed that I was either worth a great deal or nothing at all!

I asked if I could be armed. "Not necessary," said the senior man. "You have excellent skills in unarmed combat. Looking down, and shuffling papers in front of him, he asked, "Did you actually poke that fellow's eyes with your two fingers when you were in Canada?" I remembered the incident (the fellow recovered), but I didn't reply.

As the briefing continued I told them that I didn't speak one word of Hungarian and knew very little about the country. "Doesn't matter," he said. "They will be watching our people but nobody will suspect you because you are in prison."

I knew that was the reason for the charade, but all of this would not have been necessary if my cover had not been blown. Evidently I was known to the enemy, but would this be possible if someone within the department had not been furnishing information to the

Soviets? I had no idea at the time who the mole could possibly be, but there was one, as I was to learn later, and the detailed information that was being channeled to the Soviets included the identity of agents.

After the briefing I was given a false passport, clothing to take with me ... not much ... just the usual needs for a short business trip. There were a few items that James Bond fans would appreciate: a leather case which could hide papers and microfilm with a double lid that could not be detected. There was a hiding place in the heel of my shoe for a small compass and survival pills. The heel was strong and secure, but could be opened with a quick twist.

As I boarded the flight to Vienna my appearance was altered: my mustache was scraggly, I wore heavy rimmed glasses and my hair had been cut differently. I wore a brown suit with quiet checks, and a hat pulled at an angle. When I saw my reflection in a mirror my face seemed unfamiliar as I had padding between my upper gums and lip. All in all I certainly looked unmilitary.

A 'business associate' who met me in Vienna told me that I had a day to rest. At my request, I was directed to St. Stephan's Cathedral where I was able to pray and meditate for an hour and ask that my loved ones be kept safe. Despite all the assurances I was not so sure that I would see them again.

I was introduced to a young Hungarian couple, alert and intelligent University students, who spoke perfect English and would be my guides and interpreters in Budapest. We drove several hours to the border and then on to Budapest in a battered, old Mercedes that ran very smoothly. They told me that the situation there was very tense. When WWII ended, the Soviet Union kept Hungary firmly in its grasp. They placed Matyas Rakosi at the head of government, a dictator in the Stalin mold, whose secret police the AVH, were feared and hated. Under Rakosi, Hungary's economy declined until finally, the Soviets replaced him with Imre Nagy, an old line Communist, but who was more humane. Nagy disagreed with almost everything that Rakosi had done, but he lasted only a year and a half until the Soviets decided he was too liberal. They returned Rakosi to power, much to the dismay of most Hungarians, especially the students. My two young guides told me the city was about to explode.

My hotel room was pleasant, with wood paneled walls. I always locked the door of my room, but I knew a locked door would not be enough to prevent Hungarian or Soviet agents from entering if they had reason. There were various false leads in my luggage designed to reinforce my cover: family photographs including one of an older woman, supposedly my mother, and documents to confirm my businessman profile.

Despite my supposed fame for poking people in the eyes with two fingers I would have been much more comfortable being armed. I was able to buy a pistol from an old man in the hotel. He proudly told me that he had owned it since WWI. It was a beautifully oiled 9mm Mauser automatic, a model brought out in 1916. With great feeling the old man said that he hoped I would use it against the Russians. It was not small, but I tucked it into the back of my belt and I could feel the oil seeping through my shirt.

I was to wait for my two contacts and in the meantime I walked about the city which was alive with rumors and tension.

Budapest is a beautiful city with the Danube flowing through the center dividing Buda from Pest. It still bore the scars of war; the retreating German army had blown up all the bridges. Only one had been repaired by the Red Army mainly for its own troop movements.

Without drawing attention I tried to pick up as much information as I could. It was clear that the unrest was coming from the young people, especially encouraged by the students. Although most of them were Communists they objected to the secret police, puppet dictators like Rakosi, and Soviet troops in Hungary. Even though the Hungarian army was under Soviet control, the feeling was that they would not fire on their own people. There was also the belief that if tanks came in, help would be forthcoming from the United Nations, or even from President Eisenhower. "After all. The President was a great general, wasn't he?"

The situation came to a head on the night of October 23 when a demonstration was held in Parliament Square. I went as close as I could, without being in danger, to see what would happen. Rakosi had been brought back from his country home to replace Imry Nagy. He tried to address the crowd but it was difficult to hear him. The students wanted answers to their demands, not soothing words. The main demand was 'Ruski haza'! (Russians go home). Leaflets carrying the list of demands had been printed by an underground press and were everywhere. When the authorities turned out the lights to quiet the crowd, the students rolled up the leaflets to make improvised torches and held them until the lights went back on. It was an inspiring and dramatic sight.

That evening, some students invaded the government radio station and were promptly met by the secret police. The rally turned into a bloodbath when the students returned fire on the police who were using fire hoses, tear gas, and finally opened fire. An angry crowd moved into Stalin Square where a giant bronze statue of the dictator stood. They tried to topple it with ropes hitched to a large truck, but it would not budge. Finally workers with blow torches were able to cut through the statue at the knees. As the statue fell with an enormous crash the only thing left were a pair of bronze boots standing on the pedestal. Some demonstrators took little pieces of metal as souvenirs and somehow a sign saying, 'dead end' was found and tied to the head of the statue. The tension was dangerously high. I heard people murmuring, "Tomorrow we strike." By now spontaneous riots were breaking out all over the city.

When I walked into my hotel an impatient man rushed towards me so quickly that I almost pulled out the Mauser. "I was to meet with you sooner, Sir," he said in English, "but the demonstrations delayed me and I must hurry because my wife is waiting alone in the car." We exchanged identities and then sat in a far corner of the lobby. He handed me a microfilm in a small container which I slipped up my sleeve. He said that he hoped to deliver more in a few days. With that he quickly left the hotel.

I went to my room, locked the door, and looked for a place to hide the film. With my small pocket knife I pried away one of the small knot holes from the paneling, tucked the vial behind it and replaced the knot, assured it would be safe there for the time being.

A few hours later, at about 2:00 A.M., Russian tanks rumbled into the city and were stationed at strategic points and key intersections. In the first show of strength, the Russians did not send any infantry along with the tanks. This gave the resistance fighters the ability to mount attacks using grenades, and Molotov cocktails. The memory of the courage of these young people struggling for their country against all odds is something that will always remain with me. They poured oil and liquid soap on the streets to impede the traction of the tanks, which began to spin helplessly. Many of these young people had been trained in sabotage for eventual war with the West. Now ironically, the tactics were being used against the Soviets. Sometimes the students were caught in crossfire and when they were down they were often run over. The sight was grisly and disgusting. Sometimes the bodies were dragged through the streets behind the tanks. Everywhere the tricolor Hungarian flag was evident, but with a hole cut in the center where the Communist symbol had been. During this uprising thousands of innocent civilians were slaughtered and the bravery of so many Hungarians is worthy of honor. In spite of the zeal of the students; in spite of the garrison at Kilian Barracks and their valiant attempt to defeat the Russians; in spite of the leadership of Colonel Pal Malater, the uprising was squelched. (The garrison were all mowed down with machine gun fire as they came outside to surrender. Malater was seized and eventually executed as was Nagy.)

In the mean time, my students had warned that it was dangerous for me to stay in the hotel and they guided me to a 'safe' apartment not more than five minutes away. I left my clothing but took the Mauser and extracted the microfilm container. I doubted that my contact would be able to bring more microfilm, but decided to stay a little longer in Budapest. Wild rumors flew: the Soviets were staying; they were leaving; the United Nations were sending a mission; the British and Americans were sending troops. Actually the Suez crisis had exploded and the Allies were preoccupied with that. Later the Eisenhower administration admitted that the Hungarian uprising had caught them by surprise, and the President explained that to send relief he would have had to send troops across neutral territory and it might have triggered a world war.

So the Hungarians were left to fight and die alone. And fight they certainly did: young boys and often girls against armored tanks. Bodies lay in the streets and food was scarce. Long lines were forming in front of bakeries and I, too stood in line for a loaf. Some people were killed while standing in line when the Soviet tanks came through and fired on them.

By now thousands were fleeing the city and thousands more were being arrested. Trains packed with prisoners were heading east to the dreaded labor camps.

For a while it looked as if the tanks were retreating and I thought my staying might have made it possible for my contact to reach me again, but the tanks were regrouping and on November 4 they returned in full force and had troops with them with orders to show no mercy. Trolleys were wrecked, overhead wires hung in clusters, and there were burned out cars everywhere.

The gods of war gave me a chance for revenge. My new apartment was supposed to be safe, but there was always the little voice reminding me of the possibility of a leak at the Foreign Office. I heard noise and splintering wood on the floor below me, and when I went out on the landing, I saw two Soviet soldiers methodically going door to door. I went back inside, drew the Mauser and left the door ajar. I flung the door open as they approached and shot them both. Four shots, two apiece. They died instantly there on the landing. I dragged the bodies into the apartment and stuffed them into a large chest near the window. I cleaned up the best I could, but cleaning up was hardly necessary as there was blood all over the city and a small amount in my room would not draw attention. I recalled how the old man had hoped that I would kill some Russians with the gun he sold me.

Soon the students came to the apartment and said that we had best get to the British Legation where we might find sanctuary until we could make our escape. We tried to make it on foot but were turned back by the heavy fighting.

I had been told by London to contact the British Consul, Joan Fish, if I found myself in trouble. I heard that she was in the Astoria Hotel and that she was trying to help stranded businessmen, but I also heard that the Soviets were taking over the hotel for their Headquarters. I decided to forego the lady's assistance if it meant contact with any Soviets. At least I had not been forgotten altogether by London. A small man, quite calm and unperturbed stood in the street and called up to the apartment window.

"Name's Fry," he raised his voice. "Leslie Fry. I'm the British

Minister here, and I've had word to look after you, if you can't get out of Budapest."

Fry had already evacuated several businessmen to his home in Buda from the Astoria where refugees were filling up the space and food was running short. Fry put me in his car and used back streets to reach his home as a way to dodge the tanks and Soviet soldiers. My students would be joining us soon to help guide me out of the city. I was fed well, offered a change of clothes, and Fry told me he would do all he could to help. Leslie Fry was eventually knighted by the Queen for the gallant part he played in the uprising.

The students arrived, still driving the battered but dependable Mercedes, and we left hoping to join the steady stream of refugees fleeing to the West. Many were on foot, some in carts, some on horses, and those of us lucky enough to have automobiles.

In the clothes that Leslie Fry had given me ... strong trousers, dark grey shirt, and a short jacket ... I looked much like everyone else. I had traded my watch for a pair of sturdy boots and I had the Mauser, a hunting knife I found in the apartment and, of course, the precious microfilm. By now some snow was falling and the temperature had dropped, but we felt we had a good chance of reaching the border and then Austria. The students were determined to accompany me and protect me and I certainly was thankful for their ability to speak English and Hungarian. After some miles we had made our way out of the city and eventually were forced to abandon the car. Along the way we came across a sad faced man with two little children. His wife had been killed in Parliament Square and now he was trying to reach Austria. He asked if he could join us and we shared some food with them. I knew I could not let anything impede me from getting the microfilm out of Hungary, but the children looked so cold and forlorn that I told my students that the man could join us if they could keep up." But tell him," I said, "that if he becomes a burden or a problem in any way, I'll kill him." The man clutched his children close and with wide eyes, nodded his head in understanding.

We passed through the town of Dorog where we were able to avoid several Soviet checkpoints. We plodded through muddy fields half covered with dirty snow. We crossed some small streams by walking on fallen tree trunks and by now we were cold, dirty, and wet. The two children had name tags pinned to their clothes and I told the father to keep the tags on and make sure they did not cry or whimper. I promised them chocolate and food when we reached our destination. The young father carried the smaller child and I carried the little girl who clutched me around the neck and buried her face in my shoulder. I could feel her shivering. I thought of my own little Anne and wondered if I would see her again.

Icy rain began to fall at the same time that rumors started circulating that the Soviets were stronger nearer the border. They were arresting or shooting the refugees with abandon ... men women and children. None of us doubted this and our band of four adults decided to take the children and move off the road for the time being. We thought we would have a better chance of moving when night came. This meant pushing through a swampy, reedy area around and on the Neusiedler See, a lake on the border.

The Soviet patrols followed the refugees into the swamp and started shooting at anything that moved. We huddled together in water up to our waists. The troops came so close that we could hear them laughing as they shot people. We kept very low just keeping our heads above the water. The father's face hovered near my shoulder and I knew that he was miserable over the death of his wife and the peril of his children. I felt for him, but I also knew that my knife was handy and if he endangered us in any way I was prepared to use it. My students said very little, but I knew that they must be suffering from the cold and wet, too.

The soldiers began firing star shells to make it easier to see. Whenever those bright lights exploded overhead we buried ourselves in the muck, or tried to crouch deeper in the reeds. The frozen mud stuck to our shoes and made walking even harder. Our hands and faces were scratched and our clothes were torn. Close to midnight the little girl I was carrying suddenly stopped her violent shivering. Beside me her father was still trudging along with the other child and I didn't tell him that his little girl had died. I was afraid his heartbroken wails would mean the end of us all.

I don't know how many hours went by. We moved in a westerly direction whenever we thought it was safe. Sometime before daylight our pitiful looking group made it across the border, safe at last and into the arms of the Austrian police. We were taken to a shelter where I finally laid the little girl down. The father knelt beside her and burst into loud weeping. I couldn't bear to look at him but I could imagine the agony on his face.

The Austrians took our frozen clothes and gave us blankets. We were given weak, warm tea which we drank and then poured some on our frozen hands. I warned the students about warming their hands too quickly. Like mine, their hands and faces were covered with scratches from the briars and reeds.

After thawing out, the students and I were taken to Vienna. Our people wanted me to part with the microfilm, but I wouldn't. I would deliver it personally to London and nothing else. They accepted this and gave me a hotel room with every comfort and two half bottles of good cognac. I drank a large slug and drew a hot bath. I stood in the bath and put iodine on my scratches, and finally emptied the rest into the bath water. I sank deeply into the water and thought that I was safe for the moment and soon would be back with my family. I knew how happy I would be to see them.

I was not sure if they would feel the same.

chapter 20

I RESTED FOR ONE day in Vienna, but knew the department was anxious for the microfilm so I flew off after saying goodbye, with regrets and thanks, to my two Hungarian students. They had been so loyal and endured so much for me. I heard later that they had been called back to Hungary and that the husband was arrested by the new regime and died at the age of twenty-six in prison. I never knew what became of the wife.

From Prestwick, I flew to Manchester where I was met by car and driven to London. I was given an intense debriefing. I told everything that I could and willingly handed over the microfilm. They seemed pleased to get it although I wondered what use it could possibly be now that the disaster had already taken place in Hungary.

I was given a few days in the country with strict orders to see no one, be seen by no one, and not to have any contact with my family. Of course I would have to return to jail to finish my sentence. After all that I had been through I protested that this was no longer necessary. My protests fell on deaf ears. "The plan must be carried out. We'll try to get you a shorter sentence, time off for good behavior, but that's all we can do."

In those days it took several hours to drive from London to the jail. As companions I had a police superintendent and a civilian driver. Both said almost nothing all the way there, except the policeman who told me that it had been arranged that I spend the rest of my sentence in an open prison. As planned we would arrive there after dark.

We climbed a steep hill and turned off onto a narrow road through the trees which brought us to the entrance of the prison. The Governor from before was standing at the gate, greeted me briefly and led me to an office. "Your prison clothes are in the washroom.

You'd better change quickly." I did so with a sinking feeling of despair and anger. How long would I have to stay in this place?

A warder came to fetch me; a stout man with a limp. "You'll be sleeping in the piggery tonight," he said. "Nobody's there now and I'll be back early in the morning to see you." We climbed the hill to a cluster of huts. Under his arm he carried a rolled blanket which he handed to me. He pointed to a small shed. "You'll have to sleep on the stack of turnips in there. Don't come out until I tell you."

I spread my blanket in the darkness trying to make my mind a blank. For a long time I lay there, thinking of home and hearing the mice scampering around. Finally I fell asleep.

I was awakened by the latch being opened. Instinctively, out of long habit, I had hidden my self in the corner and the warder must have thought that I had fled. "I'm here," I said to him as he peered in. He told me in a hard voice, "From now on you call me 'Sir',and you'll be in charge of the pigs."

There was no cruelty at the open prison, but discipline was strict. I didn't mind being in charge of feeding the pigs because I had grown up with livestock on our farm. What I did mind was not being with my family for Christmas. I knew that Audrey was having a hard time without my support. She came to visit me once and told me that our mothers had come down for a short time to help with the children while Audrey worked as a waitress in a local restaurant, but the visits did not work well: the two women didn't get along and they returned home after a short time. Money was a big problem. By mistake, two weeks after I left, Audrey threw her wages into the fire only realizing it when it was too late.

"What about the money I left for you on the bureau?"

She shook her head, and with tight lips said, "I wasn't sure where it came from." She thought it was tainted money and preferred not to touch it.

Worst of all was not being able to tell Audrey the truth about my apparent fall from grace. I did tell her I was innocent, but that was all I could say.

As the holidays approached I became even more frustrated with my confinement. I was not only worried about my family, but angry with the firm. I had carried out my assignment; risked death in Budapest and in the icy waters of the Neusiedler See; brought back their bloody microfilm; accepted the stigma of a convicted felon that I would have to carry for life. What more did they want from me? Why couldn't they release some of the earnings that they were holding?

Janet Fergussen lived just a few miles away. Since Jamie's death we had become close friends and I trusted her completely and knew that if I could contact her she would be able to give me news of my family. It was forbidden to leave the prison, but I had been trained to move quietly and swiftly so I made up my mind to try.

Behind the open prison was a steep, grassy hill that led up to a narrow road. There was a white gate there and I was hoping that there would be a cottage close by. The December days were short and the sun set early. There was a brief time in the dormitory between the evening meal and lights out. If I moved very fast I might just get out and back without being caught.

So I went: running fast up the hill, crouching low, splashing through a little stream, over the white gate and down the road until I came to a house where some light glowed. I took off my prison jacket, straightened my clothes and knocked. When the farmer opened the door I explained that my car had stalled and I needed to use his phone. He was very agreeable and in a few minutes I was talking to Janet.

"Listen carefully," I said. "I have almost no time to talk. You know the white gate above the prison? Meet me there tomorrow night at this time. No make it ten minutes sooner." She promised she would.

It was a half mile back to the gate then a swift run down hill. Just as the last inmate was leaving I went into the washroom where I had hidden a towel and toothbrush. I followed him to the dormitory and crawled into my bunk, just in time for bed check and lights out.

The next night was the same routine. When I got to the gate Janet was waiting with some food ... a welcome present as the prison fare was scant. As always, Janet was calm. She told me that Audrey was having a difficult time but was managing. "This meeting is too dangerous, Keith," she said. "If you are caught you may stay in prison even longer. It's only a matter of days or weeks now. Go back before they find you missing."

Again I ran at full speed down the hill, rolling most of the way after tripping on a rock. I hid the food Janet had brought among the turnips and would make time to eat tomorrow between chores. I crawled into my bunk at the last minute, perspiring heavily from exertion but heartened even by the brief information about the family from someone I could trust.

In January, with my sentence shortened for "good behavior" I was returned to jail. I was given back my suit and shirt which had been laundered and starched, but my socks were missing. I was ushered through the gates by the prison officer. Dangling his keys he said, "We'll see you again before long. Your type always come back."

I made my way to the bus station, wondering whether I should stop by where my contact lived. He was a Belgian, named Andre Tessant, and had lived in England for many years. I decided against it for now as I was in a hurry to get home to Audrey and the children, although I was not sure what my reception would be.

It was chillier than I expected. Audrey was sitting by the fire, both children in her lap, and looked at me with steady eyes. There were no recriminations (at least not spoken) and no tears. She hardly ever cried. I knew our marriage was in deep trouble and I could hardly blame her.

"Well, so you're back. What are you going to do now?"

I planned to return to my work as a photographer.

You'll find that difficult," she said. "Many people won't want to associate with you now."

She was right about that. More often than not, when I tried to revive old contacts I was brushed off. I had to extend the radius of my search for jobs and even then it was difficult.

One of the most distressing after-maths of my time in prison was the reaction of my paternal grandmother with whom I had always been close. She was a tiny woman who lived alone except for a single servant. As a highly principled Victorian, she was shattered when the news of my demise reached her. I visited her to try to make her understand, but to no avail. She sent me away saying, "No more lies, Keith, no more lies. I don't want to see you again." She meant what she said and when I returned the chain was on the door and the maid told me to leave.

I mentioned the incident to a close friend in the firm. He was a brave one, because he offered to go back with me and speak to my grandmother for me. "I can't tell her what really happened, you understand, but at least I can tell her that you are not lying. She will have to promise not to tell a living soul. Do you think she can be trusted?"

"I know she can," I said.

When my grandmother consented to see us my friend showed his Foreign Office credentials. "I can reveal no details," he told her, "but I can tell you this much: if Keith says he is innocent of wrongdoing, then you can believe him."

I will never forget the look of relief on my grandmother's face. From then we were close and remained that way until her death, unexplained, and soon after.

At home the coolness between Audrey and me persisted. Finally in desperation I telephoned Janet. I was feeling very sorry for myself and knew she would understand and perhaps help. In any case there was no one else in whom I could confide. "It's a miserable situation, Janet. I'm not welcome in my own home. I don't know how we can continue like this."

"You shouldn't blame Audrey, Keith. Not after all she's been through."

"I don't blame her. I blame the rotten firm, but that doesn't change anything."

There was a long pause. Then Janet said, "It's just too unfair. I've been thinking about it. I'm going to tell Audrey a little bit of the truth."

I was stunned. "My God, Janet. You can't do that. You've signed the Official Secrets Act, too. This would be a deliberate violation. You will put yourself in serious jeopardy. You mustn't. If the firm ... "

"The Hell with those bastards. They'll never find out. Who would tell them? Not you, not Audrey, certainly not I. I'm going to do it. Jamie would want me to. Don't even try to talk me out of it, Keith. I won't tell her much. Just why you aren't the criminal or the idiot you must seem. Tell Audrey to expect a call from me." She hung up.

Audrey did get a call from Janet. She did go to Janet's house and exactly what was said I never knew because neither of the women ever mentioned it. Eventually there was a softening in Audrey's flinty manner. Some, but not all, of the warmth we once had came back. I began to think perhaps our marriage could be saved after all.

I had little time to find out. I had been out of prison only about three or four weeks when I was summoned back to London. I always felt like an outsider with the people in the firm and that is exactly how I was classified. I was told that it would be a good idea for me to get out of England for a while. How about a couple of weeks in the West Indies? The microfilm that I had carried from Budapest had proven very valuable and they knew that I had risked a lot to get it. A little holiday: a token of appreciation. They would send a body guard along. Just routine, you know.

I said, "Are you telling me that the Soviets may know I was in Hungary and not in jail?"

"We don't know that," they said smoothly, "but there's a faint possibility that they do, and if so, they may come after you. They don't like it when agents operate successfully against them. You know that as well as we do. Dropping out of sight is just a precaution, that's all."

I was more than a little disturbed. If the enemy knew who and where I was there was only one way they could have found out. Now I was certain that there was someone in the organization who was feeding information and that person had to be on a very high rung of the ladder because my mission was a very closely guarded secret.

"I don't want to go to the West Indies. My wife had a rough time when I was in your bloody prison. If I have to leave I want it to be close by. I don't want to stay there long either."

In the end the idea to go abroad was shelved and I was told I could go to Dublin. "Probably not necessary at all. Just a few weeks or so while we check out some of the reports. Have you back in no time, old boy."

chapter 21

MY BODYGUARD WAS WAITING for me at the Dublin airport. He was a rugged Scot named Robbie. I had never seen him before and I am sure that I was somewhat brusque with him at first. I was not in good humor having left home with the sense that our marriage was coming together again and angry with the firm for this trip and many other reasons.

On the bright side, I had always loved Ireland, so much that at one time I had thought of retiring there. Robbie seemed tough and competent. After I got to know him better I couldn't help liking him. We talked a little of 'home' and he told me about his wife and small children in Glasgow. I decided to let him worry about my safety and I would take it easy for a few days.

We were booked into the Shelbourne Hotel with connecting rooms and where the hotel security had been told to keep an eye on me. I stayed in for two days, reading, resting, relaxing with the secure knowledge that Robbie was next door. When I went out he went with me and it began to irritate me a little to have this tall strapping baby sitter in constant attendance.

One morning I urged him to take the day off and I walked around Dublin until I came to Peterson's where I bought a pipe. I walked over the Liffey bridge, spent some time in the University and looked at the Book of Kells. I spent the rest of the day sitting in various coffee shops, breaking in my pipe and listening to the lovely, lilting voices around me. I had told Robbie not to worry: take the day off and look around Dublin; meet me for dinner and we could make our required telephone call to London. Reluctantly, he agreed.

I headed for St. Stephen's Green, a wonderful, quiet place with a pond. The pond had been drained for cleanup and at the bottom were old bottles and trash imbedded in the mud and the smell was unpleasant. I recalled how lovely it had been when the ducks floated by on the clear water. I wondered how many lives were like that … calm and lovely on the surface and strewn with unpleasantness below. Ireland produces thoughts like that because of its beauty and poetry and ugliness and violence all at the same time.

Back at the hotel we had dinner and I stayed after to smoke my new pipe and talk to some American visitors. They left after about an hour and I stayed, realizing how tired I was from doing nothing all day. I promised myself that the next day I would go to the Trinity Library and look at the Book of Kells again.

I took the lift to my room and unlocked the door. I heard the faintest sound of movement in the bedroom, maybe it was the bathroom? My sense of security vanished and I became very wary. I continued normally, even humming a little. The room was empty and nothing seemed to have been disturbed, but the door to the adjoining bedroom was ajar. I shoved the door open quickly and then with my automatic in my hand flattened myself against the wall. Almost immediately I heard a silencer cough twice and two bullets hit the wall where I had been standing. I heard the hall door from Robbie's room open and someone running down the hall. I pressed a button which immediately connected me to hotel security and said, "He's coming sown the stairs fast and armed. Wait until he's in the street and fire at his legs. Do not kill him."

"Right," said the voice at the other end.

The windows in my room looked directly over the front entrance. As I peered out I could see my would be assassin run out and immediately a Scot voice said, "Stop or I fire!" The moving man stopped, turned and fired one shot. Fortunately it hit some stone work by the front door. Another shot rang out and the running man looked up at me in surprise as he hit the pavement. No one was in sight except a couple entering the hotel. They stood petrified and the woman turned white and doubled over as the man tried to usher her hastily inside.

My door opened and Robbie rushed in still holding his.38. He said, "I'll not leave you again, Sir. I was bloody silly to let you talk me into it."

I didn't want to hear it. "Just go down and get that man off the street. I'll deal with the police when they come." (The Irish police were known to be very quick and efficient.)

I went down to the security office and looked at the man who was sprawled on the floor and I knew immediately that the bullet had severed his spine. The security man looked very shaken and I told him not to worry that I would deal with the police.

Within the hour the body had been taken away. The clothes were Irish and his identity papers matched, but I learned later that the gold inlays in the back teeth were consistent with middle European dentistry. I knew the Soviets often used Bulgarians to do their dirty work for them.

I reached London and spoke to a close friend and told him what had happened. I told him that Robbie and I would be moving out after everything was squared with The Castle, headquarters of the Irish police.

"Maybe you're safe now," my friend said. "Maybe they just sent one very good man."

"He wasn't that good and they never send just one. There must be others."

"Where are you going?"

"I'll let you know when we get there, and for God's sake, check on my family for me," I told him and hung up. I could not imagine how the killer could have tracked me to Dublin and even to the exact hotel where Robbie and I were staying. I was left with a weary disgust. Would there ever be a time when I could come in out of the cold; leave this twilight world; stop looking over my shoulder; stop killing in order not to be killed?

The next morning representation arrived from Whitehall. They were almost sure that I had been followed from Vienna. They had picked up the trail of the killer within twenty-four hours of his entry into England. Then they lost track of him and assumed he had also lost track of me, if it was me he was after, for I was in prison. Was there a leak in Vienna? They couldn't say, but they had an idea that the Soviets knew about the microfilm and were angry about it.

"Angry enough to send an executioner?" I asked.

"Oh, certainly. Liquidating a successful agent might discourage others."

"Pour encourage d'autres," the other one said, smiling at his linguistic ability.

I did not think that being the target of an assassin and finding him in my bedroom was a humorous matter. Especially if there were others.

An hour later Robbie and I were on our way in a car provided by the Irish police. A bottle of Bushmills was in one of the side pockets: a civilized touch in a mad world.

I drove and Robbie sat beside me with his .38 on his knees. It really irritated me. "Don't be so bloody dramatic and put that thing away," I told him. He just looked at me as if to say, 'I know what I'm doing,' and he turned round to look through the rear window.

We spent the night at a small inn about thirty miles north of Dublin. My plan was to cross the border and stay with friends in Ulster. Since it was easy for me to imitate an Irish accent I registered under an assumed and very Irish name. Robbie had the map of Scotland on his face and spoke with a definite Glasgow burr so I told him to keep quiet.

"I'll do the talking, Robbie. You stick to the heavy stuff."

He smiled a little but had a worried look on his face.

That night I lay awake, my mind working overtime. If they knew of my location I could not believe that the Soviets would send a single agent; they were too thorough, and probably too angry at that. Yet if I was in real danger wouldn't the firm have stepped in and flown me to the West Indies or to their remote center in western Canada? But they had not warned me about the first man. Round and round my thoughts spun through all the angles ... a constant worry and fright of undercover agents everywhere. Are my superiors really trying to help me? Or are they hoping that the enemy will kill me?

The next morning it was clear and cold as Robbie and I continued our journey. We were headed towards a town with the strange name of Hacksballscross. Ireland was as green as it was known to be and my spirits were high as we drove through the bright winter sunshine, but the nagging fear had not left me.

As we approached Hacksballscross I noticed a Mercedes that had been following us. There were three men huddled together in the front seat. I said to Robbie , "I think we have company."

He looked in a small side mirror and said tersely, "Don't let them get too close."

I pushed hard on the accelerator, but their car was faster and much more powerful. Suddenly the man on the passenger side leaned out and a moment later two bullets crashed through the rear of our car. Neither of us were hit and I said to Robbie,

"At the next turn I'm going to roll out. You try to lose them and we'll meet tonight at the post office in Dundalk." He nodded and put one hand on the wheel getting ready to take over.

As we came around the next curve I rolled out thanking my training for my ability to do it easily. I hit the ground and rolled into a hedge. I lay there still as I could with the moisture falling on me from the wet branches. The big Mercedes flashed by. Its occupants had not seen me jump. It would not be long, though, before they realized there was only one occupant in the car ahead.

I crawled along the wet hedges to the other side of the road. The sun began to disappear and a thin, chilling rain began to fall. I headed at a trot towards what seemed to be an empty cottage. As I got closer I realized that it was long since abandoned: a tree was growing through the roof where the central room had been and there was moss growing around the windows. I went inside and squatted near the old fireplace covered with soot and ashes. Overhead what was left of the second floor sagged dangerously, but at least it kept out the rain.

I waited and listened for hours and heard nothing. Finally, the skies began to clear and I eased my way up to the road. The hedgerows made it difficult to see, but I heard a car drive by slowly then move away. I was sure from the sound of the engine that it was a Mercedes. They were still looking for me, so I crouched down in the undergrowth and waited about two hours until I thought it was safe to move on.

I was wet, cold, hungry, weary and the sun was beginning to set. I had promised to meet Robbie at the Dundalk post office and there was only one way to get there: walk.

Across the road was a cart track that I noticed because of the ruts in the mud. There was a deep ditch on either side and an avenue of trees. I headed for it as I thought it would give me cover for some distance in my effort to reach Robbie. I was moving quickly, but quietly, which saved my life. The man waiting for me in the trees did not hear me coming. I didn't see him either until I was almost on top of him.

When one is surprised at close range there is not time to draw a weapon. The man flung himself at me with so much ferocity that I fell into the ditch. Instantly he was upon me hitting me in the face with such force that I was half stunned. A million lights flashed as I was hit again in the eye and given a bloody nose. Dazed and angry I lashed out with both hands. As he drew back I doubled up my legs and planted my feet firmly on his chest hurling him upwards. He landed hard on the track. As he did he reached under his armpit and I saw two spurts of flame as the semi automatic coughed. He had been in too much of a hurry; both shots missed me. I rolled into the underbrush and as I did two more shots exploded. Something in my mind registered ... four gone. I moved up the bank furiously and came at him from the side. I hit him in the face with all my strength and kicked him hard between the legs. He doubled over and dropped his pistol. I chopped him in the neck with the edge of my hand and he fell like a sack, huddled and still.

I stood over him breathing hard, cursing the pain that shot up my arm when I hit him. I tried to push him over with my foot, but he was too heavy and solid. Finally I could roll him over and his head lolled crazily. He was dead. I had broken his neck. Suddenly I had a flash of our NCO in Canada who had made us practice that karate chop. He wore a leather collar with a target painted on. We were always urged to hit that spot harder, harder. He laughed at his own joke when he said, "If you don't get this right, I'll break your neck."

I retrieved the .38 from the grass and put it in my pocket. I sat down on the stump of a tree and tried to calm my rapid breathing. If the others were near they would have heard the shots. I waited half an hour and heard nothing, but still was uneasy about moving. I certainly had proof now that I was hunted by experts. I was cold, wet, and weary and longed for some warmth. Even though there was very little pain, my right eye was swollen shut.

Finally I decided that I had to move on to Dundalk to meet Robbie. I rolled the body into the muddy ditch and looked at the strange angle of his half submerged head and felt no pity for him. No more than he would have felt for me.

I began to move along the road stumbling in the dark. After a while I came to a stone bridge. Just beyond was a turnoff and a sign that read 'Inniskeen.'4-1/2 miles.' Just as I was thinking that it would be better to stay off the main road I heard the engine of a high powered car coming from behind me, so I left the main road in the direction of Inniskeen.

A short distance up the road I came to another stone bridge. The oncoming car turned in my direction. It came fast with its headlights cutting through the dark. The bridge was solidly built and where the road rose to meet it were some rough stone steps to a field about six feet below. The car slowed as it approached and stopped on the top of the bridge. I could not see it, but I could hear the engine running as it stood. The two men were talking quietly. I could not hear the words, but could hear an Irish accent, (the local contact no doubt), and one that sounded middle European. For a moment I foolishly thought of rushing them, but realized that they would hear me coming and I would not stand a chance. If they looked over the bridge they could see me so I eased my self into the fast flowing current, biting my lips to keep from gasping as the icy water rose to my waist. I kept to the side and I knotted the .38 inside my tie to keep from losing it.

After a few minutes I heard the car moving off the bridge, but I was not able to tell how far it had gone over the noise of the rushing stream. I wondered how long I could remain in the water. The cold water was beginning to make my legs numb and soon I would have a problem climbing the bank. If the men in the car had found their dead partner they would know that I could not be far away. So I waited and moved my legs often to keep the circulation going. It was not very effective, considering the temperature of the water, and soon I was not only numb but very tired. I thought I might eventually collapse into the water and drown only to be found somewhere downstream.

As the swift current swirled around me I was hit by all sorts of debris: bits of wood, garbage, and others that I would not like to identify. Suddenly something heavy hit me, so hard that I could not push it aside and my hands started to bleed from wrestling with it. It was a large tree branch that stuck under the bridge and wedged itself from one side to the other. I was able to grasp it and hang on. What a relief: almost as if a giant hand had reached out to help me.

It gave me some support, but as time passed I became numb and disoriented. I thought of my family and wondered if I would see them again. I thought of each one and how, even though circumstances were beyond my control, they had been treated badly.

I could see my mother's face and there was strength and comfort in that. I heard strange voices and they seemed to be full of familiar quotations. Sometime near dawn I could not hold on any longer. I let go and drifted downstream. Then my world went black.

I awoke on a mud bank in the middle of the stream and was stuck above the water so that my clothes had started to dry in the wind. My legs were almost useless, but in my mind I knew that I had to keep going and meet Robbie. After some effort I was able to reach shallow water and try to heave myself up on the bank. I kept pulling at branches that kept coming away in my hands. I stood there in two feet of water, my hands bloody and numb, crying with anger and frustration. I promised my self, 'just one more try' and then I will just float down stream. I gave one mighty heave (at least it seemed mighty to me at the time) and I was on the grassy bank.

It was getting light. I massaged my legs, a mottled blue-green, and when I applied pressure they began to swell. My mind was not very clear, but I knew that my goal was to get to Dundalk and Robbie. As the skin peeled from my hands I pulled myself up the stone embankment and, using a branch as a makeshift crutch, I managed to get to the road: better than I thought possible.

It seemed forever before I arrived at the signpost for Iniskeen. I took off my shoes because they were too slippery to walk in and went on in my bare feet. In the early morning fog two cars passed me. I tried to hail them not caring who was driving, but neither stopped. Ironically, the two license plates started with the letters CIA and FBI. If only they really had been!

Finally, in the distance I saw a car moving toward me. It was going from one side of the road to the other as if the driver was drunk. The lights were on high beam and as it came close it stopped. "Is that you, Sir? Are you all right?" It was Robbie and I was so overjoyed to see him that I did not notice that his words sounded weak and slurred.

"No, I'm not all right, you bloody fool. Come give me a hand." Then I fell on the grass and waited.

He said, "I thought you were dead," and began to get out of the car slowly.

I realized that he was injured. "Stay there. I didn't know you were hurt." I crawled to the car and got into the back seat to have more room for my legs.

He turned the car around and we moved off slowly. I saw his face in the mirror, drawn and haggard. "You're driving badly Robbie. What's the matter with you?"

Slowly and deliberately he said, "After I left you the car behind kept coming. It was too powerful to outrun and I drove into the side of a hedge. I ducked through the thicket and lost them, but a bullet had caught me in the lower back ...and I'm beginning to lose feeling in my legs."

" For God's sake, why didn't you look for a doctor?"

He did not need to answer. I knew he was putting his concern for me above his own welfare and I felt terrible that I hadn't given him more thought while I was under the bridge.

He said, "Amazingly the car was not damaged when I finally came back to it. Otherwise I wouldn't be here now."

"Stop the car. Let me look at your wound."

He protested. "While the bullet is still in there won't be much bleeding. I'll wait until we get to Belfast. Then we can get help at the Royal Victoria."

I was so moved by the loyalty and bravery of this young man that my throat tightened. Even from the rear he looked shrunken and older and I knew I must get him to a hospital.

"Move over. I'm going to drive." By now I had regained some feeling in my hands and the rest of my body.

Robbie stopped the car and slid over without a word. I swung myself around on the rear door and sat at the wheel. There was a pool of blood on the leather seat. My legs were clumsy and stiff and I drove as fast as I could to safety in Northern Ireland.

The miles went by and Robbie's voice became weaker and he was rambling. I said clearly so he would understand, "Robbie, there's a bottle of whiskey in the compartment beside you. Can you reach it?" He didn't respond. He was staring into the distance as if somehow he could help me by searching the way ahead. He was dead.

There were no further incidents and the whole episode was hushed up. In Northern Ireland I made the arrangements and Robbie's body was flown home. Later with special permission from the firm I accompanied a Chief Inspector of Police to visit Robbie's wife. She was a simple girl from the Highlands and took it stoically. I did my best to assure her that he had died bravely and on important duty. She just nodded her understanding. We left her in the care of her mother. There was a small notice in the Ulster newspaper saying, "A Sergeant in the Glasgow Police has died in an accident while on holiday in Northern Ireland." How senseless: three men were dead and the world was no better for it. No better at all.

I was kept in the Royal Victoria Hospital in Belfast for a week. I was flown to London and met by two men who whisked me away under strong security where I faced a stormy debriefing. I was so angry at the way the whole incident had been mishandled and asserted myself for the first time letting them know how I felt.

"How in Hell did the enemy know that I was in Ireland? Why hadn't you given me more security?" On and on I went. They had a magnificent way of not admitting they were wrong ... ever. By going on the offensive they had a way of making you feel the failure was your fault.

"You are only a cog in the wheel. You would do well to remember that. Who are you to tell us what was and was not adequate security? Didn't you manage to get one of our men killed? Why did you allow that to happen?"

I said in a fury, "We killed two of theirs. These were no ordinary thugs. They were skilled professionals. And what about my family? Suppose the swine went after them?"

"Not likely," I was told. "Anyway they will have extra security when you've gone."

"Gone," I said. "Gone where?"

"To East Germany, Laddie," said one. "That's the last place they will be looking for you, right under their noses ... eh? Now here's what we want you to do."

chapter 22

ONLY DAYS AFTER MY return from Northern Ireland I was in Eindhoven, Holland where I was assigned to a company of electrical engineers. They made precision instruments and I was to be one of their representatives demonstrating equipment to the East Germans. On the surface I was a harmless businessman carrying the usual briefcase. The case was not 'usual' at all. Hidden inside was a special compartment with enough rigidity to keep secret papers from rustling. At the top of the briefcase just under the handle was another compartment, wafer thin, for concealed microfilm. Neither of these compartments could be detected unless the case was taken to pieces. If this happened the contents would be destroyed by a fast chemical reaction. It could also be exploded if I pressed one of two buttons on my trousers. The detonating wire followed a chain which ran from the handle of my briefcase, up my right arm to a strong and light harness around my chest under my shirt. If pressed, the other button would also release the brief case from the chain and there was a delay of seven seconds to allow the agent to move way. If this device was discovered by the East German secret police (Stasi) I was briefed to say that the instruments were so valuable and so unique that my employers preferred having them destroyed to having them stolen. I might be held by the police, but the microfilm was more important.

Two of us had been assigned for this operation. My companion was a tall Brit with a craggy face and a deceptively casual manner. His name was Edwin. That's all. I understood that his job was to protect me and the contents of the case. I thought of Robbie and hoped he would have better luck. As "businessmen" neither of us carried conventional weapons but I had a device which looked like a harmless mechanical pencil. Concealed alongside the lead was a thin blade made of surgical steel, razor sharp that could be made to protrude about three inches from the tip of the pencil. I did not expect that I would have to use this. My hands were my best weapon. They were lethal enough!

As usual before an assignment I was on edge.

Our cover was good, our instructions were clear, and in a day or two we would be back in Holland. There seemed to be nothing to worry about. However, my past and my experience in Ireland made me wary and on guard, but not wary enough!

We arrived in Dresden on a cold, bright morning. The city had suffered severe bombing during the war. It had been cleaned up with typical German efficiency, but there was still evidence of the devastation.

Edwin and I had a meeting at a hotel where I was to turn over my briefcase to people authorized to receive it.

It was early afternoon as we walked along the street near the hotel. Neither of us were prepared for what happened. A car appeared at high speed and as it screeched to a halt a young man leaped out and, from a distance of about ten yards, hurled an object at both of us. I remember wondering if he had played cricket for his arm was kept stiff in the way the bowler would. For a split second I thought the object was a grenade. It wasn't, but almost as deadly: a petrol bomb designed to explode on contact. It hit my chest and immediately three jets of flaming petrol shot out. One engulfed my arm and the briefcase. Another caught Edwin on the leg and his trousers were set on fire. He shouted to me in a strangled voice, "Detonate." Unfortunately at the same time in an effort to drag me away from the flames he seized my left arm and swung me around. Therefore I couldn't reach for the button with my left hand. My right arm and jacket were in flames and the case was burning, too. I was able to wrench my left hand from my partner's grip, pulled my jacket over my head to wrap it around my right arm. I fell to the ground in a successful effort to smother the flames.

As I sat there coughing from the smoke, the young man from the car sprang forward and severed the chain with a pair of metal cutters. Quickly he was back in the car as it sped away. In seconds we were surrounded by tough looking men in plain clothes who were obviously police. Edwin and I were in pain, but his condition was worse than mine. I could smell burned wool and burned flesh. We were made to stand with legs spread as we were searched with automatics pressed to our head. I knew they were in league with the bomb thrower. They were ready for us if we had managed to run and avoid the bomb. The fact is they had been alerted. They had been waiting. They knew we were coming. I had been betrayed from within the department. Again!!

A vehicle drew up beside us and the back door opened. We were pointed towards it and Edwin hit his head in the process of being pushed in. His face had been contorted with pain and I saw now that his expression had softened and I knew that he was unconscious. My arm felt on fire and my uncovered hand was worse. It had started to blister. Two men hovered over us gripping a bar that went along the roof the length of the van. Their pistols were pointed at us the whole fifteen or twenty minutes until we came to a walled yard. The van was backed up to a door that was about three feet above the floor of the vehicle. We were goaded by the pistols to enter. I still have a small scar made from something sharp against my back, but the pain from whatever it was paled in comparison to the pain from the burns.

Once inside we were ordered to lie with our hands behind our heads. When my partner failed to comply he was kicked in the side until he did. For the next 10 minutes we were beaten .We also faced an Alsation snarling on a short chain. He was so close to my face that I could smell his breath. Edwin passed out twice during this ordeal and the blackened area on his leg became lacerated from the kicking and punching. This was all done in comparative silence and I knew that we were being softened up for further interrogation. At one time I had been told by someone in the firm that if one was captured by the Communists a prison term of five years was usual. I did not think I could even survive one year in the custody of these men.

At last we were taken to some sort of medical facility. Edwin was placed, clothes and all, into a tub with a greenish liquid. My arm and hand were soaked in the same liquid. The stinging was almost intolerable, but the curative action was amazing. Without it I know I would have suffered more.

Finally, bandaged and dressed in hospital gowns we were led to a small room. It was clean with two beds about twelve feet apart and had barred windows. There were two locked doors across the room from each other and both were opened electronically. One lead to a large ward and the other to a grassy area. As the door to the ward opened I could see a uniformed guard on either side. I could see that one was armed and I assumed the other was, too.

We never left this room and we were careful not to speak much or exchange signals because we were certain that the room was bugged as well as monitored from a two way mirror over the wash basin. Edwin was in bad shape but bore his pain stoically. I knew little about him except that he was one of us, (at least I hoped so!) had been a member of SAS (Special Air Services) and might still be. At one time I asked him how he was and he responded weakly, "I'm fine." From the look on his face I knew he was better than his voice implied. We were somewhat comforted at being kept together, but I'm sure it was for the possibility of gaining information from us.

At one point I said to him, "I hope we have someone to represent us with these problems."

He nodded and said,"Lor' I hope so, too."

Both prearranged signals telling one another to react quickly if the opportunity arose.

Late one day a medical orderly looked in. I had used a sponge to blot up excessive perspiration and said to him, "Bitte, bringen Sie mir noch Schwamm." (Please bring me another sponge) He walked away without saying another word and returned a few minutes later with a sponge in a small dish.

"Danke," I said and lifted the sponge and saw something written in the center of the dish: in English in small fading letters: Be ready at 4:00 P.M. The garden door will open. Make for the car waiting on the other side of the hedge.

I could hardly believe it. Was this some kind of trap, or had the staff been bribed? The orderly moved to the other bed and Edwin's expression did not change as he read the message. A quick flicker of his eyes and I knew he had understood. We had no watches so judging the passage of time was difficult.

I lay back and tried to concentrate and summon strength for the dash that we would have to make. To ease the tension I spoke of inconsequential things to my partner. I imagined that we had been let alone for so long because the Stasi were trying to identify us and were having difficulty because of the various diversions that had been set up over time. As I was to find out, the Soviets knew very well who I was, but the information had not been shared with the East Germans.

At what must have been 4:00 we heard a click and the door leading to the garden opened just a fraction. I shot out of bed, reached Edwin's bed and hooked his good arm over my shoulder. It must have been agonizing for him, but he didn't make a sound. I opened the door gently so that it would not slam back on us and then we were outside on the grass. No one was in sight. Beyond the hedge a few yards away I could see the top of a car. We ran for it as fast as we could, Edwin hopping along with amazing agility. How amusing a sight we must have made, hopping along with our gowns flapping open at the back and nothing underneath. A driver sat behind the wheel, head lowered and his body hunched over. I know he did not want to see what the outcome of our escape across the lawn might be. One of the doors was open and we crawled in quickly. Immediately the car moved off slowly towards the main entrance of the facility. Once outside it still moved at a slow pace, obeying lights and traffic signs. The driver still kept his face averted from us. After about five minutes we pulled into a side street and were transferred to a very battered and ordinary looking Citroen. Again the same cautious driving until we got to the outskirts of Dresden where there were two cars waiting. We were separated and my car gained speed and headed west towards the border. The car in which I was riding had been modified so that there was a special compartment under the back seat just barely large enough for me. I assumed that Edwin was in a similar car. I squeezed in and was able to breathe through a vent close to my face. It had a fine mesh screen to filter out road dust. There was a button that would release the cover on my hiding place and there were times between checkpoints when my driver allowed me to sit on the back seat, stretch my legs and nurse my sore arm and hand. These reprieves never lasted long and I would hear a sudden "Schnell! Schnell!" and back down I went.

Finally we came to the West German border which we crossed safely. We followed a route that was a closely guarded secret then and probably for many years to come. My partner and I were flown to England. On the way we were tended by a medic who gave us shots for pain ... a very welcome treatment. We were both a mess, but grateful to be alive, free, and back on British soil.

As was the normal procedure, Edwin and I were debriefed separately and filed our reports separately.

There were no recriminations for the loss of the briefcase. That made me wonder if it included false information that was intended to mislead the East Germans. I would never know nor would I know who betrayed us. The department was vague and evasive. "There is no need for you to know. Didn't we arrange your escape?" I couldn't quarrel with that.

I was allowed to go home for a few days. Audrey was appalled at the sight of me. She didn't ask any questions just dressed my burns as well as any nurse. My stay was all too short; just enough time for my hand to heal and me to regain some equilibrium.

In the spring I was summoned to London for further orders and I was sure that something would be worked out for me that would improve things for Audrey and the children. Perhaps between us we could continue the good feelings that had begun before I left for Ireland.

I was being naive. The department had no interest in me as a person nor in my marriage. That was confirmed when they told me of my next assignment. I could hardly believe my ears.

I was to return to East Germany. Not just any place in East Germany: Dresden.

chapter 23

AT THIS POINT IN my story I am sure that some, no many, are asking themselves: Why didn't he just say, "That is an impossible assignment and I simply cannot return to East Germany. It would be suicide." That isn't the way it works. I would not even like to dwell on the consequences. Outsiders have no idea of the threat that exists when one is disobedient. My government is not different from others in this respect. Also spy thriller enthusiasts may not realize how little information an agent has before he starts an assignment. The rule is: the less known the better. Then if he is captured or compromised in some way he or she cannot do any but minimal damage, either to his contacts or his home office. He is under orders to destroy either the information he is carrying or himself.

I have said before that sometimes agents are called upon to obey orders that seem illogical, senseless, and yes, preposterous. Never before had I been given an assignment that struck me as suicidal. Returning so soon to Dresden did seem suicidal.

I said so with every ounce of conviction I had.

In return I had flattery and soothing words. "You are one of our best chaps. You have proved your courage under fire and your ability to withstand pain. Your loyalty is beyond question. There are not many field agents like you. We need you for this most important job." On and on it went.

The department had learned from other sources that the Stasi had tried and failed to identify me. I was assured that my cover was intact.

"I doubt that very much," I shouted. "Besides I have a damaged hand and I can't even use it properly."

"You won't need to use it," I was told. "You'll be in and out in

177

no time. Just carry on as usual. Keep meeting your contact in Lyons Corner House. He'll tell you when to return to Holland."

I left the meeting with very uncomfortable feelings that somewhere something was very, very wrong. I knew that I had loyal friends in the department, but what of my enemies who thought that I knew too much? Could they be behind this current assignment? This return to Dresden had to have come from high up. What if it was from one of those who had the most to fear from my knowledge? Worse: what if such a person was an agent of the KGB working in British Intelligence? Questions, questions running through my mind over and over. Even then some of us knew there was a mole and thought we knew his identity. Years later an inquiry would clear this man of charges, but such verdicts were very suspect. This man was knighted by the Queen and retired on full pension because the British government does not want mistakes bared. There were other high placed moles: Blake, Philby, Burgess, Maclean, and others whose names would surface as the years passed. If any of these knew of my second Dresden assignment then the Soviets would know, too.

I was tense and distressed and needed to talk to someone. Not to my wife nor to Janet, for confiding in them would put them in jeopardy. Certainly not to anyone in the department either, for I was not to break silence and my talking would have to be reported.

I had an old friend, formerly in Intelligence and now a Catholic priest. Discussing my predicament with him would be a clear violation of the Official Secrets Act, but at least my discussion would be protected by his vow of silence. Even then I would have to be circumspect, but I knew just talking would lessen the tension and anxiety. He was a splendid man: wise, gentle, and very intuitive.

I went to the church and asked for Father Bruce. Soon this tall, thin friend appeared, greeted me warmly, and took me to his room. Here we could talk privately among the clutter and the piles of omnipresent books. I admired him so much because of his strong convictions and his ability to leave the shadowy world that held me prisoner. I apologized for the possibility of putting him at risk, but he just smiled and gazed out the window hands folded, while I unburdened myself.

"I certainly can understand why you don't want to accept this assignment. It sounds dangerous. Aren't they placing themselves at risk as well by putting you under such pressures? But you must go where they send you, unless perhaps you feign illness?" He looked at me questioningly.

"That wouldn't work," I said flatly. "They would send me to their own doctors to examine me. It's an impossible situation. I'm a coward if I don't go and a dead man if I do."

With a faint smile he said, "I think I would prefer to be a live coward, but knowing you as I do, I think you will go. You just needed me to help you let off some steam. Perhaps they are right that your cover is still intact. In the meantime, there's one thing that I can do. I will pray for you."

I left and tried to pull myself together. I met my contact at Lyons Corner House where he was waiting and learned that I was to report to Eindhoven in a week.

Once again: a white lie to Audrey about a photography assignment out of town and I was off.

It was a rough crossing from Harwich to the Hook of Holland, so tough I was seasick which was unusual for me. Seasickness can be depressing and I found my self thinking of my family living under basic conditions. Audrey was still augmenting our income as a waitress and the children were beginning to feel the stigma of my false imprisonment. I made up my mind that somehow things were to be put right for them and the company would have to start releasing my pay in some way or another.

The train carried me to Eindhoven and to a safe house where I was given instructions to leave for Dresden. I was again assured it was only a question of taking microfilm, concealed in the usual manner. By this time my face was padded and I wore contact lenses making my eyes brown. I was given clothes to alter my appearance and with a raincoat and a shapeless brimmed hat I could have been anyone or no one.

My papers were in order and my passport claimed that I was Neil MacDonald Smith a New Zealander of Scots descent. My story was that I had come to England after the War to study. That failed and I went into business in Europe. It was plausible enough, yet I could not rid myself of the feeling for the second time that I was about to enter

the lion's den. I thought of Father Bruce's promise to pray for me and
I remembered a line from the bible, "The prayer of a righteous man
availeth much," and I tried to be positive.

I arrived in Dresden unobtrusively. I was to meet my contact
in the afternoon, but he failed to appear and there was no signal of
any kind. I convinced my self that there was no need for concern.
Agents were delayed sometimes. I returned to my hotel and had a
light dinner as I did not like to eat too much when I was working.

The next morning after rolls and coffee I walked a short distance
and suddenly without any warning I was flat on my face on the
pavement with three men holding me down. They knew their
business well: I could not move at all. One said in Russian as if I
were a thing,"Handle it carefully." A car pulled up beside us and the
passing people hurried by quickly so as not to seem involved. I was
pushed into the car and my hands were manacled. There was a man
on either side of me and a third in the passenger seat in front facing
me. As the car pulled away this man gave me a punch in the nose
and I could hear it crunch. I was stunned and my face was suddenly
covered with blood. The men on each side of me moved away to
avoid the unwelcome flow. One gave me an oily rag to wipe the blood
away. By the time we reached our destination I was a mess and my
nose felt four times its normal size.

I was marched from the car and put in a cold, damp cell. Finally
a bucket of water was brought and I was able to clean up a little bit
with my handkerchief. A terrible feeling of hopelessness and loneliness overcame me. Also there was a strange kind of relief. The scenario
I had feared most had happened. At least the uncertainty was gone.
Soon the microfilm that I carried was found.

Interrogation began almost at once, and I was astounded by the
information that they had about me. There was no doubt whatever
that I had been betrayed by someone within the system who had
access to my confidential files. The chief interrogator who spoke good
English with a German accent had full knowledge of my activities
and cover.

"A wonderful cover," he said, "but you did not have us fooled for
long. You are a clever man and you must realize that the game is over.
Your government will disown you for certain. You are all alone now

and at our mercy, so you may as well confess your guilt and tell us everything we want to know. It is foolish to resist, as soon you will be made to talk, whether you want to or not."

I was stunned to realize that they knew of my activities and perhaps they had only found out recently, or perhaps they had watched me hoping that I would lead them to more important contacts. I was trained to keep my mouth shut, and I did. I was not brave but probably cussed. This cost me a few beatings and I prayed to God to give me the strength to die with dignity if it came to that.

I was told, "A delegation from Moscow will be sent to try you. The British government has never heard of you and you can expect no help from them."

The 'trial' was held in a long, dark, paneled room with a raised dais at one end. On the dais sat the judges. The one in the middle was a severe woman, middle aged, with grey hair and an air of authority. The whole scene was an eerie echo of the Gestapo trial in Arnhem, and my emotions were much the same: a mixture of anger, fear, and defiance.

A list of questions and answers had been pinned to a kind of lectern in front of me. They amounted to a confession and I was told to read the answers aloud as a part of my testimony. I refused. I would not be forced to incriminate myself. The woman president of the court pointed her finger at me and said, "You will do as you are told or you will suffer the consequences." When I still refused I was escorted from the court and beaten with a flexible rubber truncheon: a coiled metal spring covered in leather, about two feet long. When a blow descended on my shoulders the club curled around my neck and struck the top or my spine with tremendous force and it grew worse with each blow as the bruised area became more sensitive. Twice in this 'democratic people's society' I refused to answer the questions and I suffered for it. After the second session the pain was so severe that I yielded and read the answers cursing myself for my weakness.

The answers became part of their official record. I swore to myself I would not be weak again. The most unexpected evidence against me was given by a shopkeeper that I had known. I could hardly believe that this supposedly ordinary tradesman was anything but what he had appeared. Yet here he was in East Germany giving incriminating evidence against me. He did not know everything, but enough to enable him to tell about me being in contact with certain people in the area. He never looked at me, but gave his evidence in good German, in a flat, unemotional voice. I found this almost casual betrayal the most disheartening of all. Yet, I was to find out that one of those who really betrayed me was responsible for the arrest of no less than three hundred agents in Europe. Today, if he is still alive, he lives in retirement in Moscow.

A verdict was reached quickly: ten years imprisonment. The first two to be served in solitary confinement, the rest in Vladimir, a notorious labor camp about one hundred miles north of Moscow.

From Dresden I was flown to Moscow and taken to the dreaded Lubyanka Prison. Chained hands and feet, head shaved, wearing a drab prison uniform with a number on the top of the pocket, I was led down endless corridors, dark and icy cold, with alcoves set at intervals. At last we came to a heavy door with a small spy hole about five feet from the ground. The door opened and I was pushed inside. The door slammed shut, sounding my doom.

The cell was about five by ten feet. It was lit by a single dim electric bulb set behind thick glass in the ceiling. The light never went out which made it almost impossible to judge the passage of time. In one corner was a can for human waste. In one wall there were four iron rings supposedly to support a bed of some kind. There was no bed. I shouted angrily through the door and when the guards came I told them in limited Russian that I wanted some bedding. They left me with a bruised face and I made myself laugh defiantly, but I felt far from defiant. Eventually I learned to sleep with my back braced against the wall and my legs braced apart on the cold stone floor.

There was a microphone to record every sound that I made: every sob, every groan, every outcry. Within a short distance was Red Square, and the Kremlin. Close to the Kremlin was the British Embassy where my countrymen had denied any knowledge of me. Not far away, too was the Church of the Mother of God; called the " joy of all who sorrow." What irony!

The human mind is accustomed to having stimuli. There was no noise, no change from dark to light and nothing for the eye to see except the can in the corner and the four rings on the wall. My hands and feet remained manacled through a chain around my waist and it seemed very unnecessary because I certainly wasn't going anywhere. It did have the effect of reminding me that I was in this situation completely under control of my captors. It served as further humiliation and weakening of my will. Those chains were a constant reminder that I would never escape, that I had no control over my own destiny. Even so some small spark glowed in the back of my mind and I knew that it was a hatred for those who had betrayed me, and also a desire for revenge.

Almost at once the questioning began. I was led along dark corridors to the examination room. If another prisoner was in the corridor I was shoved into an alcove until they passed. Therefor none of us could be identified. The examiners were all fluent in English. They were officers in the secret police but had nothing in the way of the spit and polish of the Germans that I remembered from Arnhem. At first the pressures were mostly psychological. I was impressed and discouraged by the amount of information they knew of me, the department, everything. I was forced to stand for endless periods of time while lights were focused on me and the questions were battered at me. If I fell down, I was picked up, my face slapped and the questions continued.

Sometimes I was quizzed on the signals we agents used to contact each other. Sometimes they wanted sensitive information about the Gehlen organization. At times they just taunted me about our political system, our religions. There were times when food and drink was brought in for them and I had to watch them eat.

Before the physical abuse began I was able to defend myself to a small degree. "Tell us about 'so and so' in the Foreign Office. We know all about his affair with that senior officer's wife."

I protested that I was an outsider and knew little of what went on in the office. "If you know all about this why ask me?"

The General in charge told me that they knew all about me. What kind of man I really was. They said that I had been forced into this business and had little stomach for it. "We can get you out of it tomorrow if you co-operate."

When I didn't respond they tried another approach. "We heard from your parents recently and they are distressed that you are in trouble again. They think you have been arrested for smuggling. They are ashamed of your behavior. They want you to tell the truth."

"Balls," I said emphatically.

"Perhaps your department is worried about you. Why don't you write them a letter and tell them how you are being treated?"

"Go to Putney," I said.

Putney is a superb of London across the Thames River and the phrase is an invitation to jump in the river.

"Portney," the general said. "What is this Portney?"

I answered, "It is an island resort in the Outer Hebrides ... very pleasant indeed."

He seemed to be making notes and the idea that this ridiculous conversation was being recorded struck me as extremely amusing. When I was taken back to my cell I cried and laughed to myself and caused the guard to open the spy hole and look in suspiciously.

As the interrogations continued I tried to confuse them with false information telling what I hoped were plausible lies. Back in my cell I would sing hymns or smutty songs, recite nursery rhymes or Irish limericks, and make obscene gestures in the direction of where I thought the cameras were. Later I was told that the Soviets thought that I was cracking up much earlier than most prisoners and perhaps that is why they turned to physical torture while they felt I was still capable of being coherent.

The sessions became severe. At times I was stood on a wooden block with my hands chained to the wall. When the block was kicked away I was beaten around my shoulders and between my legs and sometimes hosed with cold water. My keepers had a preference for abusing the genitalia, and their preferred instruments were electric and burning wax tapers. Another form of torture was something that I have difficulty thinking about even today. I was taken from my cell and put into a smaller one: rectangular and with one wall that seemed to be made of some flexible metallic material. After a while there was a muffled sound of machinery and the wall began to move towards me slowly making the space smaller and smaller. It was terrifying not knowing if, and when, the wall would stop moving. The lights went out and the wall kept moving until I stood with my back flattened against the opposite wall. Still it kept moving until the wall pressed against my chest and I could hardly breathe. Anyone suffering from claustrophobia would have gone mad by now. I refused to scream and bit my tongue until it bled. I don't know how long this lasted but, I kept thinking of the good Father who was praying for me back in London and tried to lock my mind around this and think of nothing else. Finally, a grinding noise and the wall started to recede and soon I was taken back to my cell.

Slowly, my condition deteriorated. Sores appeared on my body, and a rash started on my head. The lower part of my body became black and swollen. It was difficult to walk except with an exaggerated waddle. Of course, there was no medical treatment. At one time I was given injections that increased my sensitivity to pain so that even the slightest tap was excruciating. One guard took great pleasure in stepping on my bare feet with his heavy boots. I thought if by some power of thought I could kill this man I would. We had been taught how to endure pain: fix your eyes on a point above the torturer's head; visualize some pleasant scene from the past; fill your consciousness with some compelling image. Pain can be diminished to some extent, but pain is still pain. I was given pentothol and I have no idea what I said under the influence of that drug.

Gradually I was losing my grip on reality and as the pressures continued, I hoped and prayed that I would die, and I remember apologizing to God for this death wish. I was slumped against the wall on my knees (too weak to even stand) and knew I was ceasing to be a man; just a thing meant to live with pain. Tears streamed down my face and I was thankful that there was no one to see me cry.

Soon after I prayed to die there were strange occurrences: things that I cannot explain, only describe. Wishful thinking, hallucinations? Maybe. The conditions were ripe for delusions of all kinds.

I know that I was leaning against the wall of my cell and saying to my self, "I cannot possibly take any more of this." I fell into an exhausted sleep and I dreamed. My mother came to me and I know that she was in the cell beside me. She explained that although she had not understood, now she knew what my life was like and that she would pray that I be given the strength to endure. The whole cell was filled with peace. As she spoke the pain seemed to recede and I knew a great determination and strength. When I awoke my attitude was dif-

ferent and the despair was gone. Even the guards noticed. Although
my mother had no awareness of these events the same thing happened
to one of my brothers who developed malaria while in Africa.

After this I was left alone in my cell for what must have been
several days. Perhaps the Soviets thought I was too battered to endure
more questioning. While one is in solitary confinement it is necessary to invent some sort of mental diversion. Of course, we had been
trained for this and I began to create a house on the wall in my cell
… mentally, not with any writing instrument. I placed all the rooms,
furniture, etc. Sometimes I would decide to replace or reconfigure
the windows or doors. I would add foliage and picture it in the different seasons. I would place a horse and carriage in the stables; or a
dog sitting happily by the front door. As the time passed I became
very familiar with every inch of this phantom house and even today I
could draw a complete diagram of it.

Another technique that we had been taught was to create dia-
logues with unseen relatives or friends. I often had these conversations
with family, Janet, or my old vicar. I took both parts and always out
loud. I also asked questions of my old vicar and Father Bruce. I asked
questions about prayer, faith and how they sustained theirs. I began
to notice something strange. Whenever I asked questions of a religious nature, the answers did not seem to be coming from me. They
were too rapid, too certain. I wanted to ask for a sign, but looking
over my past life I didn't feel worthy of any sign, but sometimes it is
to the unworthy that signs are given and far away a righteous man
was praying for me.

The interrogations ceased. Perhaps my captors thought they had
extracted all they could from me. I was given a wooden bed sus-
pended from the rings in the wall. It was hard, but infinitely better
than the stone floor and I thought that there must have been some
reason to keep me alive a little longer.

Weeks and months had passed in a blur and one day my cell door
opened and a man entered. He looked familiar and I realized he was
the one who had posted the questions and answers on the lectern at
the 'trial' in Dresden. He looked at me and said, "You are going to be
transferred."

I assumed he meant to the labor camp at Vladimir.

I responded, "I am quite happy right here, thank you."

He might have laughed at such a strange suggestion, but he said simply, " Don't worry, you are not going anywhere unpleasant."

I was unchained and taken to see the Russian general who smiled at me and in heavy English said, "You are goink home. You are beink eschange. Now what can we do for you?"

I asked for a bath, the first in months and I remember how the water came up to my navel warm and delicious. As my skin peeled away it reminded me of a newborn baby. I looked at my legs and I was reminded of Sir Winston Churchill and his pink cheeks and I started to laugh.

I was given some coffee that tasted delicious and then I was asked to sign papers. It was a statement saying that I had been well treated in prison. The papers were given to me by a guard standing by me with a rubber hose in one hand. I looked at the guard and I signed the papers knowing that they would not convince anyone.

With an escort, I was flown to East Berlin, wondering the whole way if this was some sort of trick. I had been given clothes to wear and shoes that were several sizes larger because my feet were too swollen to fit into my own. I wore dark glasses because the light was so uncomfortable to my eyes. In East Berlin I waited in a room with several other men. One spoke to me in English with an American accent and said that in about an hour I would be handed over to the British. "We wish you well and hope we don't see you again. We are very sorry you are not a Soviet because you would be very useful on this side of the fence." He offered his hand and said that he had spent years in the United States.

I replied, "That's obvious."

The Berlin Wall was not yet built when I was driven to the checkpoint, but markings were on the pavement to make the separation between the East and West very obvious. It was a cold day and I was wearing an overcoat and a large brimmed hat to help shade my eyes even more from the bright light.

I heard a telephone ring in the guardhouse and someone saying,"Ja'" then "Nein das gefait mir nicht. Wie lange daurt es?" (No, I don't like that. How long will it take?)

Then I was told that there had been a delay and I would have to wait another hour. I was driven back to a comfortable room and waited again for what seemed forever. Here I was only a few yards from freedom, but what if someone had changed his mind? What if I never made it out? Would I have to go back to Lubyanka? I swore to myself that I would not let that happen.

After an eternity the Russian escort stood up and said, "Now we go again." As we approached the crossing I could see a black limousine stop on the other side of the divide. Two men left the rear of the car and one stayed at the open door. Soon I saw the man dressed almost exactly as I was: overcoat, dark glasses, and hat with the brim pulled down. We passed close enough to touch and neither of us looked at the other. Telephones rang again and the Russian said, "Goodbye, Sir. I admire you. It is unfortunate that you work for the wrong side." I silently thought ... thank God. I squared my shoulders in spite of the persistent pain at the top of my spine and began the long walk to freedom. I was prepared for a bullet to my back and could almost hear the shot, but at that point I almost didn't care. I was thirty-three years old; I had lived too long with pain; I had lived too long with fear, and with death.

Ahead I saw a small group of faces and one man stepped forward. It was Maurice Oldfield. He placed a hand on my shoulder and said with a mischievous smile, "My dear old chap. Where the Hell have you been?" Behind my dark glasses my eyes brimmed with tears. I knew where I had been: in solitary confinement for eleven months, two weeks, and four days.

chapter 24

As I was placed in the limousine, shaky and ill, we turned around and left the checkpoint behind. At some point doctors took charge and gave me sedatives and I slept for a very long time. I was weak and confused, but in better shape than when I was released from Buchenwald. This time I had only lost fifteen or twenty pounds.

I traveled by car and then air with three men. One was a male nurse, and Maurice Oldfield another. We talked spasmodically. He said that when I was exchanged the Soviets had included a message saying, "This man is a third rate agent and everything that he knows we know." I was willing to accept their evaluation of me as an agent, but I knew that I had been able to conceal facts from them.

I said to Maurice,"Now I suppose I will get the third degree when I arrive."

"Not at all, old chap. You're free. You're home. We fixed that for you, you know."

"They left me to rot long enough, but," I told him, "if you had anything to do with getting me home you have my thanks." Oldfield, always dragging on his cigarette, was a good man; one of the best. He died of cancer some years later with a shadow over his name, perhaps contrived by people who wished to discredit him. Evidently I was not the only one with enemies in the system.

In London I was taken to a private nursing home with thin, unobtrusive bars on the windows. The doctors and nurses could not have been kinder nor more patient. My thoughts were sometimes erratic and my memory was spotty. My ability to concentrate was minimal and at times I was not sure who I was.

As had happened before, colors were intense and certain noises frightened me. On my first outing with my nurse, again a 'red monster rushed at me' and I had to stand still to control the panic. The male nurse assured me it was only a London bus.

I remember that outing well. I felt like a complete stranger who saw familiar landmarks that I could not remember: Hatchards, Simpson's where I had shopped for shirts and clothes and often had lunch, the 'In and Out Club' (Army&Navy) which I knew so well. All around me businessmen walked briskly and well dressed women carried shopping bags. The world had not stopped while I was away nor had it even noticed.

My caretaker and I walked over to Simpson's to have coffee and suddenly standing beside me was a smiling face saying, "Hello, Keith. What are you doing here? Up from the country for a few days?"

I had no idea who this tall blond man was, but I said, "Good to see you. Do sit down and have a coffee."

He hesitated and said, "Are you feeling all right, Keith? It's me, Thomas."

It was indeed my cousin, full of good cheer and laughter as ever. He told me that I could do with a decent meal and invited me to lunch. I declined and said that I had much to do in London. We talked of other members of the family, but I had difficulty remembering them. I did not introduce the nurse who approached and took my arm as we left. As we left Thomas stared after me completely puzzled. I was too exhausted to care and slept that afternoon and through the night.

In my debriefing sessions I tried to relate in detail what had happened at the Dresden trial and later in the days that followed. My de-briefers had a hard time accepting some of the odd experiences in my cell. More important, the Soviets let slip the name of a friend of mine in the department who they said was working for them. This information had stunned me, but I reported it anyway. I was told not to concern myself with this and to forget about it.

Later that respected and successful man was knighted, pensioned, and eventually raised to the peerage. I was again reminded to forget it, but I could not, and never will.

I was asked by an official who must have had access to my confidential file which enemy I considered more cruel and brutal, the Gestapo or the KGB. I replied that there was little difference. No matter what the Nazis did to me at least they did not go after my family in England. This was not true of the Soviets as they were capable of going after anyone and anywhere that they wanted.

Although most of my interviews were normal, one or two were exceptionally severe. One senior person said quite harshly, "You know if you did talk too much in the Lubyanka, we'll put you away for much longer than the Soviets did. Mark my words." I reacted angrily and told him if he was taking that line I wouldn't answer any more damn questions. He gave me a wintry smile, coughed, and said that I had misunderstood him. I had not.

I recall clearly one conversation with a Brigadier I had known from my early days in SOE. He was a sallow faced man of medium height, bald except for a fringe of grey hair. He told me amiably that the department was pleased that I had not told the Soviets anything that they had not known already.

"Of course, now your cover's blown, we won't be sending you back to that part of the world." I suspected this, but it was a relief to hear it confirmed.

I asked the Brigadier about my family and he answered casually, "Really, they are doing quite well."

The truth was that the department had done nothing to help Audrey and the children and she had been too proud to ask anyone else for help. She had continued to work and the family was barely getting by.

After more talks, the Brigadier took me into the adjoining annex that served as a conference and dining room. "I've arranged a little refreshment," he said. "If I recall you don't smoke and not a good idea to have a drink, I suppose. Tummy not quite up to it yet ... eh what?"

I washed up in a small bathroom and stared back at myself in the mirror. The image that I saw was haggard, thin, with deep set eyes surrounded by dark circles. I straightened my tie around a collar that was much too large. I returned to the dining table where the Brigadier was sitting with a glass of wine in his hand.

"Good stuff," he said. "Pity you can't join me."

"I think I will, thank you."

I did and enjoyed it, but after a few sips I felt very light-headed.

I thought to myself ... how well these blighters live: beautiful food, cold chicken, salad, cheese, biscuits, and wine.

I had to eat slowly and ate very little. When it was time to leave my male nurse led me to the car and soon I was back in the nursing home.

Gradually my condition improved. The nightmares, sweats, and periods of confusion became less frequent and I was told that I could go home soon. I began to wonder if now that I had 'come in from the cold' I would be permitted to visit my older son. Now was the time for the department to grant such a concession if they felt they owed me anything. When I brought it up there was a disapproving look and noncommittal reply, but not an outright 'no'.

My return home was awkward as it was bound to be. The children had almost forgotten me and Audrey and I were little more than strangers. As I could tell nothing of my experience in Russia the department suggested I say that since our marriage had been rocky I had gone away to sort things out. What a poor and inadequate excuse! I knew that Audrey didn't believe me, but she didn't press me for details. I was allowed to tell her that I had accomplished a successful business venture during my time away. I did have money: ten thousand pounds in cash. A sizable amount in those days, but part of my accumulated back pay. Evidently the department did feel they owed me something and sent me home with a briefcase with five hundred twenty pound notes. This was no big favor: I had earned it!

The money made it possible for us to begin a new life. We bought a delightful Elizabethan house in a fishing village. Built in the late six-teenth century, the thick brick walls sometimes seeped with salt from the sea sand used in the mortar. We were all delighted with it and it made me happy to see my family at peace and free from want at last. My wife no longer had to work outside the home and the children could go to better schools. I often stood on the edge of the cliffs in the wind and rain and thanked God.

I was obliged to see the doctors occasionally as I still had night-mares. Some times I wakened soaked in perspiration feeling again the excruciating pain of blows to my neck and the dreadful tiredness of being kept awake for hours with the bright lights and barrage of questions. It took months, but gradually the torments diminished and I was feeling and behaving rationally.

Always in my rehab I had been told to forget and to try to block out all memories of Lubyanka. I was to say nothing, even forget for the moment that I spoke a little Russian. The indoctrination was so thorough that even today when I try to recall words in that beautiful language a red light flashes in my mind warning me that this is forbidden territory.

I wasn't given any new assignments, but I knew the department would want to use me again in one form or another.

Although I was expressly forbidden to discuss Lubyanka with anyone, I knew I could trust Bruce and the new religious awareness that I had experienced made me want to visit him. I not only wanted to thank him because I knew that his prayers had played a large part in my survival during some almost unbearable situations, but I needed to confide thoughts which were troubling me deeply. He could be trusted and he would understand. I tried haltingly to explain to him how the religious experience that I had in that underground Hell had left me profoundly changed. It not only kept me sane and strengthened me in the face of torture, but left me morally sensitized for the first time in many years. I had promised God to love and follow his teachings for the rest of my life. How was this possible in a profession where religion was scorned, morality was non-existent; where even the code of discipline and loyalty to the state seemed to be breaking down? There was a rot in the system. I could sense it but was certainly not going to be able to prove it. Burgess and Maclean had already defected, but there were others. Where the moles were I didn't know, but they were there and their presence became more obvious in the years to come. They were not working for King and Country: they were working hard against it. Their power to inflict harm was growing and little could, nor was, being done about it. I told Bruce that I wanted to sever ties to my old life and lead a normal existence; have a normal family life. If I continued working for the department there was a good chance that I would not survive for long. So far I had been very fortunate, but how much longer would that good fortune last? The Soviets had come after me in Northern Ireland with no success. They were willing to release me from the Lubyanka only in exchange for one of theirs but that didn't mean that I was no longer on their list.

"No," said Bruce emphatically, "I wouldn't count on that at all if I were you."

" It's a rotten business, Bruce," I said. "You know this as well as anyone. You were a part of it. By rights I should have been dead long ago. I have no wish to die and every good reason to live. How can I resolve this?"

He thought for a while sitting there, hands folded in his dusty cassock and looking down at his shabby shoes. A clock ticked in the quiet room and I saw through the window a double-decker bus that not too long ago had frightened me. I felt the calm and inner goodness that surrounded this old friend and finally he spoke.

"I don't think the danger in your work is the important issue. You accepted that when you signed on during the war. That's not really a valid reason to call it quits now."

He paused and looked at me steadily. "If you really feel your work is immoral you must resign."

"That would be difficult," I said. "It may not even be possible. You remember Claude Dansey who died in June '47? When he was very ill I went to visit him in the Lansdowne Nursing Home in Bath. It was soon after he was given a knighthood. He was dying, simply worn out by the tremendous pressures and responsibilities of the war. He spoke to me more as a friend than the tough martinet who had recruited me a few years earlier. He said to me then, and I remember it very clearly, "You have to be very careful from now on, Keith, because they'll never let you off the hook. They will never let you go. You know too much."

Uncle Claude, as he was known to some, was a brilliant man who knew the game inside out. What if he was right?

I tried anyway. That night I composed a carefully worded resignation to the Foreign Office. In it I said that I was weary, had been through too much, and could not go on. I had been a faithful foot soldier for a decade and a half. To the best of my ability I had kept my vow of loyalty and silence and would continue to do so. I had given the decision careful thought and my mind was made up. I owed it to my family and myself and therefore I wished to resign.

The next morning I handed the resignation to my immediate boss. He read it and stared at me with a painful look. Surely I could not have meant what I had written. It was just my reaction to the terrible times I had been through. Understandably indeed ... I was still under stress. It was nothing that two or three months rest and fresh air wouldn't cure.

"Just take some leave," he said. "Take as much time as you want. We do have plans for you and you are important to the success of these plans, but there's no hurry. Do take this silly piece of paper, like a good fellow, and tear it up. We'll forget all about it and you can, too."

I didn't take the paper and asked that it be forwarded to higher authority as was my right. My words brought the temperature down and there was a distinct chill as I left without my resignation.

A few days later I was taken to dinner by two of the senior men in the department. My resignation had been passed along, but had been rejected. They had great plans for me and there was no reason why I couldn't rise quite high in the organization ... there might even be an honor somewhere down the road. When I felt I could return to work a flat would be made available in London where I could live decently as a retired man with a pension and some independent means. With this as a cover I could be quite valuable. Why ... they even had plans for sending me to school.

Suspiciously I asked, "What kind of school?"

The senior man sipped his wine and said, "No need to know just yet, but with your fondness for the theater I am quite sure that you'll find it fascinating when the time comes."

They talked on and on and mixed flattery with promises and I found myself wondering what would happen if I told them the truth: that my decision to resign was an ethical one based on a religious experience while I was in Moscow and a conviction that my work was offensive to God.

I didn't have to wonder what their reaction would be: "The man's become a religious fanatic and as such he will be a threat to our organization. A state of affairs which cannot be tolerated."

Over brandy and coffee the senior man produced my resignation and handed it to me.

"There's nothing on record about this. Why not take it home and tear it up?"

I took the paper reluctantly. With a sinking feeling of cowardice and self betrayal I put it in my pocket. Claude Dansey had been right. I knew that if I persisted it would mean the end for me. I needed to provide for my family before I died and leave them something of worth. Any doubts were dispelled when dinner was over and we were about to separate. The younger man placed his hand on my shoulder and looked me straight in the eye. "Don't worry, Sir. You can leave us anytime you want to." Then he smiled and added two words. "Feet first."

chapter 25

IT WAS AN OVERCAST day as I stood in the Sabena terminal in Heathrow waiting for my flight to Belgium. I wondered how the weather would be in Brussels: a diversion so that I could stop my wondering about how I would be received and perceived. I was elated and nervous at the same time.

I was on my way to see my thirteen year old son, Stephen. He still lived with his grandparents in the suburbs of Forêt. I had seen him a few times over the years always telling him that I was a friend of the family who had known his mother and father. Now, at last, I had permission from the department to tell him who I was.

The permission had not come easily. It was pointed out to me that the department had gone to great lengths to eliminate all records of my marriage and even changed Stephen's surname on his birth certificate in Somerset House so that his paternity could not be traced to me. I was assured that his ignorance of our relationship was to protect him. If it became known that I was his father forces on the other side might use the information to pressure or blackmail me. This posed a host of questions in my mind which I could not raise. Who in the department could be trusted? I was warned that there were cases where children of agents had been held hostage or met with 'accidents'.

In return I had some arguments of my own: Stephen was my son, the child of a woman I had loved dearly. He deserved to know about his mother and how bravely she lived and died. I had given my utmost for my country and I felt that they owed me at least this much. I doubt if this swayed my superiors, but in the end they granted my request with conditions. I could visit Stephen and tell him who I was and that was all. To make sure that I followed these conditions and did not 'overstep the mark' another agent who knew the family well would be present at the gathering. He was currently stationed in Brussels and I had known him for a long time. His name was George Hastings.

George met me at the airport and we taxied to the suburb where the family lived. "Stephen is a fine boy," George told me as we sped along. "Very sensitive, very bright. He's been kept in the dark, of course. He thinks his mother disappeared in one of the forced labor roundups during the war, and that his father was a Belgian officer killed in action, but you know all of this. All those records are fault-less. During my last few visits I have tried to pave the way for you a bit. I told him that you knew his parents well and wanted to tell him more about them. So perhaps this meeting will not be too much of a surprise. Of course, he will need to appreciate the need for security and I'm sure that he's capable of that."

I turned to George, "I'm nervous as Hell, George." And I certainly was.

We came at last to the large stone house. The main door opened and I saw Arlette's mother and father come forward with great smiles of welcome. I had deep affection for these lovely people who had lived with so much suffering in their lives. Over the years I would talk to them by telephone or visit briefly when I was in Belgium and they would report to me lovingly of the everyday events in the life of my son. Although they were among the very few people who knew about my life and work they never asked questions and never wavered in their love for me. They had willingly shared their daughter with me and knew that our short time together had been happy. Having Stephen with them had been some sort of compensation and now here they were: my father-in-law tall and dignified as ever with his wife by his side, smaller and older, but with Arlette's beautiful eyes. As we moved through the hall and into the study I became increasingly nervous. I wanted so much to know my son, but I was prepared not to expect too much too soon.

The family had a chauffeur-butler-handyman named Wim who had become a great friend of Stephen's. He was waiting in the study and said to my father-in-law, "Shall I call the young man in, Sir?"

"Yes, please do, Wim," he said and was obviously nervous himself and walked over to the fireplace quickly and lit his pipe.

In a few minutes Stephen came into the room. His eyes took

in the whole scene quickly. He shook hands with George then with me.

" I remember you, Sir. We met when I was ten years old and you took me to Anvers for the day."

I did, I did. How well you remember I thought. Just then lunch was served and a gong sounded in the hall. I had given them that Burmese bell when they lived in London during the war and it was very similar to the one we had at home booming out lunch or dinner to bring us from the surrounding fields or gardens. That warm familiar sound helped me to relax a little bit.

My father-in-law sat at the head of the table and I to his right. Stephen sat next to me and seemed such a friendly boy eager to talk of his previous conversations with George. "He said that you might be able to tell me about my father. Is that right?"

"Yes, I believe I know more about him than anyone else. Perhaps after lunch I may share with you what I know, but you must keep it in strict confidence."

"Oh, I will, I will. I would not even tell Wim."

The simple lunch of cold meats, salad, and cheeses did not last very long and over strong coffee I looked to the head of the table and got a nod from my father-in-law. Why don't you and Stephen go into my study ... just the two of you? The rest of us will just stay here and talk."

As we walked into the study Stephen smiled at me and said, "I thought you might be able to tell me more."

Briefly he talked of his friends and school work and I knew that he must be doing well because of his enthusiasm.

He had some of my characteristics, but mostly he looked like his mother, and I told him so. I wanted to tell him so much of his mother: how gallant she was, how proud he should be of her, but the words stuck in my throat. How could I tell this child of his mother's sudden and violent death?

Stephen sat quietly with his eyes fixed on me. Finally he said,"You know I don't think my mother is ever far away. I have often felt her in this house."

It startled me because in this quiet room I could feel her presence, too.

Stephen hesitated and then said, "I wonder if you loved my mother. You don't say much about her and yet,"... his voice trailed away.

He stood up, went to the window where there was a sudden burst of sunshine and said. "I think you are my father. I wish you were. Please tell me."

"Yes, Stephen. I am your father. And yes, I did love your mother. And yes I do believe she is very close to both of us at this moment."

I was unable to continue and together we walked out into the garden. The air was crisp and clear and the lawns and shrubs were vivid green and God was in His Heaven and all was right with the world. Suddenly everything was worthwhile: the pain, grief and sorrow, misunderstandings, agonies, and moments of despair, all redeemed by this one moment of blessing.

As we walked I told Stephen of his mother's role in the Resistance and how very soon after he was born she returned to Nazi occupied France. I told him how she was captured in a fierce fight and then handed over to the police. (I omitted the Gestapo.) At the very least her time in captivity was brief. I told him that she was far more courageous than I and she died bravely for her country without fear or regret.

I did not say much about myself just that I had a complicated security job and that I had lived in the shadows. I made light of the difficulty that this entailed. He had now replaced a phantom father with a real flesh and blood one and that is what mattered most to him. I was not allowed to tell him of my remarriage or his half brother and sister. For the moment he just wanted to know as much about me as I could share. His mind was so like his mother's: curious, questioning, and sensitive to others. It was such a joy; a bonding that I hoped would withstand any future misunderstandings.

As we returned to the study the large ornate clock was just striking four. There was the smell of tobacco in the dining room where the others still sat talking and wonderful aromas from the kitchen. My mother-in-law announced tea. It was a custom that they had continued from their days in London during the war.

After tea, George said that he had to be getting home and he asked me to call him the next day at the Palais de Justice.

"Take Stephen away for a few days, old friend. Just the two of you. I think I can persuade the department for permission." And he added with a smile, "Maybe after you've gone." He gave me a quick handshake and left.

That evening, Arlette's brother and his wife came to dinner. Henri had been too young for the war but he remembered vividly the journey they had all taken across the sea when they were escaping the Nazis. It was Arlette who kept their spirits high.It was she who produced dry socks and a half bottle of cognac she had wrapped with other bits in an oil cloth tied around her waist. It was she who spotted the British trawler in the fog. Stephen listened to these stories with shining eyes.

As Henri and his wife left he said, "I always wondered if you were involved in government." It was a statement and a question. I didn't reply. We were all tired and as Stephen climbed the stairway he turned and gave my hand a very firm shake. The rest of us remained in the library and I tried to express my gratitude for all they had done for our son but my words were quite inadequate. It was then that my British reserve disappeared and the three of us stood in front of the fire and held hands. Great tears welled in my mother-in-law's eyes. The tension of the years seemed to be resolved and this marked a new phase in our lives.

After church on Sunday, we sat at the same table and in the same places, but it all seemed different. In the afternoon we planned the journey Stephen and I would take. My father-in-law would lend us his Peugeot and we would drive down the Loire Valley visiting churches and chateaux along that lovely river. Stephen was on holiday from school and I could manage almost a week. When I checked in with George he told me all was well and that I was to check in daily ... a promise I was glad to make and glad to keep. Those four days passed swiftly and happily. Stephen was fascinated by ancient castles and their moats, especially the vast chateaux at Sully sur Loire. We stayed in a lovely auberge close to the castle. As one picturesque view after another appeared along the route Stephen would leave the car to take pictures to share with his grandparents. Once he hesitated, "I suppose that I should not take any pictures of you?"

"Perhaps not," I replied, "but Grandpère has one of me from the old days. I know he will give it to you." That seemed to satisfy him.

As we traveled on we stayed in small inns and ate in cafes. In Poitiers we dined in the shadow of the cathedral in a large restaurant with an open fire place. On our way home we paused in Le Mans where I showed Stephen the road used for the famous auto race. For five minutes I let the Peugeot speed to see what it could do and to impress my son with my driving ability. When I slowed down Stephen said enthusiastically, "That was really good driving, Father." I was absurdly pleased with his praise and use of the name 'Father'.

We drove on through Rouen, Amiens, Arras, Lille, Mons, and back to Brussels. I had to part with those I loved, but promised that I would return for another vacation when circumstances made it possible. If only I could share him with my family in England, but I knew he was being cared for by loving grandparents. Parting was lightened by the fact that I knew my son at last and I felt that he had some affection for me. It was only to grow stronger and deeper in the years left to us.

chapter 26

IN THOSE DAYS AFTER Lubyanka I was in a conflicted state of mind. The religious experience that occurred while I was in prison was very real to me and I was trying to keep my life in accord with the goodness I had felt there. Outwardly, I had accepted that the department would not let me go, but within, a slow burn of rebellion was rising. I wanted to be able to think and act for myself. The conviction that something was very wrong within the system persisted and yet I was a prisoner within that system. Nobody wanted to know about the problem or be involved in fighting back: it would be too dangerous. When I raised these issues I was always put off with soothing words, "The damage is being contained. We are dealing with it. Don't worry about it."

I did worry about it. Who were these traitors hurting my beloved country? What was being done about it? Why wasn't I who had suffered because of them not entitled to know? The answers always came back smooth, bland, and impenetrable: forget it. I knew what was being done: nothing. Over time this core of anger within me became fiercer. One day I was expressing this to an acquaintance in the system who I knew and whose sharp mind and wit I admired. He was a slender man in his mid thirties with reddish hair and a slightly mocking and supercilious manner, as if everything amused him.

"Oh, well, you know," he said, "we do catch up with those chaps from time to time. Try them quickly 'in camera' with no mess, no fuss, no bother; get a confession usually. Then deal with 'em one way or another."

"What do you mean," I asked, "one way or another?"

"Oh, some we retire on a decent pension. Gets them out of the way, you know. No questions in Parliament. No beastly publicity. Sometimes we allow them to go to Russia. After all that's their adopted country, isn't it? Matter of fact we're holding one fellow right now who's scheduled to go to Moscow. Friend of yours ... actually," and he told me the man's name.

I stared at him unbelievingly. This man was a product of one of England's finest schools and had been an officer in the British Army. I had heard him express some pessimistic thoughts about the future of the Empire, but how could he possibly be a traitor?

"Oh, he's a traitor all right," my red-headed informant said. "Betrayed many of us, even you ... d'ya see? It all came out at the trial. Not only did he confess, but seemed proud of it, too, but he'll soon be back with his Russkie friends. Good riddance, eh?"

I made sure that my expression didn't change, but I felt that core of rage within me begin to grow into a white hot fury.

"Where are you holding him?"

"Oh, dear me. Couldn't possibly tell you that, ol' boy. Said too much already."

"I'd like the information and am prepared to pay for it ... and your silence."

He looked surprised for a moment then was thoughtful. "Ah," he finally said, "in that case ..."

It took him a few days to consider but in the end he did talk and I did pay.

I made my preparations quickly because I didn't have much time.

On a wooded hillside not far from Lulworth Cove, Dorset, I lay on my stomach, shaded by small trees and beneath brush. My dark clothes blended with the surroundings and there was a slight chill in the air as the sun started to set. It was late summer of 1958 and nine months after my release from the Lubyanka. I was not fully recovered from that ordeal but considered myself fit enough for what I planned to do. About fifty yards from where I was were a row of dilapidated and apparently abandoned buildings. Beyond these was a stockade type of enclosure surrounded by a ten foot barbed wire fence. The top was angled outward at the top to make access more difficult. I knew that wires were stretched across the top carrying an electric charge strong enough to stun a man, if not kill him.

Inside the fence were several small huts. This was a restricted area under the jurisdiction of the Ministry of Defense. I had been told that the man I was seeking was being held there until arrangements could be made to send him to the Soviet Union.

My car was parked about two miles away in a grove of trees. I had driven over from my great aunt's home in Ilminster where I had been visiting for a few days. She was delighted to spend time with me and it made a good base for what I had in mind.

In a specially fitted drawer under the driver's seat of my car I carried some of the paraphernalia used in covert action: binoculars, compass, light metallic blanket, and a balaclava I had bought in Harrods.

Early in the afternoon I used the binoculars to watch the comings and goings within the stockade. I could see just a few guards and attendants patrolling now and then. My information was that very few prisoners were being guarded ... perhaps only one. Security didn't appear to be very tight. One point: the inmates or inmate had no interest in escaping, and it was probably thought that no one would attempt to break in.

My informant had told me that the man I was seeking was confined in one of the huts for twenty-three hours a day, but in the late afternoon was outside for a walk or to sit in the fresh air. As I watched I finally saw him appear and made note of the time. At that distance I couldn't see his features distinctly, but he was wearing a scarf with the colors of a famous English public school and that was identification enough. He walked up and down for a while and then sat on a wooden bench between two of the huts. A guard came up and spoke to him briefly, then moved away. As the sun set he pulled his overcoat closer around him, then finally went inside.

Now I knew all I needed to know and went quickly and quietly back to my car. Although I had checked, I hoped the good weather would last at least another day.

The major preparation involved building a wooden ladder, hinged to form a bridge. It could be easily folded and carried. Working fast, I made it in the small workshop I had at home. The ladder was very narrow and therefor very light. It was designed so that when it was fully extended the top half could fold out and over and then descend on the other side of the fence, leaving a platform across and above the electric wires. With rubber gloves and rubber soled shoes an active man could scale the fence, I hoped, without triggering an alarm. A mechanism worked the hinges so I could withdraw the ladder once I had re-crossed the fence. The uprights were greased to make them slide easily and I was quite sure once I had started I could cross the fence in fifteen or twenty-seconds. The folded ladder was hidden in the trunk of my car.

The next day I was on the hillside, consulting my watch now and then, and keeping my eye on the cloud bank developing to the Northwest. I was not concerned by the clouds, but the rain that might follow and create a hazard on a wet and slippery ladder.

As the minutes ticked by I made myself relax. I was calm and I told my self that it was necessary for me to confront this man face to face and satisfy my curiosity. That was all: find out what I could and perhaps learn the identity of others who had conspired to betray so many of us. Possibly I could gain some insight into the motivation causing an upper class, well educated Englishman to forsake his country.

Mere curiosity is hardly a sufficient driving force to impel a man to scale a ten foot electric fence, with the chance of being shot, or at least being severely punished if caught. There had to be a much more powerful motive. One was my growing desire to establish some degree of independence from the department. I didn't know it then, but this impulse towards rebellion was the beginning of a long road that would eventually lead me to a break with my superiors. The second motive was simply the smoldering anger that I had carried since my arrest in Dresden two years ago. Someone had betrayed me to the Communists and the thought that he would simply be deported to Russia, getting away with everything, almost rewarded for his treachery, was intolerable. In reality there were two, maybe even three, personalities inside the black clad figure waiting on the hillside.

At almost the same time as before, the man emerged from the hut. Again wearing an overcoat and the blue and white scarf around his neck, he walked back and forth along the perimeter of the stockade for exactly twenty-one minutes. Then he sat down on the wooden bench facing west and gazed towards the sunset. I had already selected my point of entry close to one of the uprights which supported the fence and where I could not be seen unless the man looked around. Once over the fence I would walk around the back of the hut and approach from the other side. If he thought that I was a visitor who had come in the main gate so much the better.

An open space of at least eighty yards separated the foot of the hill from the abandoned buildings. I was trained to move swiftly and lightly and I covered the distance and crouched in a shallow ditch behind the buildings. With the ladder beside me I waited and listened. I moved to the door in one of the buildings and found to my surprise the whole structure was a dummy made of painted fabric and camouflage cloth. The door too was a fake and swung easily leaving an opening just wide enough to get my ladder through.

The ladder worked perfectly. I climbed like a cat, crossing the live wires, dropping on the far side and drawing the ladder after me, putting it on the ground in shadows. I pulled off my hood and gloves, donned an old tweed cap and opened my dark jacket at the top so my shirt and tie were visible. I looked like any casual visitor.

I walked around the hut and straight up to the bench where the man was sitting. With his old school scarf he looked like some prematurely aging schoolboy. He stared at me in amazement.

"Good lor'... good God," he sputtered. "What the Hell are you doing here?"

Now that I was face to face with him my anger seemed to be replaced with more contempt than fury.

"I've come to see you," I said. "As I'm sure you know the Soviets caught me in Dresden and sent me to the Lubyanka for almost a year. They gave me a hard time and I want to know if you were responsible for that?"

He gave a quick shrug and I knew that he was willing to tell the truth as he had nothing to lose by doing so.

"Perhaps I was ... among others, but you were lucky. You got back, didn't you now? Sorry if it was unpleasant, but that's just part of the bloody game ol' boy."

I hit him then with my left hand. It was quite strange because it seemed to move of its own volition. I hit him a downward backhand slash on the side of the neck with the weight of my body behind it. It traveled no more than twelve inches and killed him instantly. His head sagged sideways into the scarf and he would have fallen from the bench had not one hand caught in the arm rest and held him in place. He stayed there almost as if he had fallen asleep and I felt no regard for him, no remorse whatever. I felt an enormous inner relief as if an unbearable pressure had been removed or some invisible scales had been brought into balance for myself and others. However, I was startled at what I had done: my hand had acted faster than my brain.

Pausing long enough to put on my hood and gloves I went back over the fence as easily as I had come. I folded the ladder, put one arm through it and slung it over my shoulder at the point of balance where I had added padding to make it easier to carry. In a few seconds I sped over the open space and into the trees where I had been only a few short minutes ago. From there I returned to my car and ultimately to my great aunt's home in Ilminster.

I drove to London early the next morning. My contact was waiting for me at my club with orders for me to appear at Headquarters. As I had expected, the department was furious and they had their accusations ready.

"What the bloody Hell did you think you were doing?" My actions were going to ruin some well laid plans. The Soviets were going to be furious!

I said, "They probably will be if you are frightened of them."

There was outrage at the highest level. I wanted to get my word in and I said, "Are the Soviets dictating to send a traitor there, when he should be locked up here? Who's running the damn show?"

"Now listen carefully to me ... you'd better curb your tongue, or you'll be in deep trouble. You cannot make statements that you cannot substantiate."

"I'm well aware of that. You'll charge me with telling the truth."

"You know bloody well," the senior man yelled, "you killed that man," ... and he named him.

"If that bastard's dead, I'm delighted, but what makes you so sure that I had anything to do with it?"

"Nobody but you could have done it," he shouted rising from his chair. (This was not true. There were others in the system who were just as able.) "You got into that compound somehow and murdered that man. You killed him in cold blood."

"My, my. Look who's talking about cold blood."

"Admit it. You did it. Admit it."

"Prove it," I said, knowing they couldn't.

And they knew it, too. It would be too embarrassing to try anyway. In the end, despite additional accusations, threats, and denunciations, no formal charges were brought. It was believed within the inner circle that I was the culprit. There were a few who believed this and thought I deserved a medal, not a reprimand, but I had no doubt from that time on I had made a few additional enemies. I sure didn't need any more.

chapter 27

DAVID KNOWLES, THE HAWK faced little soldier who had carried me to shelter during the intense German mortar barrage within yards of the Utrecht-Arnhem crossroads, came out of the war, recovered from his wounds, and was ready to go wherever money or women were to be found. I could not understand why women fell over David, but they certainly did. Blonde, brunette, single or married it made no difference. When it came to holding a job or behaving responsibly he was hopeless, but as a ladies man he was fantastic.

I met him only a few times after the war before he sailed for Kenya where he was soon in trouble for bouncing checks and chasing other mens' wives. He became entangled with a very senior government official's wife and was placed on an airplane bound for England with orders never to return. The British Criminal Investigation Department was not happy to have him back and they warned him when he stepped off the plane that he had better behave himself. He assured them that he would.

By then I had the promised apartment in London, and a substantial clothing allowance. I was working in London and acting as a courier abroad. As intended, I was sent to school: a school for the blind. I had several weeks of intensive training learning how to act blind or as a partially blind man would. This is more difficult than one would suppose. It was not just a matter of wearing glasses and carrying a cane. The deception demands and involves learning many mannerisms and details until they seem quite natural. The idea was that most people regard blind people as objects. They will talk more freely if they think they are not being observed and it is true that a blind person can monitor conversations a sighted person might not be allowed to hear. My assignment was to take advantage of this by listening for moles and subversives at various levels of London society.

The deception was an elaborate one that I detested. I wore contact lenses that made my eyes seem cloudy and, although I could see through them, I could not see well. The department insisted that I was a fine actor and my part had to be played convincingly. Attending classes with sightless people who had no idea that I could see was another aspect of a bizarre life where the unreal was almost the norm.

One day I was called back to Headquarters and told by my contacts that David was back in England. They had been keeping an eye on him and they believed he had been approached by agents of a foreign power who wanted him to use his former friendship with me to ascertain whether I was still employed by the department. It was suggested that perhaps agents wanted to recruit me to work for them. Or perhaps, for one reason or another, they wanted me dead. My assignment was to meet Knowles' by accident' to find out what it was all about and to convince him that I was no longer in the 'spy' business.

In addition I was to try to learn who was employing him, why, and discover his source of income. The department admitted that this was a depressing situation: that a man who once had saved my life might now betray me. Obviously he had been chosen because it was known that I owed him a debt of honor and that I wouldn't be suspicious. It was not difficult to run across Knowles 'accidentally' one day as he emerged from a grocery store in South Kensington. We greeted one another with surprise and apparent delight and our wartime experience was soon renewed. Knowles became a frequent visitor at my London flat and I was pressed to invite him to my home. This triggered warning bells, for I had tried so hard to keep my other life apart. While staying with us Audrey took a dim view of his drinking and philandering.

The department was placing us at risk. Almost at once he became involved with the wife of an army officer who was serving overseas. He was a very irritating guest, even more so when he borrowed my car and parked it all night outside the 'lady's' house. My grandfather's gold cufflinks disappeared only to appear on Knowles later in London where I was able to retrieve them. My long suffering wife did not appreciate any of this and questioned my relationship with the 'stinker' and, of course, I couldn't explain anything.

I realized that it was a risk allowing Knowles to come so close to my family, although I didn't think that he would harm them. Soon it was clear that I was being tested in various ways, but Knowles was not a professional and I was able to parry most of his queries. I reported to the department to arrange to keep Knowles under surveillance when he returned to London.

One afternoon he was followed to a hotel in Basil Street where he met an attractive woman. They greeted each other with affection and had tea together. One of the several lip readers in the department sat nearby and 'overheard' their conversation quite easily. Knowles told the woman that he was sure my connection with the undercover world had ceased years before. The woman said that she and her colleagues were not persuaded and he was to continue his efforts to ascertain all he could concerning my activities. Knowles protested that he needed more money. After all, he could not live on air. He was told that he would get paid more on completion of his assignment, and not before. Until then he would continue to do exactly as he was told. They smiled at one another through the whole of their conversation, although it was obvious that neither was satisfied with the direction it had gone. Finally they separated, completely unaware that their whole conversation had been monitored.

A few days later Knowles telephoned me. It was a Friday and he asked me when I was returning home. I told him that I planned to leave later in the day and I would stay through the following week. He asked me if I would be there on Monday. He asked again, "Are you sure you're going to be there then?"

There was a curious urgency in his voice and a small warning bell rang in my head. "Yes, I'll be there. Why do you ask?"

"Oh," he said and sounded flustered and embarrassed, "I just thought I might come and join you for a couple of days, if that's all right?"

Reluctantly, I told him it would be satisfactory, but the moment I hung up I called the department on a private line. "Knowles is trying to make certain that I will be at home next week. I don't know what's going on, but there's a chance he's trying to set me up and I don't want my wife and children in any danger. Do you hear me? I want full coverage down there, and I want it right away. The whole thing doesn't feel or smell right. You're taking a bloody risk with our lives."

In response they said two people on whom I could call if necessary were already in that vicinity, and they named both. One was a retired Brigadier, a neighbor who lived almost next door. The other was 'Pip' Hargreaves, a fisherman and painter of sorts, who lived on the outskirts of Stoke Fleming. "We'll have a word with them both," they said.

"That's not good enough," I said forcefully. "Retired people cannot handle this. I want the best we have. I want the house watched twenty-four hours a day; someone needs to keep an eye out for strangers in the village. I want this given an immediate priority."

After more discussion, they agreed to send some security specialists from Exeter. "But really," they countered with some irritation, "you've always been able to take care of your self. Why all this sudden alarm?"

"Because my wife and children are down there." I rang off.

As always I took precaution and my car windows were already darkened so I could not be seen. I drove out of London using the radio telephone in my car several times before reaching the Exeter bypass. Each time London claimed to have no knowledge of impending trouble. I should have been reassured by them, but that sixth sense of danger persisted.

More questions without answers: Why were these men stalking me? Was it because I killed their man in the stockade? Was it retribution for someone else's deed? Was I over-reacting? I gripped the wheel and drove faster.

When I arrived home everything appeared peaceful. Was it truly the haven that I had tried so hard to make for them?

At five o'clock a message from the Brigadier was brought to my door. "Come and have a drink ol' fellow. We need to talk privately."

Telling Audrey that I would return soon, I walked the short distance. A voice of modified thunder came from the kitchen. "Come in and sit ye down. Pour yourself a drink me dear chap." It was the Brigadier's wife who had a heart of gold-but who frightened the villagers with her direct and gruff manner. Surely she was more of a combat commander than the Brigadier himself! "Bill's in the bath. Be right down," she bellowed.

I poured myself a drink and soon Bill came down, ruddy faced and smiling. He glanced towards the kitchen to make sure that his wife was out of earshot, and said, "Had a call from an old friend in London. Put me in the picture and said I was to help in any way I can. Your fellows want to use my house for watching yours ... and a Special Branch fellow is arriving here tonight."

I said, "I didn't know that, but I'm relieved to hear it."

Bill moved over and poured himself a drink. He cleared his throat, coughed, and said, "I had a job in a similar thing once, so I know approximately what's what. You'll probably have a caller or two yourself in the morning."

He sat down and lit a large pipe. "You never told me that they called you 'Vapor' and I had a good laugh when they told me why."

I said, "Vapor, whatever. The name seems to have stuck."

We talked a bit more, then I went home, passing through the kitchen to say,"goodbye" to Mrs. Brig. They were both staunch and solid friends and I was glad to have them on my side.

The next morning, shortly after the postman, a man came to the door saying that he was from Exeter and wanted to discuss an insurance policy I had. I knew who he was as these preliminaries were for anyone who might be listening.

I was still wary, even after he had come in and identified himself as from the Special Branch. I kept my hand close to the .38 I had carried ever since leaving London. He noticed and told me later that he had the unpleasant feeling that if he had made the slightest false move I would have shot him.

He told me a man was posted in the woods and called him on the radio intercom. The man reported that all was quiet and he saw no sign of danger. My 'insurance' man said that the village was also covered and he would stop by the following day, Sunday, just to check that all was well. We agreed on hand signals to use under unusual circumstances. I told him that if anything did happen we should try to take at least one of them alive. We needed to know who was behind all of this. He agreed, and we shook hands firmly as he left.

He did stop by the next day and said that all was well.

"Keep a very close watch tomorrow," I told him. "If they are coming at all it will probably be then."

Even though it was calm on Monday morning, I decided to call London to see if there were any new developments. When I called the department I used a telephone box. There was one on the way to Pip's house on the other side of the river. To reach it I took the little Kingswear Ferry which shuttled across the Dart River and took only a few minutes. I saw my 'insurance' man standing by a house on the right of the slipway. We ignored one another, although I was relieved to see him on the job. I parked my car and waited for the ferry and when it docked I boarded. Just then I turned and saw my man give a sudden urgent signal, then vanish into the trees. As he did two men appeared walking rapidly intent on catching the ferry just as it was to leave. They were too late and had to step back to avoid the churning water. I knew that I had just missed a close call and I prayed that my man was on his way to alert the men guarding my family.

I was certain that they were after me and would continue until successful. It was unusually rough and the trip took a little longer than usual as the ferry turned in the swift current. I knew if I could reach the telephone box at the top of the causeway I could call for additional help. I thought of the danger that my family might be in and I thought of Knowles and wished him in Hell.

Before the ferry was tied up I was off and running up the slippery cobblestones. At the phone box I dialed my special number and the call went through immediately.

" I want help and damn quick. I'm going to try to get to Hargreaves one way or another. There are at least two of the bastards on my trail."

Pip's was too far for me to reach quickly on foot so I ran to a row of parked cars checking for keys left in the ignition. On the fourth one I was in luck. As I got in and started the engine the owner came running towards me waving and shouting. I shot forward barely missing him. As I picked up speed along the waterfront a police constable stepped into the road with his hand raised but I blew the horn, swore at him and kept going. About one hundred yards farther on a car came out of a driveway blocking my way. I hit it a glancing blow and it spun around in the opposite direction

I left Dartmouth by the Stoke Fleming road at a speed that did the car no good at all. On a bend in the hill before coming to the village my front tire went flat. I left the car and decided to run for it and as I went on up the hill I heard a crash. The unattended car had run backwards, gone through a frail wooden fence, and dropped over the sheer cliff. The owner won't thank me for that, I thought, but at least he'll get a new car out of it.

No one was at home at Hargreaves' and I let myself in through the back door and went straight to the telephone. When the operator came on I snapped at her that this was an emergency call and I gave her the number. Seconds later I had an answer, but the line was bad and I could hardly hear. I said, "Get someone out here fast. I can't manage on my own. See if the Navy or the Coast Guard can send a helicopter. It will be easier to see them from the air and we want them in one piece. Alert the police in Dartmouth and Kingsbridge." There was a crackle of static and I could only hope that my message was understood.

I was perspiring profusely and dropped into a chair with my .38 in my hand. As I sat there the front door opened and in came Pip. He looked surprise and greeted me with, "Still in trouble, Vapor? I knew you hadn't given it up. What in God's name are you doing here?"

I was told that Pip had been alerted. What was going on? I told him that at any minute all Hell might break loose and asked where his wife and daughter were.

"They're in the village. Perhaps I can head them off." He sat down by the telephone, seeming like a pirate with his bushy, black beard and distinct aroma of fish. He spoke to his wife and told her to stay in the village until he came for them. It was starting to rain and he didn't want them to get wet. "Just stay at the Robinsons and wait for me. Don't come home until I fetch you. Now ... do as I say. It's too far to walk in this weather." He put the phone down and said, "Now what's this all about?"

I told him as much as I thought I could and should, then asked if he had any firearms in the house. He had his service revolver and a .12 gauge shotgun. He brought them down from upstairs and produced boxes of ammunition.

It was early afternoon and the rain was coming down hard. While we waited, hoping the police would arrive, we talked of people we had known in the past including our friend who had lost his fingers to the Gestapo. We had not seen one another for thirteen years. I knew Pip wanted to stay on after the war but the Intelligence Service would not have him. I recalled that immediately after the war he had been drinking and was considered a risk.

"Too easy to see us in here," Pip said, and he walked over to close the curtains. As he did a silencer coughed outside and the glass splintered under the impact of a bullet. It missed Pip, who ducked back and leaped for his shotgun. As he did, another shot was fired from the rear of the house and into the kitchen. So there were at least two of them. I was sure they would rush the house if we did not fire back. I said to Pip, "Cover the doors if they try to come in and I'll go out the side door and see if I can work behind them."

I slipped out into the small garden that was surrounded by shrubs. Through the hedge I saw movement at the rear of the house. Picking up a heavy stake from a pile near the entrance to the garden, I worked my way around to a point where I could see two men lying about twelve feet apart. As I watched, one of them stood up and moved closer to the house while the other covered him, still lying down. I moved quickly across the space separating me from this second man. As he turned I kicked him in the face with my heavy walking shoe breaking his jaw. I hit him with the stake and the gun flew out of his hand. The other man whirled around and came towards me firing fast as he ran. I fired two shots in turn, and the second hit him in the nose and passed through his brain. The first man was writhing in pain, his jaw looked grotesque and the stake had broken his arm. I dragged the dead man across him so he would be unable to move, then made my way cautiously to the back door of the house. I called Pip by name, and there was nothing but silence. A broom was standing in the kitchen and I used the handle to open the living room door. Still no sound so I entered the room to find Pip in his chair holding his chest, his hands wet with blood. He looked at me and said weakly, "Vapor ... I'm dying. Only to ask one thing: make the damn government look after Betty and Ann." Before I could reply, he fell forward.

I was used to death and dying, but the thought that my loyal friend had been killed trying to protect me filled me with rage and overwhelming sadness. I wrenched open the door and saw a third assassin running down the road to he village.

Where in God's name were the police? Through the soaking rain I ran after him. When he saw me coming he scrambled over a dry stonewall, and moving fast, took off across a field. The red Devon earth stuck to my heavy shoes as I ran, but I was determined to take this one alive and again I was filled with anger at the injustices of this mad world. I paused and fired three shots at the man's legs. All missed. He came to the top of a rise, vaulted a stone wall about three feet high, and fled to his right. When he came to a gap in the stone wall he turned and fired at me in the open. I dropped to the sodden earth where a long hillock gave me temporary refuge.

Behind me I could hear the thud of a helicopter but it was above the low clouds and mist. I couldn't see it and it certainly wasn't able to see us. Then a megaphone from a police car crackled and an indistinct voice in the wind said, "Come back to the road. We have the fields covered. He can't escape." The police called me by name and repeated the message.

I had no intention of following their orders. I was concerned that they might kill the man, and I was determined to take him alive. My breath coming in short gasps,

I stood and sprinted for the wall. As I reached it and jumped over, I saw the man no more than thirty yards away, making for a stand of trees. I shot him above the left knee and he went down hard. I was concerned that he might try to kill himself so I ran forward as he was struggling to stand. I wrestled him to the ground and took the automatic from him. It was empty and he tried to get up but collapsed in pain with his face in the mud. Some police came and carried him away covered with red mud and blood. I followed with others to the police station in Dartmouth. The chief constable of Devon County, Lt. Colonel Lacon and a Special Branch officer took charge and I was told that the whole incident would be dealt with, which meant without any publicity whatever. We shook hands and he sped away and the whole affair disappeared in silence.

How an incident involving the police force of two counties, leaving two men dead, and two others injured could go unreported in the press might seem incomprehensible to the average citizen. What the average citizen does not know is that a 'D' notice from one of Britain's secret services could completely silence newspapers, reporters, and even the police. Not even a commissioner of police could disobey when told under the Official Secrets Act that he is to say nothing, explain nothing, reveal nothing.

Pip's widow was told as much as she could be told. I never met her, but she was given a substantial pension. A few of us had to fight with the department for her as Pip was not currently employed. Knowles was picked up for questioning in London. Nothing specific could be pinned on him, even though he spent some uncomfortable weeks in prison waiting for help. It was decided to set him free so that his activities could be monitored in the hope of getting more information. The two surviving assassins were Hungarians. After a brief prison term they were deported to Hungary partly as a result of intensive pressure from their government. Their story was that they were simply tourists who happened to be in the Dartmouth area on that bloody Monday and were set upon by some British madman. Nonsense! They had guns. None of their excuses could hold up and they were lucky not to be spending years in prison.

The 'British madman' was taken home by the police, somewhat cleaned up, but still mud-stained. My wife was in the kitchen and when I came in she called out,"Is that you Keith? You're a bit late. What kept you?"

"Nothing much," I called back. I thought of poor Pip and thanked God that I was safely home.

chapter 28

IT WAS 1961, A year after Pip' death, and I had been in London for months, sometimes traveling back and forth to Europe as a courier, sometimes in my role as a retired officer with independent means. I led a fairly quiet life in the city occasionally dining with friends, attending various functions and serving on the board of a small club. I also continued my friendship with Father Bruce, visiting him now and then, always making sure that I was not observed.

My special place for Sunday worship was the old Anglican church within the grounds of the Royal Chelsea Hospital. They had, and probably still have, a fine choir. Before and afterwards I would enjoy meeting people. The hospital was founded by Nell Gwynne, the famous mistress of King Charles the Second, and was a place where many retired veterans lived: elderly men, very proud and easily distinguished by their red coats.

One of the important occasions at the hospital was Founder's Day, when usually one of the Royal Family came to review the parade and distinguished officers and others gave receptions. At one of these functions I was introduced to Colonel Reginald Squibb and his wife Kay, who lived within the walls of Windsor Castle due to his position as the Senior Military Knight. We became close friends and I was often invited to their home in Windsor, where ultimately a small apartment was placed at my disposal. I was urged to come and go as I pleased and it was here that I met some fascinating people: Lord Mountbatten, Haile Selassie, (the diminutive emperor of Ethiopia proudly wearing the Order of the Garter), King Michael of Romania and many others. The firm was not happy with the connections that I was establishing at Windsor, but I claimed that they enhanced my cover and I'm sure they did.

One happy consequence was that I was able to invite my parents and Audrey (introducing her as a sister-in-law) to the colorful ceremony of the Order of the Garter . On these occasions I wore my decorations and my mother and father were able to recognize that I had played some part of consequence during the war and was accepted in a small circle of people close to the monarchs; a circle most carefully screened and limited.

One evening I was asked by one of my friends to dine at a new restaurant in Mayfair. It was a pleasant occasion; we were all formally dressed and given a good table. The plan was to return to our host's London home, within walking distance, for brandies after dinner.

After coffee I excused myself and went to the washroom. As I stood washing my hands I noticed a man standing close by looking at me intensely. He said, "I must say, it's been a pleasant evening." Somewhat surprised I merely nodded. He looked straight at the wall and said in a different tone, "I know exactly who you are and I want to make you an offer, quickly, if you'll listen." I stared at him suddenly alert and on the defensive. I was not frightened by him, but the whole thing had caught me completely by surprise.

Smiling the whole time, he stood facing me, "I have good friends who would pay you well to work for them. More money than you've ever had in your life. Almost anything you ask for, I'm authorized to say ... "

"Who the Hell are you?" I demanded.

He stepped past me and locked the door. "Now we're all right for the moment," said this dapper, intense man. He looked me right in the eye, "I represent a worldwide organization run from Moscow. They know almost everything there is to know about you. Everything you've done since your return from prison in Moscow. We have excellent terms for you and your family in the country. They would be included, of course."

I took a deep breath, "KGB, I suppose?"

"Something along those lines," he said. "I should consider it very carefully, if I were you. I'll be back here in four days exactly. Same time. I suggest you be here, too. Don't bring anyone with you or your family will suffer."

He left quickly, closing the door behind him. I stood there for a moment, sorting out my reactions to this extraordinary meeting. By the time I followed there was no sign of him in the restaurant, and a look both ways from the front door revealed nothing either.

I returned to the table and, of course, said nothing. Soon after we walked back to our host's house where we were offered brandy, but I had no taste for it.

With my mind in a whirl, I returned to my flat, sat down and wrote a note of thanks to my host, but could get no further than the salutation. I went out and walked the streets for an hour, staying alert, but there seemed to be no one following me.

The next morning I walked into Knightsbridge and used the telephone in a Danish cafe to call my special number. "It's important that you meet me today. Come for a drink at the club today at six." I rang off knowing that my request would be heeded.

At six o'clock I was sitting in the bar and looking out the French windows at the garden below when my contact came in. We shook hands, he sat down beside me and I told him what had happened the night before. I added urgently, "I want double protection on my family. You can understand why."

He said soothingly, "Don't worry about that. The security around your family is quite adequate. This has been rather a shock for you, I know. What did this fellow look like?"

I described the man as best I could and emphasized the threats he made where my family was concerned. "Even if you can get a line on him don't pick him up until I can meet him again and find out what he has to say. I'm going to refuse the offer, of course. Don't ask me to do otherwise." I said this because often the firm considered such an offer a golden opportunity to plant an agent inside the KGB.

He spread his hands and said a bit vaguely, "Those days are over now, of course. We'll have him tailed after he meets you."

I said, "For Heaven's sake. Don't let your boys bumble it. These people are not fools, you know. They'll assume I've talked to you." I put my hand on his arm and said, "The main thing, the absolutely crucial thing, is to protect my family when they know I'm not going to work for them."

He said, "We'll do our best." Then he added, "We cannot work bloody wonders, you know."

I took my hand off his arm. "You better had," I said.

On the fourth night after the encounter in the washroom I returned to the restaurant again. The firm had arranged that I go as a host of a small party of three couples. Outwardly we looked like a congenial group out for a pleasant dinner. All of us were from the department, and trained for action if there was a need. At exactly nine-thirty I left the others and went again to the washroom. It was empty. As I washed my hands I noticed a piece of paper stuck in the corner of the mirror. It was a note: "Colonel: meet me tomorrow at 1:00 p.m, Kensington Park opposite Albert Hall. Wear dark suit, carry Daily Telegraph." On the back were two words printed in bold capitals: "NO FRIENDS."

I slipped the note into my pocket for our laboratory chaps and returned to my friends. We chatted for another fifteen minutes and then the two men and I took a cab to one of the safe houses, an apartment off Marble Arch. There we discussed the note and it was decided that I should meet the man the next day. The area would be carefully staked out and the encounter would be photographed by telescopic lens.

The next day, dressed in my dark suit and carrying the newspaper, I took the underground to Kensington High Street and walked back toward Kensington Park. It was very crowded: some people eating lunch on benches others strolling around. I saw no one who looked even remotely like an agent, of course, but before long a man wearing a baggy raincoat came up alongside me and put his hand companionably on my shoulder. "Hello, Colonel," he said. "Haven't seen you for weeks."

I had not seen him before in my life, but knew he was the man. He looked down at the grass and said, "No time to waste. What's your answer?"

"Who are you? Who's making me this offer?"

"Talk about details later. Is it yes or no?"

"No deal," I said curtly.

His expression didn't change. He said, "Not much point in asking you to reconsider. We know you. Very foolish, if I may say so. You know your family'll suffer. Is that really your final decision?"

I nodded and he moved off toward the road where a double-decker bus was pulling away. He leaped aboard with his raincoat over his arm. He was wearing a dark suit as the photographer showed later and he looked remarkably like me from a distance. The officers watching from a short distance away were confused and thought I was the one boarding the bus and the man got away.

Later I complained bitterly to the department, "The bastard made fools of all of us."

" Oh," they said easily, "we've an idea who he is. We'll pick him up later." If they did I was never told.

All I could do now was make sure that my family was safe. My mother and father seemed happy enough when I called them that evening. When I spoke to my siblings all was well with them. I called my contact in Brussels and asked permission to speak with Stephen's grandparents. He said it would only worry them, that they were fine and there was security on them. I was still worried but gradually my over-worked nerves began to relax.

Some days later one of the firm said to me with a smile, "There's really no need to make all those phone calls. All your family are safe." I had made those calls without their knowledge, but still somehow they knew, and yet again I realized that I had no life of my own.

Three weeks later I had word from my contact to meet him at the club. When I did he looked grave. He told me that Stephen had been struck by a taxi outside the Gare Central in Brussels. He was in a hospital there, critically injured. He might survive; or he might not.

Five hours later I stood in a Brussels hospital looking down at the broken body of my son. Stephen was in a deep coma, many fractured bones, tubes and traction devices everywhere. With me were his grief stricken grandparents. Doctors said that if he could cling to life for a few days he might survive, but they were far from hopeful. I was filled with anguish for the suffering of this boy, who had done nothing to merit this pain. There was the possibility that I had perhaps been to blame for insisting that I reveal my relationship to him. I had no proof that the Soviets were responsible and my colleagues in the firm insisted that I was paranoid to harbor such thoughts. The security on Stephen had been adequate, they said.

But some deep instinct in me knew who was responsible.

Day after day I sat at Stephen's bedside, praying, summoning him back to life. Perhaps it was fanciful, but I could feel his mother's presence on the other side of the bed. On the fourth day the doctors said that Stephen would not make it through the night, but somehow the spark refused to go out and he rallied, gradually and painfully.

Stephen had no recollection of the accident. News of it was suppressed but one witness said that he had just stepped off the curb and was waiting for the traffic to pass. That was when the taxi hit him, but not just a glancing blow. The driver wrenched the wheel so that the vehicle mounted the curb driving Stephen back against a nearby wall. It was no accident; it was deliberate.

The firm insisted that there was no proof so I decided to get proof of my own. I went to my friends at the Gehlen organization which had infiltrators throughout the Soviet Union. They did their own checking and reported that there was a ninety-five percent chance that the accident had been planned and carried out under orders from the Kremlin, and issued to the chief of Foreign Espionage Service. There had evidently been discussion about where I was most vulnerable, and Stephen had been chosen as the target. Injury or death to him would punish me, as threatened, for not accepting their offer, and to soften me up for any further offers they might make.

When I took this information back to the department they were angry that I had sought it elsewhere, but finally admitted that they had received the same reports. "Anyway," they said, "the boy is recovering, isn't he? We're glad about that."

Stephen did partially recover and two years later entered a branch of the University of Heidelberg to study engineering. Suddenly, he was stricken with a complication resulting from the old taxi accident and his life ebbed away and finally ended in June. It had taken a few years, but he was finally murdered after all.

It is painful to see a loved one disintegrate before your eyes and I never got over it. On the day of his death, I looked down at my son with eyes blinded with tears and pledged to fight Communism with whatever means necessary. I thought of the productive years stolen from him and my grief seemed too much to bear.

He would have grown to be a fine man.

He was just twenty years old.

chapter 29

IT IS AN ELEMENTARY principle that if you need to destroy a person's credibility or to weaken faith in his or her reliability, the best way is to launch a character assassination. If one can be smeared with false charges, and smeared successfully, whatever they say or do can be challenged for veracity. Some good friends may even turn away in embarrassment. There were those in the department (all these years later) who had good reason to fear what I might reveal about the betrayal in N Section in WWII. So in the early 1960s some of the experts in character assassination began their move against me.

There began a series of incidents, small in monetary value, but huge in the consequences to my life and reputation. For example, I spent three months in jail for supposedly stealing a small packet of dried fish, worth under two pounds, from a local store. I had been accused of stealing pants from Marshall and Snelgrove which appeared in the trunk of my car as I returned to it one afternoon. And of course, the local police already had me on their radar as a suspicious fellow due to my supposed theft before I went to Hungary.

The impact on my family was severe and although Audrey believed my protestations of innocence she began to withdraw and masked her feelings with silence. My children were treated unkindly in school and we were asked to resign from the local yacht club where we had enjoyed many happy hours. The house that Audrey had loved so much became a sort of prison and we moved to another town closer to the channel where I was often sent to NATO headquarters at Fontainebleau: still employed, strangely enough.

Audrey opened a small boutique with money that came from a surprising source. The German government decided to pay compensation to survivors of the concentration camps. The amount awarded was measured by the amount of 'pain and suffering.' I was called to

London and handed slightly over six hundred pounds in five pound notes, instead of a check. As usual the department wanted nothing on the record as far as I was concerned.

In the mid sixties I not only kept up my role as a retired man living in London, but was withdrawn frequently and sent to various hotspots around the world, usually carrying documents or microfilm. I was sent to the former Belgian Congo and also South Africa. Some legitimate investments that I had made there were frozen in retaliation for my refusal to work for their Gestapo oriented security system called BOSS. In Uganda I met the infamous Idi Amin who offered me employment on his security force, which I quickly turned down. By that time he had slaughtered thousands of his people and my department was giving serious thought to assassinating him.

Some of the missions were dangerous as there were often violent factions working against the established government. Sometimes these rebel forces were not sure which side you favored and your life could be in jeopardy.

In the early sixties I was sent to Algeria with microfilm for Mohammed Seghir Neccache, the Minister for Foreign Affairs, and another film for Abderrahmane Cherif, the Minister of Justice. As a mere courier I had no knowledge of what the films contained; it was just my job to deliver them. One had been placed in the stay of my shirt collar and another was in the back of my wristwatch. The department insisted that I not arrive in Algeria with any arms as it might cause complications with the French government. The French had half a million men trying to contain the rebellious populace who felt that the Europeans were keeping them subjugated and stealing their best land.

I did have a pen in my pocket that could project a jet of fluid that could temporarily blind a man and a pencil with a sharp blade where the lead would be.

I was told that murders were common in Algiers and I believed it. At the airport I was met by two Frenchmen and driven to a hotel in the center of the city. It was obvious that security at the hotel was tight: no one was allowed to use the stairs, only the elevators. I was told that I could expect a body guard, but none appeared. I was uneasy because I was sure that my arrival in a police car could not be missed. There was little I could do about it except be alert and wary during the time I was in North Africa.

My room was one story up from the lobby with a partial view of the city. Down the corridor and around a corner was a flight of stairs which were off limits. As always, I checked carefully to make sure that the windows did not offer access to climbers. My bed faced the door and there were wooden shutters that I could close across the French windows allowing me to see without being seen. I decided to shrug off the uncomfortable sense of impending danger and go to dinner in the small hotel dining room.

My comfort was always to choose a corner table where I could watch the room and the entrance. It was a warm evening and the dining room was not full. The cuisine was excellent; Algerian with French accents. I drank a good amount of bottled water and allowed myself one glass of wine contrary to my usual practice when on assignment. As I finished the dinner I was approached by a large rumpled man in dark clothing who spoke to me in good English with a French accent. His credentials proved him to be a senior police officer and he offered to help me help in any way. I was surprised when he showed me an automatic pistol and placed it on the table before me.

" You will need this here in my city," he said, "for no one is completely safe. Allow me to offer it to you ... for a small consideration. We know that you do not have one of your own."

I declined politely and told him that if my government had thought it necessary they would have provided one for me. He insisted saying that it would be foolish to be without it. It was an excellent small weapon and he wanted me to have it for two hundred pounds. "And I do believe that you have that amount with you," he said with a crooked smile.

I handed him the money although the automatic was not worth more than fifty pounds. When I pointed this out he shrugged and said, "It is difficult to obtain a legal weapon here, Sir. If you take it you have my authority to use it. You are safe." He hesitated, "Of course if you tell anyone I sold it to you, it would be my unpleasant necessity of saying you are a liar." By then the money had passed into his hands. I had hesitated wondering how I might justify such an extravagance when I returned to London as I would have to account for every penny.

It was too late; I had bought it. I checked to make sure that I had the correct ammunition, then wedged it into my belt. The large man stood and walked away with a debonair flourish of his right hand as he wished me, "Bon voyage, mon ami." I watched him as he disappeared sure that he was more interested in my money than my welfare.

Back in my room I tried to read for a while but was restless and a little sad for I missed my family. At home my marriage seemed to be failing. Audrey had retreated behind a wall of coolness and silence I could seldom penetrate. My contacts at Windsor were still strong, but there too my life was based on lies and deceptions. None in that circle knew that I was involved with the Foreign Office and none knew that I had a family in the country.

At last I fell asleep with the narrow rolled pillow propping me up against the headboard and the loaded automatic between my legs under the sheets. I slept fitfully and wakened a few times hearing cries in the streets and sometimes noises of distant gun shots. The Algerians were a fierce and violent people and only a few years earlier there had been violent battles in Algiers and Oran where thousands died.

The next morning I was awake at 6:30. I showered in what masqueraded for a bathroom and dried myself with a towel the size of a washcloth as the tap water spat brown and tepid water into the basin where I shaved. Dressed and ready for breakfast I went into the hall and closed the door behind me. As I did I was overwhelmed by a sudden sense that something was wrong. It is hard to describe this psychic occurrence, but it happened to me several times in my career and it had saved my life before and was about to do so again. Standing there alert, I heard a faint sound coming from the stairway which was hidden from me by a bend in the hallway. Automatic in my hand I moved to the corner and saw an armed man climbing the stairs. He was wearing a white head dress and when he saw me aimed his gun immediately in my direction. I shot rapidly and the force of the bullet knocked him backwards against a second man who was right behind him. That man fired at me, but the jostling of the first man caused the bullet to go wild. My second shot hit him, too.

A third man turned and ran down the stairs. My third and fourth bullets caught him in the back and he was thrown all the way to the bottom. I leaped to where the first two lay, apparently dead, but just in case kept my finger on the trigger, thinking the gun was worth every penny of those two hundred pounds. I checked all three bodies for other hidden weapons and was just about to wrap what I found in the white head cloth of the first shooter when the screaming employees ran through the door from the lobby. I knew that they would have called the police and very shortly they arrived. I surrendered my gun and tried to give an explanation, but I was hand-cuffed and taken for a ride to a police station and then pushed into a small and smelly cell. Within a short time the two Frenchmen who had met me at the airport came to release me. They had identified the three dead men. I had killed two known terrorists, they said, and the nephew of one of them.

"They have many deaths to their credit and you have saved us the trouble of killing them. Of course, we would have caught them in time."

Why were they after me? There were many shrugs. Perhaps they wanted to rob a rich Englishman. Perhaps they were interested in the film I was carrying. Who could say. What the police could not understand was how I knew they were coming up the stairs around the corner. I told them I had acted upon instinct, but they were not satisfied and seemed convinced that I knew something I was not telling them. "And the pistol," they said. "You did not have such a weapon when you arrived. It is French and the serial number is missing. Where did you get it?" Now it was my turn to shrug.

"Well, why don't you keep it," one of the officers said. I thanked him and said I would.

That afternoon I met the representatives who, when Identified, took the microfilm from me. After the necessary preliminaries I gave them my shirt and my watch. Soon my shirt was returned to me as if it had not been touched and I was given an identical watch.

"We will suggest to your government that you not return here," were the last words.

I flew back to Paris and then on to London for debriefing. During the flight I thought over the numerous skirmishes in which I had been involved when by rights I should have lost my life. I knew that unless I was able to escape from the department more would lie ahead and I wondered if I would continue to be spared, but it was a question that had no answer.

That was the end of the Algerian episode, but as traumatic as it had been I remember thinking that I would rather face a physical assassin than the invisible forces who were steadfastly trying to undermine my reputation and discredit my character.

Just after the hearing on the Marshall and Snelgrove episode where I was coerced into branding myself as a petty thief, I paused on my way home to see Janet. I knew if I told her the truth she would believe me. I not only told her what had happened, but showed her the ugly bruise on my shoulder where I had 'fallen' in the cell.

Janet said nothing for a moment, then walked to the bookcase and pulled down a volume of Shakespeare to show me a passage from Othello.

> Who steals my purse steals trash; 'tis something. nothing.
> Twas mine,'tis his, and has been a slave to thousands.
> But he that filches from me my good name
> Robs me of that which not enriches him,
> And makes me poor indeed.

She said, "Things haven't changed much in four hundred years, have they old friend?"

"No," I replied. "Evidently not."

Merely sharing with her was a relief.

chapter 30

LOOKING BACK, I THINK the most difficult part of being a member of the Department was not the danger or the deception, nor the ruthlessness built into that way of life. It wasn't even the ever present threat of capture, torture, or brain washing by friend or foe. The most difficult part was the inner loneliness that comes from trusting no one, confiding in no one, nor revealing true feelings or depth of emotion unless you are alone and unobserved. We hear of those who have 'come in from the cold.' This is where the cold is bleakest: the words you may never utter, the memories you may never share, the searing events that are buried in your mind and must remain so, perhaps forever.

Now and then over the years when the pressures and repressed emotions began to seem unbearable I would go by myself to some place where associations were especially strong. One of those was St. Paul's Church in Knightsbridge where Arlette and I were married and also the memorial to the women who died in SOE, where her name has been omitted. Once a pilgrimage like that took me deeper into the past than I anticipated.

I was in the Netherlands, in Utrecht, where my work had taken me, and decided to put aside a day to have time to visit the cemetery at Oosterbeek, near Arnhem, where so many fallen soldiers lay. It is a quiet place down a lane of trees about five minutes walk from the bus stop and about twenty-five minutes from Arnhem.

It was a grey day in January, windy and cold. I had taken the train from Utrecht and arrived at Arnhem station where there was a little flower shop. I bought two bunches of flowers and some string and made my way to the taxi rank. I told the driver where I wanted to go and asked that he wait for me as the weather was too cold for a long visit.

We left the station and rode parallel to the Neder Rijn, the Dutch Rhine. On our left was the former Headquarters of the Gestapo, and I gave it a long look recalling the time I had spent there before going to Buchenwald. Soon we passed the Saint Elisabeth Hospital where I had been recovering when the Gestapo found me.

It was beginning to snow as we pulled up to the iron gates that led to the cemetery. The flakes came down faster and began to settle on the rows of headstones where so many soldiers of all ranks had been laid to rest. Some graves had names; others merely were marked "A Soldier."

The graves at Oosterbeek are tended with great care. I don't know if the custom continues, but after the war local Dutch children were assigned a grave to tend: one to a child. They would bring flowers and in some cases correspond with the fallen soldier's next of kin.

There was shelter near the entrance and I stopped there to find the location of the graves I was looking for. As I did I noticed a tall man in a dark overcoat watching me with interest. This annoyed me as the whole purpose of my visit was to be alone with my memories. I ignored him and went into the snow and found the first grave. I tied my bouquet to the headstone and said a silent prayer. I noticed the man watching me with interest, but turned my back on him and went to the second grave. After tying my flowers to the headstone I stood back and read the inscription. As I did I noticed a single carnation lying in the snow at the foot of the marker. The inscription gave the real name of the man I had known as Ian Elliot, the victim of the German machine gunners in the garden behind the house at Oosterbeek. I stood there silently watching the snow falling so gently on the graves of these men who had died so violently. Twenty years had passed and the anger was gone, but not the sadness and the terrible sense of futility and loss. I said a prayer for them, for myself, for the whole suffering world.

As I left and reached the gate the tall young man approached me. I watched him warily, but he came forward slowly and said in English with a Dutch accent, "Excuse me, Sir, but may I ask if you knew some of these soldiers?" I answered somewhat abruptly that I did. (Why should this man be concerned? He was far too young to be in the war.)

"Well, Sir," he said, "I saw you standing beside that grave. Did you know this man also? I always put flowers on his grave whenever I can."

That softened me a bit. "That's kind of you. Yes, I fought with him. All these men died in a battle we thought we were gong to win; instead, it was a great disaster. Why is still something of a mystery, but it was."

By now we had reached my taxi and I asked him where he lived. He told me not far away in Oosterbeek. I offered him a lift home and he gave the driver an address.

As we drove along he said, "Had you known the Major a long time, sir?"

"No, a very short time."

He hesitated,"For a while the Major's body was buried in the garden of our house, along with another British soldier, a sergeant. After the war they were moved to the cemetery. I can remember that terrible day; my grandfather was killed, too. I know that the soldiers were trying to protect my mother and me. That is why I bring flowers to the grave."

I leaned forward and asked the driver to pull over. I needed air. I opened the window and took some deep breaths. After a while I said ... and I remember saying it very slowly ..., "You don't remember me, but I am the man who picked you up and carried you to your mother. It is most extraordinary that we meet like this, but I believe that there is a reason why such things happen. I cannot pretend to understand why, but it gives me so much happiness to see you again. I have often wondered what happened to you and your mother."

I motioned the driver to move on and as we drove along the sun came out suddenly and the roads and the fields were dazzling white. The man beside me said nothing, but his eyes never left my face. When we arrived at the house he motioned me to follow. It still had the panes of glass that I remembered. The young man said, "Please wait in the hall. I will tell my mother about you and I know she will want to see you."

While I waited I could see the door at the end of the passage leading to the garden and I remembered the bright orange carrots that had been unearthed by machine gun fire.

Shortly the mother came from the kitchen: about sixty and typically Dutch: stout, dressed in black and wearing furry slippers. She took my hands and held them for a moment without speaking. Finally she said in halting English, "You are most welcome in our house, Sir. You come this time under much happier reasons. We are grateful to you." She smiled suddenly and said, "And now I am giving you some English tea."

She served the tea and we talked for half an hour or so. I supplied a few Dutch words when she could not find English ones. Her son spoke quite well and he was proud to tell me that they had great faith in God and tried to live by His word.

When I stood to leave he shook my hand and his mother put her arms around my neck. There were tears in her eyes and I was too moved to say anything. I left quickly for the waiting taxi and went back to the train station.

I don't suppose I will see them again.

chapter 31

FROM THE MOMENT WHEN my friends in the Gehlen organization reported that the 'accident' to my son was no accident at all, and my superiors in the Department confirmed it to be an act of reprisal by the Soviets, I worried constantly about the safety of my wife and children: Nigel 15 and Anne 12. At that time we were living close to the Dorset and Hampshire line. I tried to get home as often as I could, which was not very often.

It was hard to impress on the children the need for caution: always being sure the doors were locked, always being wary of strangers, without telling them why in order not to instill fear.

I arrived home unexpectedly that spring planning to spend a long weekend with the family, although the Department preferred that I stay in London and be close and available for any assignment. No one knew of my intentions as I drove south early one Friday evening and I was greeted happily by all.

At about this time Nigel was going through a difficult period, one not uncommon in adolescent boys. Basically he was a gentle, quiet, and industrious young man. His transgressions were not serious: the usual infractions of curfew and disobedience, but I felt he was exposed to danger and sometimes I reacted too sternly. Audrey tried to be the peacemaker and pointed out that I was not home most of the time and she was the one to cope with the children. Indeed she managed admirably over the years and credit is more than due. By now ours was a marriage in name only and we certainly did not communicate well at all.

Nigel was clever with his hands and sometimes made extra money rebuilding old bicycles. When I arrived there was one in pieces on the kitchen floor and I complimented him on his ingenuity. A short passage between the kitchen and the back door led to

236

the garden. This door had a frosted glass window and the door was always locked.

Early the next morning Nigel was busy with his bicycle work and Anne and Audrey were upstairs. I was sitting in the living room in an easy chair reading the paper when Nigel came into the room with a troubled look on his face. He said, "Someone's at the garden door. They didn't knock, just tried the handle."

The thought that someone who didn't know that I was there was attempting to enter my house sent a jolt through me. My greatest fear was for the safety of the family and I reacted instantly. I shot out of my chair and ran to the kitchen stopping only long enough to open a linen closet and reach my automatic from behind a stack of sheets. Behind the glass in the door I saw the silhouettes of two figures. I had no idea who they were, but I was sure they were there to do damage of some kind. As I lunged for the door I reached a small radio communicator and twice pressed a button that would alert the Dorset and Hampshire police that I needed help. This signal was to be used only in dire emergencies. In one motion I reached the door, turned the key and wrenched it open. Two men in dark clothing turned and ran.

Our house was protected by a stone wall on one side and an iron fence on the other. In the rear was a garden house where we stored out of season equipment and beyond it bushes and trees. A path surrounded the main house on three sides.

Both men headed rapidly toward the little garden house and the trees beyond. I might have let them go, but one turned and fired at me with a weapon with a silencer, the bullet hitting the stonework of the house. Knowing what the intruders had in mind I shot him in the hip and as he fell to the ground I shot again and put a bullet through his head. By now, his companion had almost reached the shelter of the trees, but he too turned and fired: the bullet was very close. I fired once hitting him below the left eye; he was dead before he hit the ground. My breath was coming in short gasps and I turned and saw Nigel standing behind me, petrified at the sight of two men dead in his back garden. I knew the boy was in shock and my first thought was somehow to shield him. A doctor who lived nearby could be trusted to keep silent and I was hoping that he could prescribe a sedative for Nigel who by now was trembling violently and who did not answer when I spoke to him. With my weapon still in my hand I gently moved Nigel toward the house. As I did so, a man in civilian clothes appeared from the direction of the garden house pointing a pistol at me.

He shouted, "Drop your weapon or I'll shoot."

I called back angrily,"Drop yours or I'll kill you!"

Although I was fairly sure that he was police I wasn't certain and without any identification was ready to disarm him. As I spoke, other men also in plain clothes appeared from the bushes in the back. They had arrived with extraordinary speed and one stepped forward with his hand extended indicating that I should surrender my gun, but I put it firmly in my pocket and buttoned my jacket over it. I had two emotions at that moment: concern for Nigel, and fury with the department whose protection of my family I had counted on and who had failed me again. I had no clue about the intention of the intruders: was it to kidnap one of the children or do harm to the whole family thinking I was not at home? In any case, the two men were dead, my family was safe, and I was still alive ... at least for the moment.

The officer in charge of the detail wanted me to accompany him to headquarters. He was calm and respectful and assured me that an officer would be left behind to guard the house. Reluctantly, after delivering Nigel to his mother and assuring her and Anne that all was well, I went with him. At police headquarters I was well treated and complimented the men on their speedy response to my radio alert. The dead men were carried away; I was told later that one was a Hungarian and the other strangely, an Englishman. My own headquarters in London reacted with some consternation admitting no fault, but promising triple security around the house. If any further attempts were made they must have been intercepted and dealt with. I heard nothing more.

Nigel's reaction to this episode was to block it out of his mind completely and almost at once he became more withdrawn than before. He became rebellious of parental authority and particularly resentful of me. Once after one altercation he left home altogether and was gone for several days. Audrey was frantic. I hated to involve the authorities, but I was also afraid that he might have been kidnapped. The horror of my older son's death haunted me and I finally asked the police to put out a call to search for Nigel.

Late one night they told me that Nigel had been seen in a bowling alley not far away. I drove there at once and as I entered, Nigel saw me before I saw him and he shot past me and out the door. In those days I could run very fast and I took off after him, across a main road, fortunately fairly empty at that time of night. Ahead of me I saw him dart into a multi level parking garage that was still under construction. He vaulted a barrier marked 'Danger' and disappeared into the darkness. When I followed I could hear his footsteps running up the concrete stairs as if the Devil was after him. I called, but there was no response as I chased after him.

The chase ended on top of the unfinished building where broken pieces of concrete, unused lumber and other debris lay everywhere. No barrier existed around the edge and it was toward this edge that Nigel was backing, his eyes fixed on me as I stood frozen at the top of the stairs. I could hear his breath coming in sobs as he moved away and toward the dark abyss behind him.

I said,"Don't be afraid, Nigel. We have been worried about you and just want you to come home."

He said nothing, but at least now he had stopped moving, even though close to the edge. I said, "Truly, Nigel there's no problem. Your mother is terribly worried about you. Let's go home and tell her that you are all right."

"I don't want to go home," he sobbed. "I have no freedom there. Every time you come home it's 'Do this. Don't do this.' Nobody understands. I might as well be dead."

He looked over his shoulder at the blackness behind him and I felt my heart stop. I could not believe that Nigel really wanted to kill himself, but who could tell what a distraught teenager would do?

I said, "It's all right, Niigel. It's all right."

He asked, "Will you promise to change if I do come home? Will you promise that things will be different?"

I replied that I would listen to his grievances and do what I could, but I could not make promises under circumstances like these. As I spoke I was looking for a way to get around him and block his path to the edge. To the right there was nothing but emptiness, but to the left there was a partial barrier attached to a large pillar. I thought if I could get him to move in that direction I might get to him. So I kept talking quietly and inching slowly to my right and as he shifted away from me I moved very quickly and place myself between him and the edge. He backed into the large pillar and stood there trembling. I came up to him and placed my hand very gently on his shoulder. As I did, the resistance seemed to drain out of him. He was still angry, but without further protest he came down those concrete steps with me. I thanked God every step of the way for his safety. I remember thinking, too that I could not in all honesty blame the Soviets for Nigel's behavior. It would have to be placed between those in MI6 and myself: for living the life they had decided for me and myself for being the person that they had schooled me to become.

chapter 32

BY NOW I HAD established myself as a convivial retired officer, unmarried, whose eye problems had been cured by surgery in Switzerland. I was living in a flat in Chelsea that could be a 'safe house' for the department to use in a variety of ways.

One of my main assignments was to look for subversives and report these people to the department on a regular basis. Sometimes the firm would give me the names of people they wanted me to cultivate.

One evening I went to a dinner party given by two good friends of mine, a retired RAF Group Captain and his wife. One of the other guests was their niece, an attractive, unmarried flight attendant who flew between London and far off places and had just returned from Hong Kong. Her name was Karen and she looked to be in her mid twenties. I was seated next to her at dinner and when the party ended I offered to drive her home. She lived not far from me, in Chelsea, in a flat shared with two other young women. I did drive her home, we exchanged polite good nights and I promptly put her out of my mind.

In those days I was under considerable strain. There had been a burglary at my flat and I lost an amount of valuable things, both monetary and sentimental: heirlooms from my grandmother's estate, official letters of commendation, and other irreplaceable documents. There was no sign of forcible entry. The alarm system was elaborate and complex and only a few people knew how to deactivate it. The intruders had found ... or had previous knowledge of ... a wall safe hidden within a cupboard and had been able to open it. It was a baffling and disturbing event.

In addition I had been involved in a sharp confrontation with the firm about my efforts involving the Official Secret Acts. They had demanded that I cease all efforts, threatening me with dismissal and loss of pension rights if I persisted. My financial future was entirely in their hands as they still held payments in a special account for me, too. At last I acquiesced and promised to remove my self from that arena.

To these events was added the constant strain of leading two lives: one in London and Windsor, the other in the country with my family. The years of deception and evasion were beginning to take their toll. My nerves were stretched too thin and I began drinking to relax. I dwelt on many previous assignments with regret and guilt.

A few weeks after I met Karen she telephoned me. She asked if I remembered her and I responded that I did. "I have just returned from South Africa and want to know if you can join me and some friends for dinner later in the week." I did join them and had a pleasant evening with her friends, all married couples.

As was my custom, I turned my past two weeks activities in to the firm including all the people that I had met. A bit later when I was in the office I was asked casually what I knew of Karen Fitch, the young woman with whom I had dined recently.

I replied, "Nothing much. She is the niece of some friends of mine. It's as simple as that."

In the department was a man named Maitland, a calculating person if there ever was one. I didn't like him and I am sure that it was mutual. It was he who opened the door to a project that never should have been undertaken. Not by me; not by anyone.

The next morning I had a call from Maitland who wanted to drop by and discuss something with me. I had no good reason for refusing him, so he came around. I offered him coffee and he came right to the point.

"I've done some checking on Karen Fitch," he said. "As you know, she travels a great deal in her job. She's bright, speaks three or four languages, and could be very useful to us, meeting contacts abroad, taking information out and bringing it back, that sort of thing. We've lost six couriers lately, four men and two women. They became known so we had to stop using them. Now we need replacements. This girl seems quite reliable. She's ..."

"Wait a minute. What are you suggesting?"

He put down his coffee cup. "Well you've already met her. You're a friend of the family, so she would be inclined to trust you. We thought you might, er, cultivate her friendship a bit and then ..."

"No!" I said emphatically. "I never mix business with my personal life. You know that. Besides I've been down that road before, thanks to you all, and I promised myself never again. So you can just forget ..."

"You mean Pauline Harrison? That didn't turn out so badly. You had some fun, and she ..."

"Shut up!" I said through clenched teeth. I wanted to punch him.

He gave a little shrug. "All right. But that was a totally different situation. The Harrison woman was playing games with the Commies. This girl seems quite straight forward. No dubious politics. No messy love affairs. Just the sort we need because no one will suspect her. Now, Vapor, be reasonable. We know she invited you to dinner so she must be a little interested in you. Just take it from there. What's so dreadful about all this? She will be doing something useful for her country, and you will be doing something that might boost your stock with the firm. And if you don't mind my saying so, it could do with a little boosting."

"No," I said flatly. "Absolutely no. You have casanovas in the office. Use one of them."

"You already have one foot in the door. Anyone else would have to start from scratch. No, you are the logical person." He stood up and gave me a thin smile. "Think about it." At the door he paused. "Why not talk to JR about it? He's a friend of yours. I've already discussed it with him."

"John Russell Smith was indeed a friend of mine. He had been on my staff when I was at British Rhine Headquarters. When I sought him out I found that he agreed with Maitland. "There's nothing to it, Keith. You won't have to get in over your head the way you did with the Harrison woman. Just keep this one interested, but at arm's length. If you do the job well it could improve your standing around here."

"JR," I said a little desperately, "this is a nice girl. I hate to see her get involved with us. If she learns too much it could put her in a dangerous position. Besides, she's not just any girl. She's a niece of friends of mine. I don't have the right to do this."

JR laughed. "Just when did you get the idea that people like us have any rights at all? Do the job, Keith," he paused and looked at me searchingly, "How are you feeling these days? Everything under control?"

I hesitated. Inside the firm one never knew in whom one could confide. But I did know that he was my friend, so I said, "To tell you the truth I have been feeling rotten lately. Can't seem to concentrate at times; disoriented almost. Sometimes I wonder who the Hell I am. Feel like a worn out old shoe, if you know what I mean."

"Not too surprising," he said. "You've lasted a lot longer than most agents and you've been through some rough times. Have you checked with the quacks?"

"No," I said. "You know how it is. If they feel you are beginning to be a security risk they will report it and then God only knows what will happen."

"I know," He said. "It's a cruel world, isn't it? But humor Maitland with this airline hostess thing. Do a good job and they may ... who knows? decide to let you off the hook entirely."

"If I could believe that I would agree to almost anything."

So I called Maitland and, hating myself for giving in, told him I would do what I could about Karen.

As I spoke to him I had an uneasy foreboding. To be sure that was the beginning of a long slide into disaster. By now Karen had been assigned to the South American run which pleased Maitland because the firm had important contacts in Buenos Aires. "But don't rush things with her. Go slowly at first. We don't want her to suspect anything."

As it turned out I was not the one to rush things: it was Karen. The third time we met for dinner she told me that she was just getting over an unhappy love affair. Right now there was no man in her life. I smiled in sympathy and she suddenly asked me to come to Shropshire for the weekend at her Aunt and Uncle's; they would be glad to have me as a guest and it would be 'lots of fun.' She would be flying off on Monday and gone for ten days.

I remember looking at her and remembering what had happened with Pauline, but said that I would be happy to accept.

The house was huge and rambling. The Group Captain and his wife welcomed me cordially and it was plain that they looked upon Karen almost as a daughter and that they approved of her interest in me. Some neighbors came for dinner and Karen entertained everyone with tales of her adventures in far off places. She was a sparkling girl, full of animation and humor. I did not consider myself God's gift to women, but I have to admit that I was flattered by Karen's attention.

The dinner ended, the guests went home and the four of us sat around the fire with our brandies. We all said goodnight and went to our respective rooms.

Mine had a great, gloomy four poster bed, and I lay awake for a while, going over in my mind the plans that the firm had for Karen. They were quite simple, really: when the time was right and I was sure that she would not refuse, I was to ask her if she could help me with some financial dealings in places where her flights would take her. I had funds frozen there, I would say, and she could help me retrieve them by taking a confidential letter from me to certain contacts, who in turn would give her cash to take back to London.

The firm would prepare these letters for my signature, and if Karen opened them, they would appear to be what I had told her, but concealed in the paper would be microfilm containing sensitive information which the contacts would extract. Karen would be given sizable amounts of pounds and the money delivered to me in turn would be given to the firm. Karen would know nothing about the microfilm, nor would I know anything about its contents. It would be a one way operation only, with nothing coming back except the money. No one would suspect Karen of being a courier and she would not be suspicious, either. True she would unknowingly meet some of the firm's contacts overseas, but only think they were friends of mine being helpful with my money problems. They would be glad to take an attractive girl to dinner and thank her for her assistance. As I drifted off to sleep I assured my self that nothing could go wrong.

Some time later I was awakened by the slow turning of the doorknob. A figure moved slowly toward the bed and quickly removed a robe and slid in beside me. Her face close to mine, her body close against me, Karen whispered, "You're not going to throw me out, are you, Keith?"

Actually I was. And, gently as possible, I did.

Soon Karen was agreeable to almost anything I asked and she agreed readily to help me retrieve some of my funds. Her first mission went off without a hitch and the firm was pleased, of course.

From my point of view the trouble was that Karen wanted a husband, not a romance. When she returned from her trips she would ring the bell of my flat and when the door opened would call out, "Hello darling" for all to hear. Frequently she brought gifts for me: silk ties from Hong Kong, Ivory figures from Africa, etc. She also brought unused liquor from the galley and other delicacies; a practice that I am sure was not permitted. When I let her into the flat she headed straight for the bedroom and left a trail of clothes along the way.

My assignment was to keep the girl happy and devoted, but it did not take much effort. Once or twice I took her to Windsor where my friends were delighted to see me escorting an unmarried woman. In London I sometimes took her to restaurants, but she preferred that we be alone in my flat.

While Karen was in London a momentum developed to our so called courtship that left me little time to think. When she was away a host of unwelcome thoughts crept in. The tenseness and stress that I had been experiencing for some time was becoming worse. I was having alarming dreams. In one, I was on one side of a two way mirror looking into an interrogation room, but when the tormented woman inside looked up it was not Pauline, but Karen. Some of the nightmares that I suffered after Buchenwald and Lubyanka returned. To escape from these things and the guilt that I had about my family I began to drink too much. I tried to ask myself what was wrong and when I did I came up with two plausible, but unsatisfactory answers.

The first was that spark of ethics that had never really died. This was the quiet voice that reminded me that adultery was wrong even when carried out in the interests of the State. I could hear Father Bruce's voice saying, "Personal danger is not sufficient reason for going back on your commitment to your work, but if you think it is offensive to God, then you must get out."

I wanted to get out; I wanted to escape from the whole dirty business, but I didn't know how to transform my wish into reality.

The other was a deep seated fear that I carried with me for years: the fear that my own countrymen, who had betrayed me twice were perfectly capable of betraying me again. Winston Churchill himself had sent me to be captured and tortured by the Nazis and I had been betrayed to the Soviets in Dresden. If at any time my colleagues became sufficiently displeased with me, the third and final betrayal could be death.

The conflicting emotions ... the desire to leave and the fear of leaving ... set up a tension that I felt was pushing me towards some sort of break down. I knew that I was not supposed to have any qualms about deceiving Karen. I had been trained not to think twice about such things, but I did care about the girl's welfare and the memory of Pauline haunted me and the parallel between the two situations was unmistakable. I wanted to get Karen out of her role before she made a mistake or the firm got tired of her and decided that she was no longer of any use to them.

There was no one I could talk to about such things. Certainly not Audrey who I still saw at intervals. To confide in Janet, one of my oldest and most trusted friends, would put her at risk. I had talked to her, of course, about my desire to resign or retire, but she was always pessimistic about that.

"They'll never let you go, Keith, not voluntarily. They can keep you by simply threatening to withhold your pension and accumulated funds. Besides, if you did leave, where would you go and what would you do?"

"Oh," I replied, half jokingly, "to some peaceful place and write my memoirs, I suppose."

"If you did, nobody would believe you. The firm would disown you and brand you a liar and you'd have no way of proving what you wrote. They've obliterated your record so completely that you would never be able to document anything."

"If I told the truth," I answered, "perhaps some people would believe me."

Janet shook her head. "If you told nothing but the truth, you might not be around to read your own book."

Janet had not been enthusiastic about my efforts to affect changes to the Official Secrets Act either. "The people who have that power will never let it go. If the heads of government right up to the prime minister want to retain it in its original form, who are we to question their judgment?"

I responded, "I am a citizen of a democracy, and in a democracy the citizens can question or challenge the judgment of its leaders."

"As long as the OSA is in effect," Janet said almost sadly, "you're not living in a democracy. None of us are."

Years later when I was living in what amounted to exile in Israel, Moshe Dayan expressed almost the same thought to me. "Pretty arrogant," he said, "for one man to take on a whole government."

"What if a man is right?" I asked him.

"Still arrogant," he said.

Perhaps I was. Or foolish. Or both.

Karen's next surprise was her unexpected arrival at my flat with her suitcases packed with clothes from the flat she shared with two other girls.

"What's this?" I asked.

"Oh, I have a splendid idea. I'm moving in with you."

In vain I pointed out the disadvantages of such an arrangement.

"We're engaged, aren't we? We can discuss it over the weekend in Shropshire." She was driving down that afternoon with her uncle and aunt. I should follow by train on Friday.

When I arrived she had another surprise waiting for me: an engagement party! Ours. Her aunt and uncle were delighted and had planned a large party on Sunday.

I stared at her. "But that's impossible."

"Too late to call it off now, Darling. The guests are all invited."

And so they were. They came with handshakes, congratulations, and toasts. Karen was radiant and I was numb. This whole thing was getting out of hand and I had visions of an announcement in the Times of London or the Daily Telegraph which would be read by someone who knew that I already had a wife. My reaction was to drink too much at the reception and return to London early the following day.

I went to see two very old friends, Marilyn and David Hobbson, who had known me for years and knew all about Audrey and the children. When I told them what had happened they were aghast.

"My God Keith," said David, "you must be mad!" They had met Karen a few times, but knew nothing about her connection to the firm.

"Well,"I said, "I think you're right. I am mad, but, what am I to do?"

"You must tell Karen that you are married. That's the least you can do. When she learns that you have been deceiving her she will let you off the hook."

"It should at least slow her down a bit," said Marilyn. "And she sounds like a girl who could do with some slowing down."

"She's coming up to London tomorrow. Could I bring her here for dinner? I'll need some moral support when I tell her. I'd be most grateful ... "

The Hobbsons were loyal friends. They said that I could bring Karen to dinner. They did more than that. When we arrived, Marilyn who was a take charge sort of person, drew Karen aside and bluntly told her the truth while David and I were pouring the drinks.

Karen's reaction surprised us all. She said that if I loved her ... and she knew that I did ... it didn't matter if I was married or not. I could get a divorce; it was as simple as that. She could understand if I never told her of this shadowy family whom I rarely saw, if ever. She knew that I would tell her eventually. She was leaving for Cape Town in the morning and when she returned we could work out the details of the divorce and then everything could work out as planned. This was said so calmly and with such conviction that none of us had any reply. We continued with a dinner that seemed almost surreal. Karen chatted away as if noting unusual had happened. The Hobbsons were civilized people and carried it off very well. As we left, David murmured to me, "Guess you're not out of deep water yet, ol' boy." He was right about that.

The situation was impossible. Karen was smothering me and if I didn't break off with her disaster loomed. If I did the firm would be furious; without knowing it she had become an important part of their communications network. When Karen went to Cape Town I was left with this dilemma, and I felt as if I was back in that peculiar cell in Lubyanka with the walls closing in. Even if I drank quite heavily, I could not sleep. I consulted a doctor, a private one because

I was afraid to consult any from the firm. I told him that I was very stressed and was unable to sleep. He prescribed some sort of tranquilizer and cautioned me about mixing it with alcohol.

By the time Karen came back from Cape Town I had decided to tell her the truth about everything. This was a horrifying breach of policy. I had never done such a thing before, and I knew the firm would be furious, but in my confused and desperate state of mind I could see no alternative.

So I told her. I told her that we had been using her in a dirty and dangerous game and that she ought to walk away from it and me while she still could. At first she was inclined to disbelieve me altogether, "You're making all this up, aren't you Keith? Because you're tired of me and want to get rid of me."

" I'm not making anything up," I said. "Do you need proof? Well, do you remember being taken to dinner by my friend in Nairobi? Do you remember what you talked about? I can tell you, because every word you said was recorded, and I've listened to the tape. You told him about a cocker spaniel you once had named Penny. You told him ..."

I didn't go on because she turned very pale.

"Now do you believe me?" I said. "You have to get out of this Karen. And for God's sake never open your mouth about what I've just told you. Not to your uncle and aunt. Not to anyone. Do you understand?" (A warning that proved to carry little weight with Karen.)

She was angry now. "I understand that you've been making a fool of me. You implied you loved me. They say married men always go back to their wives. Is that what you're planning to do?"

There were more words, bitter ones. I felt desperately sorry for her and for the situation into which she had been led, but I also knew that Karen was tough, that she would overcome her anger and humiliation if she realized that I was very concerned for her safety. How wrong I was! In the days that followed she visited old friends, her relatives, even Audrey, and quizzed them about me, complained about me, and made life generally unpleasant. How my desire to spare her was turned against me and how far her vitriol spread! I had been trying to do the decent thing while not living a decent life.

Of all the emotions churning inside me, the strongest was fear: fear of what might happen if the firm learned that I had broken the code by telling Karen the truth. I had placed her in extreme danger.

It was this fear that drove me, a few days later to Father Bruce. I had not seen him for some time, but he was one of the few people I could trust, the only one who could really understand what my tormented life was like. In my confused state he seemed like the only line to God. I knew mine was badly frayed.

It was late when I arrived and the door was locked. I banged and shouted that I had to see Father Bruce. Finally the door was opened and he stood there behind the doorkeeper. "Bruce," I babbled, "for God's sake let me in. Help me"

Without a word, he took me by the arm and up the stairs to his room. "I'm breaking all the rules, Keith," he said, "but come in and tell me what's wrong."

I must have talked for hours because I cannot recall when I stopped talking, only that I woke up with daylight streaming through the window, stretched on the floor with a blanket over me. Bruce came in, his cassock as dusty and untidy as ever. He brought me coffee. Then he said he had thought deeply and believed I should tell the firm what I had done and face the consequences. "They'll find out sooner or later," he said. "It's almost certain that the girl will tell someone to explain why you jilted her. And that person will tell someone else. In the meantime, I can see that you are in very bad shape emotionally. You must try to get all this behind you. If you don't, something is going to snap, Keith, I'm sure of it."

He said a prayer over me and sent me back to my flat where I tried to pull myself together and do what had to be done. I sat by the telephone for a long time. Finally, I called my contact at the firm and said that it was most urgent that I talk to a senior person right away. I used a code that I knew would bring him quickly, and it did. Within an hour the Brigadier in charge of my section was in my living room, looking at me somberly.

His expression did not change as I told him what I had done. I said that I regretted deeply having broken the cardinal rule, but that I had remembered what had happened to Pauline and I was afraid that something similar might happen to Karen. I argued that Karen was an innocent person who did not deserve to be hurt and I wanted to protect her.

"You idiot," the Brigadier bellowed. "You're the one who has put her in jeopardy by doing what you have done." He picked up my telephone, spoke a few words, and within ten minutes two men who I knew as members of the firm opened the door and stepped into the flat. I was instructed to wait in another room while they conferred. Then I was called back.

It was almost like a court martial, ominous and grim. I was a bloody fool. I knew the rules. If I had problems why had I not come to them? Did I realize how much damage I had done? By disobeying orders I had imperiled a vital network and an important operation of which I knew nothing. I had also left my own reliability in doubt. How could they ever trust me again? A decision would be made later about what to do with me. I might face charges of violating the Official Secrets Act. I might be censured and lose important benefits. They did not specify which benefits, but I knew they were talking about my pension and the funds built through the years that the firm was holding for me.

Almost worse than these threats was the atmosphere of icy disapproval bordering on contempt. High ranking British officers can be very good at this. My state of mind prevented me from rising to my own defense or mustering any anger at their accusations. I knew that they represented a powerful force and were capable of making things intolerable for those who incurred their displeasure or stood in their way. In the face of such power I was helpless. It made no difference that I had been pressured into taking the assignment and that this was the first time in all the years that I had broken faith with the firm.

I was left alone with firm orders not to leave the flat until I heard from them. I had a feeling that I would be left to dangle for some time ... part of the punishment ... but there was nothing to do but wait. When the men were gone I poured my self half a tumbler of whiskey and drank it. When that gave me no relief I poured another.

At about noon the telephone rang and it was Audrey. We no longer pretended to have a real marriage, but I had asked her to call now and then with news of the children. By now I was too drunk to make sense and she became worried. She sensed that I was in trouble and decided to come to London to help. I remember telling her not to come (it was against rules for her to be there ... she had never been before), but she ignored my protestations and arrived with Anne.

When they arrived I was in a sorry state. Audrey knew better than to ask questions, but she managed to get me fed and then into bed. I was grateful for her concern and would tell her so in the morning. But in the morning things were very different.

I felt the chill the instant I walked into the kitchen. When I asked what was wrong, Audrey told me they would be leaving for home right away. After some questioning I discovered what was wrong and my heart sank to my shoes. Anne, being inquisitive about me and my work, had started rifling through my desk and found letters from Karen. As I said before, Karen was not shy nor reticent in her protestations of affection. Anne went right to her mother with the evidence of my dallying and the impact was devastating. Although we had been estranged, Audrey was horrified of this proof of my supposed infidelity. The look on my daughter's face was painful. I had tried for so long to maintain the respect of my children and now it was gone, perhaps forever.

When the door closed behind them I was unable to stand the silence. I tried to telephone Janet, but no one answered. I took one of the pills and washed it down with whiskey. The rest of the morning I sat and drank steadily trying to blot out the sense of guilt, failure, and remorse. I had wrecked my career, betrayed my family, and brought unhappiness to many others. I tried to recall prayers, but none came. In an attempt to dull the pain I took another pill ... forgetting the doctor's warning.

Finally I staggered to my bedroom where I kept my .38caliber automatic. Suicides were common in my profession; why not just one more? Over the years I had taken many lives, why not add one more? Suddenly I remembered Father Bruce's voice, "Something is going to snap, Keith, I'm sure of it." I moved toward the telephone to talk to him and suddenly everything went black.

I have no awareness of how long I was unconscious, but when I was able to raise my head, I seemed half paralyzed. After what seemed hours I dragged my self to the phone on the floor nearby and pressed my direct emergency number to the department.

After a while I heard the sound of splintering wood and the door was broken and four men stood over me. I tried to speak, but was unable to mouth words. One of the men who seemed to be a doctor, leaned over me, felt my pulse and looked into my eyes. Another sniffed the empty glass and said, "Looks drunk to me." I was propped up on some pillows and a blanket was thrown over me. I thought they would take me to a hospital, but they didn't. I was given an injection and then the doctor and two others left. The fourth stayed and put me to bed giving me hot milk and some food he found in the kitchen.

The next morning I felt somewhat improved and was able to talk a little. The doctor came and examined me and I could hear him reporting on the telephone: "Damn near killed himself mixing tranquilizers and alcohol. Tough customer. Probably all right." I was told to 'rest up' and not leave the flat.

At the end of that time I was visited by a member of the firm who told me curtly that I was in disgrace and would be sent out of the country for an indeterminate period while my case was under review. He gave me a paper to sign saying that Karen had been recruited with no knowledge on her part and had been unaware of the contents of the letters she had carried. I asked if that meant that she would be free from prosecution or from being detained in any way. He gave me a cold stare and said,"Such things are no longer of any concern to you." I asked where I was being sent and he answered with one word: "Italy."

My departure to Heathrow airport was with an escort of two silent policemen. A seat had been reserved for me on an Alitalia flight to Rome. I was given a ticket and some money and allowed to keep my special passport. We sat in a small room where I was confined until the flight was called then escorted to the plane and placed at the rear, boarding before any other passengers. As they left, one policeman said, "Now, no tricks. Don't try to get off. We'll be watching until he plane leaves."

I was too dispirited to think of getting off. The final words from the Brigadier were, "Stay in Italy until you hear otherwise. We'll keep track of you all the way. Don't do anything foolish. You're in enough trouble as it is."

The plane lifted off and I sat there looking at the green fields of England disappearing in the mist. I felt like a man without a country.

Perhaps I was.

chapter 33

WHEN I ARRIVED IN Rome, as instructed, I went to a pensione near the top of the Spanish Steps. Once part of a convent, it offered the quiet I so desperately needed. When I was settled I wrote to Audrey. I told her that I had been sent to Italy on assignment, a story that had a grain of truth to it.

For three days I left my room only to eat or to visit the ancient church at the top of the Spanish Steps, where I simply sat in the stillness and hoped the Presence there would touch and heal my battered spirit.

On the fourth day, as I sat in the English Tea Shop, I was approached by a man who looked Italian, but spoke perfect English. He paused by my table and said, "May I sit down, Sir? I have some information for you."

He told me that a Fiat car would be waiting for me early the next morning. There was a small job for me in a small town called Nerano, beyond Sorrento. It involved a radio tower or some sort of communication installation. I was to drive there and stay until further orders. He gave me a large sum in Italian lire, the papers for the car, and driving directions. I could collect some keys from the only store in Nerano; the owner would show me where I was to stay.

It was a long drive, and it was dark in Nerano when I arrived. I found the store and collected the keys and the directions. Then I followed a winding road until at last my headlights showed me a shuttered villa, quite large, about 50 feet below the village and about a quarter of a mile above the sea. No one was there, but obviously I was expected as cold food had been set out and one of the beds had been made. I fell into it gratefully and slept like the dead until I was wakened by sunlight streaming through the windows.

When I went down into the kitchen and out into the garden ...

full of orange and lemon trees ... I saw three people waiting there: mother father and daughter. They were to be my servants. They came every morning and departed promptly at six every afternoon, leaving my evening meal prepared. I remember thinking wryly, that I might be in disgrace, but at least it was a luxurious disgrace. In any case I decided to wait. Tend to the insignificant assignment and enjoy it. That was all I could do.

The days passed peacefully, and I felt my sanity and strength coming back. I swam near a small restaurant, where the owner's wife cooked me octopus and called me from the water when it was ready. Once a week the local police came from Sorrento to check on me and drink a glass of wine in the villa. I suppose they reported to London that I was behaving myself.

There were villas nearby that were owned by German industrialists some of whom I was sure had been SS or maybe even Gestapo. One or two sent invitations asking me to dine, but I declined. The local priest regarded me with some wariness until I said to him one day, "Father, I'm sure that when God made Nerano He stood and admired His handiwork!" After that we became quite good friends.

Three times I wrote carefully worded letters to the firm, expressing regret for my mistakes, but asking that these be balanced against past service and that I might be allowed to go quietly into retirement with my Army and Foreign Office pensions. I would trouble them no more, and specifically would not work any more to amend the Official Secrets Act. I had no reply. Once I tried to call them collect from Sorrento, but the call was not accepted. When I paid for it myself, none of the individuals I asked for were available. Finally a tired voice (tired of me, I think) said, "Really, you're being a nuisance. You'll be told when to come back." And the line went dead. I liked to think that it was the cause of the unreliable Italian telephone service.

About twelve weeks after my arrival in Nerano the summons came quite suddenly. It was an ordinary cable from a post office in Knightsbridge, "Suggest you call to see me in ten days." There was no signature; none was needed.

I drove my reliable Fiat through the Mont Blanc tunnel into France and on through Belgium into Holland where I turned in the car and caught the ferry from the Hook of Holland to Dover. From there I took the train to London. I stared out the window at the wonderful English countryside rushing past and wondered what lay ahead for me. I knew that I had enemies and detractors in the firm, but also I hoped, a few friends who still wished me well. It was a little like flipping a coin and wondering which side would come up. In the long run I always knew that it came down to "Heads we win; tails you lose."

When I arrived at the foreign office, I could hardly believe my ears. Here was I, a middle aged battle weary agent with a recent history of unreliable behavior. I had been guilty of a flagrant violation of the code of silence. Yet, now their plan was to send me to one of the most unstable and dangerous areas in Europe: Northern Ireland. I remember my first reaction: Well if they want to get rid of me, this is a perfectly good way to do it.

Their reasoning was that I knew Ireland intimately, had spent much time there, was able to communicate with the people. I had other special skills and experience, they said, that should prove useful. I would, of course, be given extensive briefing before I went and I might be gone for several months or longer.

Even today I cannot discuss details of that assignment. At times I wore my uniform; at times I didn't. I was not supposed to be involved in any police action or fighting. I was to learn all I could about certain aspects of the situation facing the British Army, write reports, make recommendations, and if possible stay out of harm's way. Once I was called back to London for discussions with Prime Minister Edward Heath and others.

In 1972, the flames of violence in Northern Ireland seemed almost out of control. A three hundred pound bomb blew up one of the two railway station in Belfast and destroyed the adjacent bus terminal as well. Another bomb planted in a restaurant caused hideous civilian casualties. I was slightly injured when I came too close to a telephone box that had been booby trapped. I was simply passing by when the unfortunate caller was blown to bits and flying glass sprayed my face and head. Had I not been wearing sunglasses I would have been blinded. Splinters had to be carefully removed from my forehead.

One area of concern was the flow of illegal arms into the area, most of them from Communist satellite countries. The majority of these shipments went to Eire and then were smuggled across the 180 mile border that separates the two countries. The government of Eire disapproved, but it was not hard to find people who would look the other way. Even when smugglers were apprehended it often was difficult to get a conviction because few people were willing to risk testifying against them. Many trials or hearings ended in acquittal and it was in the aftermath of such a hearing in Belfast that a sniper's bullet finally caught up with me.

I was standing outside the police barracks with a young Major who had been at the hearing with me. Both of us were wearing our uniforms. Across the street was a row of warehouses that were constantly checked for security; access by unauthorized persons was considered impossible. Sentries were posted along the street in front of the police buildings. The windows of the empty warehouses were so dirty that no one could see into them, but behind one of those windows was a young man with a high velocity, small bore rifle. By raising the sash a crack he could look almost straight down into the area where the Major and I were standing beside a massive oak pillar that had been set in the ground near the steps. The young man had been waiting a long time; twenty cigarette butts were found on the ground where he had crouched while the hearings went on.

To this day I do not know whether the sniper's primary mission was to eliminate me or just to kill a couple of British officers. In any case his motives made little difference, I think I had turned suddenly to react to a noise across the courtyard when, with a sound like a slap with a wet rag, the first bullet passed through the young Major's skull, killing him instantly. As he fell my instinctive reaction was to help him, so I stooped quickly. As I did, the second bullet hit the oak pillar beside me with enormous force and disintegrated into a cloud of splinters and metal fragments that sliced the upper right side of my chest. More damaging was an oak splinter, about the size of a screw driver, that was driven into the inside of my left knee, locking the joint in a crouching position. I passed out, and when I came to I knew that I had a sever pain in my knee and could not move it and that I was covered with the Major's blood. My chest and shoulder were numb. I was sure that I had been shot and I waited for the third bullet that might finish me altogether.

It didn't come, because in an effort to get a better firing angle the sniper raised the window and leaned out. One of the security forces standing in the street saw him and, considering he had only a hand gun, made a truly remarkable shot. The bullet struck the sniper in the throat and he tumbled from the window and hit the pavement, dead.

I was rushed to an operating room where the splinter was removed from my knee and my other wounds were treated. I remember coming out of anesthesia and wondering hazily if the KGB was still after me and if the sniper might have been Russian? Even more farfetched, could he have been guided by my own people? Such thoughts were unworthy and probably unlikely. Still, I had been betrayed before.

Although my stay was short, I received excellent care in the hospital. There had been an ugly incident before in this hospital when someone disguised as an orderly had entered a room and yanked the life support tubes from a wounded British officer. This death was on the mind of the British commander for Northern Ireland when he came to see me. He said that he did not want me evacuated in the normal way to a waiting ambulance. Even as he was speaking I saw that bars on the windows were being removed and soon after a helicopter had landed close by. I was passed through the window on a stretcher and rushed to the waiting helicopter. Five crew members were aboard: a pilot, a navigator, guard, and two medical corpsmen. With an injection for pain, I was flown across the Irish Sea, stopping in Wales to refuel, and finally landing in the London area. I was rushed to hospital, still under security, where I was cared for as my wounds began to heal. I was not permitted to tell anyone what had happened or where I was. I was not allowed to call Audrey.

After a while I was visited by a member of the firm who said, with cool correctness, that they regretted that I had been hurt. They wanted to speed my recovery in any way possible and they thought that in view of the possibility of further reprisals against me I should recuperate in some place distant from the British Isles.

"There is a small job in Greece that you could do while you recover. Nothing important or demanding. Mainly liaison with NATO and some defenses that are being built along the coast of Corfu." All this was said quite gently, but I knew it was an order, so I went.

In Corfu I found that my duties were almost nonexistent: two hours a day took care of them. By now I could move about painfully with two crutches, and every day I used them to propel my self across the beach and into the warm sea. I often wished that Audrey and the children could be with me because it was more like a holiday than an assignment.

It all ended somewhat abruptly when Col. George Popodopolous was deposed and Greece pulled out of NATO. I was sent then to a small town in an isolated part of France to continue my recovery. I tried to discover what the firm had in mind for me, but each time I came up against a wall of silence.

Finally I was called to London and told that a hearing had been arranged to deal with my case. A single judge, sitting 'in camera' would be authorized to make all decisions. This sounded ominous because I knew that such judges were selected primarily for their rigid views where the Official Secrets Act was concerned. The whole procedure was reminiscent of "Star Chamber" days when the will of the monarch could be imposed on a subject with no concern for individual rights at all. I would not be permitted a lawyer, I was told, because by consulting him I would be breaking the OSA, as indeed he would be too, in counseling me.

The day of the hearing an officer escorted me to a large room with no windows. When the judge came in from a door behind his chair the officer told me to rise and remain standing. Then he left and I heard the lock click behind him. After that, the silence seemed deafening.

The judge gave me a nod and a faint smile then proceded for some minutes to go through what appeared to be my records. While he did, I glanced around the room wondering if it was bugged or even covered by a camera. I saw no signs of any.

At last, the judge leaned back and closed the folder. It was clear, he said, that I had broken some very important rules. He would list some of them in a moment. I was not being formally charged he said. Therefore in my answers I could say what I wished, for it was in confidence with him alone. He would not necessarily discuss this interview with anyone else. All decisions were up to him. If I could satisfy him with my answers there might be no blemish on my ... he hesitated ... otherwise excellent record.

I had a sinking feeling that my fate had been sealed before I came into the room, but I braced myself for his questions and tried to answer them truthfully.

The chief complaint against me concerned my efforts to have the OSA amended or repealed. Such efforts, as I well knew, represented a direct disobedience of orders. I replied that I knew of some cases where the Act had been used to damage or discredit innocent people and of others where it was used to conceal treason. I admitted having worked to have the law changed but added that when ordered to desist by my superiors I had done so.

"Even so," the judge said sternly, "you were able to stir up opposition to an Act of Parliament. You did considerable damage. Some of your associates are persisting in those efforts still. This we cannot and will not tolerate!"

Another allegation was that I had revealed government secrets to a civilian (Karen) in direct defiance of regulations. I should have sought advice and discussed the problem with a higher authority rather than taking the law into my own hands. Another complaint was that I had invested monies in a foreign country (South Africa), despite this being prohibited by the rules of the firm. Finally, my recent tour of duty in Northern Ireland was not satisfactory because it had been left unfinished.

This last seemed so unreasonable and so unfair that I answered it first. "Of course the job had been left unfinished. The sniper in the warehouse had seen to that! There had been praise for my performance while I was there. I cannot believe that this is being held against me."

As for investing money in South Africa, this was common practice in the firm, as he well knew. Everyone did it, including the chief of my section. It was merely a repository for funds paid to us secretly, but legitimately, by the government. If I was guilty so were many others.

Where Karen was concerned, I tried to explain that I had been under a tremendous amount of stress and that at the time I thought the girl's life might be in danger. I added that in my opinion she was innocent of any offenses under the OSA since she had never signed it.

At this the judge's eyes flashed. "It's not for you to decide who is exempt from the Act of Parliament. It covers you and anyone else if we so decide!" He looked up at me with an air of finality. "You are an unusual case and we want to help as much as possible to rehabilitate you. But it seems we can no longer employ you in any government capacity and reluctantly must let you go."

I stared at him, unbelieving. "I may have made mistakes, but I have never betrayed my country. What about my pension? What about ..."

But he had risen from his chair and was gone.

For almost half an hour I sat there in despair. I could not leave until the door was unlocked. Finally, it opened and the officer who had escorted me entered. "Come with me, please."

I limped down the corridors after him and found myself in another office facing a man I knew quite well. He looked like a man assigned a job he did not care for. "I'm directed to inform you," he said, "that we advise you to leave the country for an indefinite period. You are no longer a member of Military Intelligence, but you will have to report to us from whatever country you are in. The country will be decided on in a few days. For the moment, the payment of any pension to you will not be considered. If in time we are pleased with your behavior, it is always open to review."

"But that's damnable," I replied. "You take people like Roger Hollis who you and I know are guilty of high treason and give them a title and a pension and send them off to the country. I've never betrayed this nation to the Soviets or anyone else. Why can't you at least release the funds for me?"

He looked out the window with a faraway stare. "No two cases are alike, Keith." I could see that he was genuinely distressed. He forced a smile. "You ought to try Psalm 146: 'Put not your trust in princes.' "Or," he added softly, "in their judges, either."

The door opened and two officers beckoned me to follow them. With one in front of me and one behind I was led through the maze of corridors to a door. It opened, then closed behind me. I was on the street.

Feeling dazed, I walked into Whitehall, past the Cenotaph Monument, and Horse Guards Parade, and on into Saint James Park.

There was a bench overlooking the pond and I sat there in the sunlight shivering a little because it was cold and I had been too distraught to retrieve my coat when I left the Foreign Office. I sat there for a long time trying to make sense of the past few hours.

I found no answers, but realized that I, like everyone else was a sum of so many experiences, good and bad. I thought to myself 'You should have been dead many times over' and here I was still alive for some unknown reason.

Suddenly I was aware of a bobby standing in front of me, looking at me with concern,"Beg pardon, Sir, is everything all right? You've been sitting there for quite some time."

I stood up shakily feeling the familiar twinge in my knee. All right? What did that mean? I was in my fifties. I had been separated from my job. I had been told to leave my country. I had little money saved and was not likely to get any more. I had wounds and scars to show for thirty years of service, but nothing else. I had an unpredictable future and an unprovable past.

But still I had the loyalty of my wife. I had two children who I loved dearly. I had the unbreakable friendship of Janet and a few others. I had fought against an unjust law and lost, but I believed, and still believe, that someday that fight will be won. The English are a fair-minded people and justice will have to prevail.

Finally I knew that I was a survivor who had lived through torture and imprisonment, betrayal, and the fringe of madness. By rights I should have been long gone from this earth, but I was still here, and perhaps there was some purpose or meaning in that.

I was a survivor and somehow would go on being a survivor.

I looked at the bobby and said, "Thank you, Constable. Everything is quite all right." I walked away with my shoulders as straight as I could hold them.